Droid™ X
FOR
DUMMIES®

by Dan Gookin

WILEY

Wiley Publishing, Inc.

Droid™ X For Dummies®

Published by
Wiley Publishing, Inc.
111 River Street
Hoboken, NJ 07030-5774

www.wiley.com

WILEY

About the Author

Dan Gookin has written more than 115 books about technology, many of them accurate. He is most famously known as the author of the original *For Dummies* book, *DOS For Dummies*, published in 1991. Additionally, Dan has achieved fame as one of the first computer radio talk show hosts, the editor of a computer magazine, a national technology spokesman, and an occasional actor on the community theater stage.

Dan still considers himself a writer and technology "guru" whose job it is to remind everyone that our electronics are not to be taken too seriously. His approach is light and humorous, yet very informative. He knows that modern gizmos can be complex and intimidating, but necessary to help people become productive and successful. Dan mixes his vast knowledge of all things high-tech with a unique, dry sense of humor that keeps everyone informed — and awake.

Dan's most recent books are *Word 2010 For Dummies, PCs For Dummies,* Windows 7 Edition, and *Laptops For Dummies*, 4th Edition. He holds a degree in communications/visual arts from the University of California, San Diego. Dan dwells in North Idaho, where he enjoys woodworking, music, theater, riding his bicycle, being with his boys, and fighting local government corruption.

Author's Acknowledgments

I would like to acknowledge Kelly Crummey and Megan Keefe, from WeberShandwick, for their helpful assistance.

Publisher's Acknowledgments

We're proud of this book; please send us your comments through our online registration form located at `http://dummies.custhelp.com`. For other comments, please contact our Customer Care Department within the U.S. at 877-762-2974, outside the U.S. at 317-572-3993, or fax 317-572-4002.

Some of the people who helped bring this book to market include the following:

Acquisitions and Editorial

Senior Project Editor: Mark Enochs

Acquisitions Editor: Katie Mohr

Copy Editor: Rebecca Whitney

Technical Editor: Stephen Worden

Editorial Manager: Leah Cameron

Editorial Assistant: Amanda Graham

Sr. Editorial Assistant: Cherie Case

Cartoons: Rich Tennant
(`www.the5thwave.com`)

Composition Services

Project Coordinator: Patrick Redmon

Layout and Graphics: Samantha K. Cherolis, Joyce Haughey, Kelly Kijovsky

Indexer: Claudia Bourbeau

Special Help: Chris Webb

Publishing and Editorial for Technology Dummies

Richard Swadley, Vice President and Executive Group Publisher

Andy Cummings, Vice President and Publisher

Mary Bednarek, Executive Acquisitions Director

Mary C. Corder, Editorial Director

Publishing for Consumer Dummies

Diane Graves Steele, Vice President and Publisher

Composition Services

Debbie Stailey, Director of Composition Services

Contents at a Glance

Table of Contents

Introduction

*T*o call the Motorola Droid X *another* cellphone is to do the gizmo a disservice. Sure, it can make phone calls. More than that, though, it's a portable technology marvel. As such, the Droid X can be a daunting device. In fact, I know a lot of people who shy away from using their cellphones beyond using its basic phone features simply because of the complexity. That's sad.

The factor that's probably most intimidating about the Droid X is that it's a *smart*phone. People don't like using devices that they believe are smarter than they are. But — trust me on this one — it isn't the phone that's smart.

Nope, even though the Droid X is an amazing piece of technology, it harbors no native intelligence. The only way to prove it to you is to write a book explaining how the Droid X works and do it in an informative, relaxing, and often humorous manner, which is exactly what this book does.

About This Book

This book is a reference. I don't intend for you to read it from cover to cover. Instead, you'll find each chapter to be its own, self-contained unit, covering a specific topic about using the Droid X phone. Each chapter is further divided into sections representing a task you perform with the phone or explaining how to get something done. Sample sections in this book include

- Typing on your phone
- Receiving a new call when you're on the phone
- Setting up Visual Voice Mail
- Taking a picture and sending it to Facebook
- Turning your phone into a deejay
- Dialing an international number
- Battery-saving tips

You have nothing to memorize, no mysterious utterances, no animal sacrifices, and definitely no PowerPoint presentations. Instead, every section explains a topic as though it's the first thing you read in this book. Nothing is assumed, and everything is cross-referenced. Technical terms and topics, when they come up, are neatly shoved to the side, where they're easily avoided. The idea here isn't to learn anything. This book's philosophy is to help you look it up, figure it out, and get back to your life.

How to Use This Book

This book follows a few conventions for using the Droid X. The main way you interact with your phone is by using its *touchscreen,* which is the glassy part of the phone as it's facing you. Buttons also adorn the Droid X, all of which are explained in Part I of this book.

There are various ways to touch the screen, which are explained and named in Chapter 3.

Chapter 4 discusses text input on the Droid X, which involves using a multi-touch keyboard on the screen. New to many smartphones in addition to the Droid X, the Swype keyboard is featured for superfast text entry. And, when you tire of typing, you can always input text on your Droid X by dictation.

This book directs you to do things on your phone by following numbered steps. Each step involves a specific activity, such as touching something on the screen. For example:

> **3. Choose Downloads.**

This step directs you to touch the text or item on the screen labeled Downloads. You might also be told to do this:

> **3. Touch Downloads.**

 Some phone options can be turned off or on, as indicated by a gray box with a green check mark in it, as shown in the margin. By touching the box on the screen, you add or remove the green check mark. When the green check mark appears, the option is on; otherwise, it's off.

 You can use the barcodes in the margins to install recommended apps. To install an app, scan its barcode using special software you install on the Droid X. Chapter 19 discusses how to add software to your phone, and Chapter 25 discusses how to use the Barcode Scanner app. You can use the app to read the barcodes.

Foolish Assumptions

Even though this book is written with the gentle handholding required by anyone who is just starting out, or who is easily intimidated, I have made a few assumptions. For example, I assume that you're a human being and not merely a cleverly disguised owl.

My biggest assumption: You have a Droid X phone by Motorola. Though you can use this book generically with any Android phone, it's specific to the things the Droid X can do.

In the United States, cellular service for the Droid X is provided by Verizon. Many things that the Droid X can do are based on the services Verizon offers, such as Visual Voice Mail or the Backup Assistant feature.

I also assume that you have a computer, either a desktop or laptop. The computer can be a PC or Windows computer or a Macintosh. Oh, I suppose it could also be a Linux computer. In any event, I refer to your computer as "your computer" throughout this book. When directions are specific to a PC or Mac, the book says so.

Programs that run on the Droid X are *apps*, which is short for *applications*. A single program is an app.

Finally, this book doesn't assume that you have a Google account, but already having one helps. Information is provided in Chapter 2 about setting up a Google account — an extremely important part of using the Droid X. Having a Google account opens up a slew of useful features, information, and programs that make using your Droid X phone more productive.

How This Book Is Organized

This book has been sliced into six parts, each of which describes a certain aspect of the Droid X or how it's used.

Part I: Hello, Droid X

This part of the book serves as your introduction to the Droid X. Chapters cover setup and orientation and familiarizing you with how the phone works. Part I is a good place to start, plus you discover things in this part that aren't obvious from just guessing how the phone works.

Part II: Your Basic Phone

Nothing is more basic for a phone to do than make calls, which is the topic of the chapters in this part of the book. The Droid X can make calls, receive calls, and serve as an answering service for calls you miss. It also manages the names of all the people you know and even those you don't want to know but have to know anyway.

Part III: Other Forms of Communication

The Droid X is about more than just telephone communications. Part III of this book explores other ways you can use your phone to stay in touch with people, the Internet, and other gizmos such as your desktop computer or a Bluetooth headset. Chapters in this part explain how to use text messaging, send and receive email, browse the Web, use social networking, and set up your phone for networking, among other things.

Part IV: O What Your Phone Can Do!

This part of the book explores those non-phone things that your phone can do. For example, your phone can find things on a map, give you verbal driving directions, take pictures, shoot videos, play music, play games, and do all sorts of wonderful things that no one would ever think that a phone can do. The chapters in this part of the book get you up to speed on those activities.

Part V: Off the Hook

The chapters in this part of the book discuss a slate of interesting topics, from taking the phone overseas and making international calls to customizing it to the necessary chores of maintenance and troubleshooting.

Part VI: The Part of Tens

Finally, this book ends with the traditional *For Dummies* Part of Tens, where each chapter lists ten items or topics. For the Droid X, the chapters include tips, tricks, shortcuts, things to remember, plus a list of some of my favorite Droid X phone apps.

Icons Used in This Book

This icon flags useful, helpful tips or shortcuts.

This icon marks a friendly reminder to do something.

This icon marks a friendly reminder *not* to do something.

This icon alerts you to overly nerdy information and technical discussions of the topic at hand. Reading the information is optional, though it may win you a pie slice in Trivial Pursuit.

Where to Go from Here

Start reading! Observe the Table of Contents and find something that interests you. Or, look up your puzzle in the index. When those suggestions don't cut it, just start reading Chapter 1.

My email address is dgookin@wambooli.com. Yes, that's my real address. I reply to all the email I get, and you'll get a quick reply if you keep your question short and specific to this book. Although I do enjoy saying Hi, I cannot answer technical support questions, resolve billing issues, or help you troubleshoot your phone. Thanks for understanding.

You can also visit my Web page for more information or as a diversion: www.wambooli.com.

 Enjoy the book and your Droid X!

Part I
Hello, Droid X

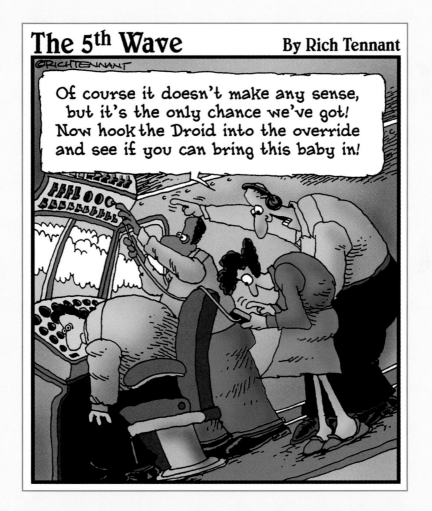

Oh give me a phone,
Yes a phone of my own,
One that's handy and not too complex
I will not bemoan
Whether G3 or roam,
'Cause it's not just a phone, it's Droid X

This first part of the book covers basic orientation of your Motorola Droid X phone, from setup and configuration, to discovering how the phone interacts with you, the human. It's your introduction to one of the few inanimate objects you'll ever own that you constantly will be saying "Hello" to.

| My Location | Music | Add App | Voice Search | Close | Calling | | Add App | Voice Search | Close | Calling | My Location | Music | Add App | Voic |

1

Your Very Own Droid X

In This Chapter

▶ Putting your phone together

▶ Charging the battery

▶ Identifying the phone's pieces parts

▶ Taking the phone with you

▶ Keeping the phone in one place

The word *droid* comes from *android*, which is used in science fiction litera-ture to refer to a robot in human form, such as the people who work the ticket counters in airports. An android differs from your run-of-the-mill robot, which may be an ugly thing that assembles cars or vacuums floors. *Android* was shortened to *droid* most notably in the *Star Wars* films. In fact, curiously, Motorola licenses the term *Droid* from Lucasfilm.

You don't have to license anything to use your Droid X phone. You do have to free it from the confines of its packaging and set the thing up. Then I recommend that you get to know your way around the Droid X, by identifying its various parts, buttons, and what-not. This chapter handles those orientation chores.

Initial Droid X Setup

Harbor no fear about your phone ringing inside its box. The ringing would be nifty, especially if you answered and heard a cheerful voice say, "Hello from your new Droid X phone!" It doesn't happen, though. That's either because someone else already set things up for you or the battery isn't installed inside the phone. It shouldn't be a big deal. When it is, just use the helpful advice found in this section.

Looking in the box

Several items come in the Droid X box. Even though you've probably opened the box already, or the people who sold you the phone have done so, I suggest that you take a moment to locate and identify each of these goodies:

- ✔ The Droid X phone
- ✔ Miscellaneous papers, the instructions, the warranty, and perhaps the *Getting Started* foldout
- ✔ The phone's battery and back cover (if the battery isn't installed)
- ✔ A micro–USB cable
- ✔ A power adapter

The Droid X may ship with a sheet of plastic over its screen, which tells you where various features are located. You can remove the plastic at this time.

Beyond the items I just listed, you might have been given a bonus package of goodies from whoever sold you the phone. If the person was classy, you have a handy little tote bag with perhaps the Verizon logo on it. If you look inside the bag, you might find these items:

- ✔ A smart-looking, leatherette belt-clip phone jacket
- ✔ A micro–USB car charger
- ✔ Headphones
- ✔ Even more random pieces of paper

The most important doodad is the phone itself, which might require some assembly before you can use it; refer to the next section for assembly directions.

I recommend keeping the instructions and other information as long as you own the phone: The phone's box makes an excellent storage place for that stuff — as well as for anything else you don't plan to use right away.

If anything is missing or appears to be damaged, contact Motorola online at

```
motorola.com/support
```

Installing the phone's battery

When your phone comes disassembled inside its box, your first duty as a new Droid X owner is to install the battery. Your second duty is to charge the battery. Installing the battery is easy, and charging it doesn't require a lightning storm and a kite.

If the nice people who sold you the phone already installed the battery, the phone is ready for charging; see the next section. Otherwise, you can install the battery yourself by following these steps:

1. **Ensure that the phone is turned off.**

   There's no need to follow this step unless you got all excited and already turned on your Droid X. If so, see Chapter 2 for information on turning off the phone.

2. **Flip the phone over so that the front (the glassy part) is facing away from you.**

   Don't remove the phone's cover when the phone is turned on. You should also disconnect any cables or the headset, if they're attached.

3. **If necessary, remove the back cover: Place both thumbs on the center part of the back cover and gently slide the back cover downward using your thumbs. Lift the back cover and set it aside.**

   A gentle push is all that's required; feel free to squeeze the phone as you push upward. The back cover slides down a wee bit, about ⅛ of an inch.

4. **If you have a new phone and the battery hasn't yet been installed, unwrap the battery and the phone's back cover.**

   Again, if they weren't installed, you'll need to free the battery and the Droid X's back cover from the confines of their plastic mummy wrap before you can complete phone setup. Also, you can remove the plastic coating from the back cover.

5. **Orient the battery so that its metallic contacts are in the lower right corner as you're looking at the back of the phone.**

   The battery is shaped like a giant, square mint cookie, the fudgy kind that the doctor advised you not to eat.

6. **Insert the bottom edge of the battery first, and then lower the top edge like you're closing the lid on a tiny box.**

   See Figure 1-1 for help in positioning and inserting the battery. Its metal contacts should be on the lower right edge as you insert the battery into the phone, as illustrated in the figure.

   When the battery is fully inserted, it snaps into place. The back of the battery is flush with the back of the phone; it doesn't stick up, not one itty bit.

7. **Replace the phone's back cover.**

   The cover has four prongs that slide into four slots on the back of the phone. Position the cover over the slots and it falls into place. Then slide up the cover with your thumbs until it snaps into place.

After the battery is installed, the next step is to charge it. Continue reading in the next section.

Figure 1-1: Inserting the phone's battery.

Charging the battery

After you insert the battery into your new phone, the next step is to charge it. It's cinchy:

1. **Plug the phone's charging adapter into a wall socket.**

2. **Plug the phone into the charger cord.**

   The charger cord plugs into the micro–USB connector, found on the phone's left side. The connector plugs in only one way.

As the phone charges, the notification light on the phone's front side lights up. When the light is orange-yellow, the phone is charging. When the light is green, the phone is fully charged.

- ✔ Wait until the notification light turns green before unplugging the phone from its power cable, especially the first time you charge the phone.

- ✔ The notification light uses three colors: amber for charging, green for fully charged, and red as the battery-low warning light.

- ✔ As the phone charges, the notification light on the phone's front side may light up. See Chapter 3 for information on reviewing notifications.

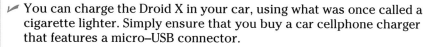

- You can use the phone while it's charging.

- The Droid X uses any standard cellphone charger. The charger must have a *micro–USB connector* to be able to plug into the phone.

- You can charge the Droid X in your car, using what was once called a cigarette lighter. Simply ensure that you buy a car cellphone charger that features a micro–USB connector.

- The phone also charges itself when it's plugged into a computer using either the USB cable that comes with the phone or any micro–USB cable attached to a computer. The computer must be on for charging to work.

- A *micro–USB* connector has a flat, trapezoid shape, which makes it different from the *mini–USB connector*, which is squat and slightly larger and used primarily on evil cellphones.

Droid X Orientation

How long has it been since you've actually dialed a phone? I don't mean since you punched in a number — I mean *used a rotary dial* to dial a phone? Are you old enough to remember how much you disliked calling people who had too many nines or zeros in their phone number? Oh, but I date myself.

A term such as *dial* a phone, or even *hang up*, is jargon from a bygone era. Here in the 21st century, new terms are required in order to describe the knobs, gizmos, and doodads that festoon a modern cellphone, such as the Droid X. Consider this your basic orientation and familiarization section.

Knowing what's what on your phone

Like all other confusing things, the Droid X attempts to intimidate you with some new terms for its features, not to mention that you may not be aware of all its available hardware features. Fret not, gentle reader.

Figure 1-2 illustrates the names of all the useful knobs and doodads on the front of your phone. Figure 1-3 illustrates the same thing, but for your phone's backside.

The terms referenced in both Figures 1-2 and 1-3 are the same as the ones used elsewhere in this book, as well as in whatever scant Droid X documentation exists.

- The phone's power button, which turns the phone off or on, is found on top of the phone, as shown in Figures 1-2 and 1-3.

- The main part of the phone is the *touchscreen* display. You use the touchscreen with one or more of your fingers to control the phone, which is where it gets the name *touch*screen.

Figure 1-2: Your phone's face.

- ✔ *Soft buttons* appear below the touch screen (refer to Figure 1-2). They have no function unless the phone is turned on.

- ✔ Yes, the main microphone is on the bottom of the phone. Even so, it still picks up your voice, loud and clear. You don't need to hold the phone at an angle for the bottom microphone to work.

- ✔ The two bonus microphones (refer to Figure 1-3) are for noise-cancelling purposes. They help reduce background noise, which means that you hear people on the phone more clearly and they hear you more clearly. You do not speak into the noise-cancelling microphones.

- ✔ The rear speaker is designed for video and other audio playback.

- ✔ You adjust the phone's volume by using the Volume button on the phone's right side (refer to Figure 1-2).

- ✔ The Volume buttons also serve as a Zoom function when using the Droid X as a camera. See Chapter 15 for additional details.

- ✔ Yes, the Droid X lacks a physical keyboard. Instead, an onscreen keyboard is used, as covered in Chapter 4.

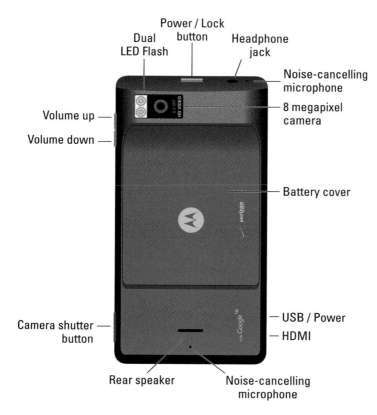

Power / Lock button
Dual LED Flash
Headphone jack
Noise-cancelling microphone
8 megapixel camera
Volume up
Volume down
Battery cover
Camera shutter button
USB / Power
HDMI
Rear speaker
Noise-cancelling microphone

Figure 1-3: Your phone's rump.

Listening with earphones

The Droid X most likely didn't come with earphones or any form of headset in the box. That's not a reason to give up on the concept. In fact, the nice people who sold you the Droid X might have tossed in a set of earbud-style earphones for you to use. If not, well then, they weren't that nice, were they?

You're probably familiar with the earbud type of earphone: The buds are set into your ears. The sharp, pointy end of the earphones — what you don't want to stick into your ear — goes into the top of the phone.

Between the earbuds and the sharp, pointy thing is often found a control noodle on which a button sits. The button can be used to mute the phone or to start or stop playback of music when the Droid X is in its music-playing mode.

You can also use the control noodle to answer the phone when it rings.

Usually, a teensy hole on the back side of the noodle serves as the phone's microphone. The hole allows you to use the earphones as a hands-free headset with the Droid X.

- You can purchase any cellphone headset for use with the Droid X. Any standard earphones work, though some headsets may feature noodle buttons that may not work on the Droid X.

- The earbuds are labeled R for right and L for left.

- You don't use the earphone's noodle to set the phone's volume, either in a call or while you're listening to music. Instead, the phone's volume is set by using the volume control buttons found on the side of the phone, as illustrated in Figures 1-2 and 1-3.

- See Chapter 17 for more information on using your Droid X as a portable music player.

- Be sure to fully insert the earphone connector into the phone. The person you're talking with cannot hear you well when the earphones are plugged in only part of the way.

- You can also use a Bluetooth headset with your phone, to listen to a call or some music. See Chapter 13 for more information on Bluetooth attachments for the Droid X.

- I find it best to fold the earphones when I don't need them, as opposed to wrapping them up in a loop: Put the earbuds and connector in one hand and then pull the wire out straight with the other hand. Fold the wire in half, and then in half again. You can then put the earphones in your pocket or on a tabletop. By folding the wires, you avoid creating the wire-ball-of-Christmas-tree-lights that would otherwise happen.

Exploring your phone's guts

It rarely happens, but occasionally you may need to examine the intricacies of your phone's innards. Unlike other cellphones, the Droid X is designed to have easily replaceable items that you can access without having to sneak around behind the manufacturer's back, pry open the phone, and alert the warranty police.

Specifically, there are two reasons you might need to open your phone:

- To install or replace the battery
- To access the MicroSD memory card

When you need to access one of these items, you can obey these steps:

1. **Turn off your phone.**

   See the section "Turning off the phone" in Chapter 2 for more information.

2. **Flip the phone over.**

3. **Use your thumbs to slide down the upper back cover.**

4. **Set aside the back cover.**

   Use Figure 1-4 to identify the phone's battery and the MicroSD memory card.

   To access the MicroSD card, you must first remove the battery.

   The battery is removed by lifting the little tab that says *Pull* (see Figure 1-4).

   To remove the MicroSD card, slide it to the right, toward the empty battery compartment. Pull the card all the way out until it's free.

   When you're done rummaging around inside your phone, you close things up:

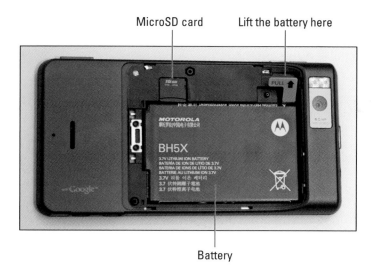

Figure 1-4: Droid X guts.

5. **Return the back cover to the phone; the little prongs on the cover fit into the four holes on either side of the phone.**

   The cover fits only one way.

6. **Slide up the cover until it snaps into position.**

You can turn on the phone again after the back cover is locked into place. See Chapter 2 for information on turning on your phone.

➤ Do not remove the MicroSD card from the Droid X unless you have first unmounted it. Refer to Chapter 13 for information on how to unmount the MicroSD card.

➤ See Chapter 22 for more information on the Droid X battery.

➤ The Droid X doesn't have or use a SIM card. Other cellphones use one to access the cellular network. The SIM, which stands for Subscriber Identity Module, identifies the phone and does other things you need not care about.

Using other phone accessories

The Droid X has available various optional accessories you can buy to enhance your mobile communications experience. In addition to various cases, holsters, and charms, two accessories worth considering are the multimedia docking station and the car mount.

The multimedia docking station

In a nutshell, the *multimedia docking station* is a base into which you can set the phone. The station features both USB and HDMI connections so that the phone can recharge inside the docking station as well as communicate with a computer or HD television.

When the Droid X is set inside the multimedia docking station, it runs a special clock application, which displays the current time and provides access to the phone's weather, music, slide show, and alarm clock features.

The multimedia docking station, which makes a helpful home for the phone (see the next section), can be used as a bedside alarm or, when connected to a stereo system, to delight you with its music.

➤ The multimedia docking station can be purchased at the same place where you obtained your Droid X or at any location where cellphone goodies are sold.

➤ When you buy the multimedia docking station, you get the handsome, high-tech-looking base and a USB cable, plus a power adapter.

➤ See Chapter 18 for more information about using your state-of-the-art cellphone as a digital clock.

➤ Chapter 17 covers playing music on the Droid X.

➤ Viewing slide shows and managing pictures with the Droid X are covered in Chapter 16.

Car mount

I suppose you don't have to use the car mount inside a car. It has a cradle for the Droid X on one end and, when properly assembled, a suction cup on the other. You could probably stick it to any flat surface, but it's a *car* mount, so I assume that it will stick to the windshield or dashboard of your favorite auto.

When you stick the Droid X into the car mount, the phone automatically switches to the Car Home screen, shown in Figure 1-5. You can read more about this screen in Chapter 3, which is your basic Droid X operations chapter.

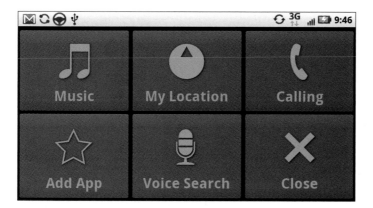

Figure 1-5: The Car Home screen.

A car charger is also available for use with the car mount. It's one of those gizmos that plugs into what was once called a cigarette lighter. The other end of the car charger plugs into your Droid X, which can be nestled in the car mount or just rattling loose inside your vehicle.

The car mount also comes with an AUX audio cable. You can plug that cable into an AUX input jack on your car radio so that you can use the car's speakers to hear your music and other noises that the Droid X makes.

✔ Yes, you can use the car charger without having to use the car mount.

✔ The car charger also features a USB connector, which can be used to power other USB devices you may tote along in your car.

✔ Gizmos such as the car charger are also available separately. Ensure that you find one that features a micro–USB connector.

✔ For the suction cup on the car mount to work properly, use a hard, flat, smooth surface. An adhesive plastic disk comes with the car mount. Use it to ensure that the suction cup has a solid surface to suck on.

✔ The Car Home screen may change when the Android operating system is updated. The new screen offers the same features but might appear differently from the one shown in Figure 1-5.

✔ The official name for the car mount is the Navigation/Music Vehicle Mount.

A Home for Your Phone

Where I grew up, the phone was always in the kitchen, on the wall. I remember that great day when my folks added a line in the living room — and then in the bedroom! You could even plug in an extension cord and take the phone outside to talk. Man, we were kings.

After charging the battery in your Droid X, you can take it anywhere. Even so, I recommend keeping a home for your phone when you're not roaming about, even if that home is in your purse or pocket.

Carrying the Droid X

The Droid X isn't the smallest cellphone, but it can still fit into a pocket or even the teensiest of party purses. It's well designed, so you can carry your phone in your pocket or purse without fear that something will accidentally turn it on, dial Mongolia, and run up a heck of a cellphone bill.

Because the Droid X features a proximity sensor, you can even keep the phone in your pocket while you're on a call or listening to music on headphones. The proximity sensor disables the touchscreen, which ensures that nothing accidentally is touched when you don't want it to be touched.

- Though it's okay to place the phone somewhere when you're making a call, be careful not to touch the phone's Power button (refer to Figure 1-3). Doing so may temporarily enable the touchscreen, which can hang up a call or mute the phone or do any of a number of other undesirable things.

- You can always store the Droid X in one of a variety of handsome carrying case accessories, some of which come in fine Naugahyde or leatherette.

- Don't forget that the phone is in your pocket, especially when it's in your coat or jacket. You might accidentally sit on the phone, or it can fly out when you take off your coat. The worst fate for the Droid X, or any cellphone, is to take a trip through the wash. I'm sure the phone has nightmares about it happening.

Storing the Droid X

I recommend that you find a place for your phone when you're not taking it with you. Make the spot consistent: on top of your desk or workstation, in the kitchen, on the nightstand — you get the idea. Phones are as prone to loss as your car keys and glasses, so consistency is the key to keeping and finding your phone in one spot.

Then again, your phone does ring, so when you lose it, you can always have someone else call your number to help you locate the phone.

- I keep the Droid X on my desk, next to my computer. Conveniently, I have the charger plugged into the computer, so I keep it plugged in, connected, and charging when I'm not using it.

- Phones on coffee tables get buried under magazines and often squished when rude people put their feet on the furniture.

- Avoid putting the Droid X in direct sunlight; heat is a bad thing for any electronic gizmo.

- Do not wash your phone in the laundry (see the preceding section). See Chapter 22 for information on properly cleaning the phone.

Setup and Configuration

I don't remember my parents ever having to fuss with setting up a new phone. After the guy from the Telephone Company left, the phone just worked. Then came our first answering machine, thus ushering in the current era of confusing features to set up and configure for a telephone.

The Droid X is more than just a telephone, and it's seriously a lot more than a cellphone. It's a *communications device.* It chats with the Internet, pays attention to satellites orbiting the earth, takes pictures and video, plays music, and does lots more things that I write about elsewhere in this book. To make all that stuff work requires a modicum of setup. It's not that difficult, but also not that obvious. This chapter helps you set up the options on your Droid X and describes the basic steps for turning it on and off.

Hello, Phone

One of the most basic operations for any gizmo is turning it on. Don't bother looking for an on–off switch: The Droid X doesn't have one. Instead, it has a *Power button.* It can be used in several ways, which is why I had to write this section to explain things.

Before you can turn on the phone, the battery must be installed. See Chapter 1.

Turning on the Droid X for the first time

To turn on the Droid X for the first time, press the Power button. You see some fancy graphics and animation. After a moment, you hear the phone say, in a robotic voice, "Droid!" Don't be alarmed. Well, at least that greeting is better than when you turn on one of those inexpensive phones and it greets you with, "You skinflint."

When you turn on your phone the first time, you have to do some setup. This required step may have been done by the folks who sold you the Droid X. If not, you can follow along here when you start the phone and the Android character prompts you to get started:

1. **Obey the instructions on the touchscreen display and touch the Android icon.**

    Instructions appear, describing your new phone and some things you can learn. Read them if you want, or just pretend to read them. There will be no test.

2. **If your Droid X has not yet been activated, you'll be directed to do so: Touch the Activate button and follow the directions on the screen.**

    You'll need to make a phone call to activate the phone. Touch the Speaker button so that you can hear the phone and use the touchscreen to input information.

    After activation, you can touch the Next button to proceed with the tutorial.

3. **Touch the Begin button to read about your phone.**

4. **Continue working through the directions on the screen.**

    You'll be asked to create or sign in to your Google account. I recommend that you do so: It's a good idea to have a Google account with your phone, especially because it says "with Google™" on the back. You just get a lot more out of the Droid X when you have the account.

    Using your computer to set up a Google account is easier than using the phone. See the later section "Account and Synchronization Setup" for more information on using a Google account with the Droid X.

    If you have multiple Google accounts, sign in to the phone using the primary account or the one that has the calendar you use most often.

5. **Touch the first text field where you enter your Google account name.**

    A keyboard appears at the bottom of the touchscreen.

6. **Use the onscreen keyboard to type your Google account name.**

    The Google account name is also the first part of your Gmail email account. For example, my Gmail account name is `dan.gookin`.

Touch the onscreen keyboard's Delete button, labeled DEL, to back up if you make a mistake.

7. **Touch the Password text box.**

8. **Type your Google account password.**

Each character in the password appears briefly as you type it, and then the character turns into a black dot, so pay attention to what you type!

Touch the keyboard's Shift key to display capital letters. The *Shift key* is the upward-pointing arrow near the lower left corner of the onscreen keyboard.

Touch the keyboard's Symbols key, labeled ?123, to see numbers and a smattering of other symbols that might dwell in your Google account password.

9. **Touch the Sign In button.**

If you can't see the Sign In button, touch the Done button on the keyboard or, if that button isn't available, touch the Back soft button, found at the bottom of the touchscreen (and shown in the margin).

You may have to wait a while for everything to sync up.

10. **If prompted, choose whether you want to use Google locations.**

You do, but you can always change this option later, after you use the phone and figure out what it means.

11. **Touch the Next button.**

12. **Touch the Finish Setup button.**

You'll be asked whether you want to use Backup Assistant.

13. **For now, touch the Skip button.**

You can read more about Backup Assistant in Chapter 22, where you can sign up for that feature.

The next screen allows you to set up other accounts for the Droid X, such as a non-Gmail email account, Facebook, Twitter, Yahoo!, and so on.

Other chapters in this book offer details on how to configure those accounts. For example, see Chapter 10 for information on setting up email; see Chapter 12 for information on setting up Facebook and Twitter.

14. **Touch the Done Adding Accounts button.**

You're now ready to start using your Droid X.

After the initial setup, you're taken to the Home screen. Chapter 3 offers more information about the Home screen, which you should probably read right away, before the temptation to play with the Droid X becomes unbearable.

- ✔ If you have more than one Google account, you have to manually add it after you initially configure your Droid X. See the later section "Setting up a Google account on your phone."

- ✔ The Droid X works closely with your Google account, sharing information you have on the Internet for your email and contacts on Gmail, appointments on Google Calendar, and other Google applications.

- ✔ A Google account is free. Google makes bazillions of dollars by selling advertising on the Web, so it doesn't charge you for your Google account or any of the fine services it offers.

- ✔ You will find that your phone has automatically synced with your Google account after its initial setup. Your contacts, calendar appointments, and Google Talk pals will already be configured for you on your Droid X.

- ✔ You can also configure your phone to work with other information sharing services, such as those offered by your company or organization. See the section "Configuring the Droid X for corporate use," later in this chapter.

Turning on the phone

Unlike turning on the phone for the first time, turning it on after that isn't complex. In fact, you probably won't turn off the phone much under normal circumstances. After you turn it off, you turn it on again by pressing and releasing the Power button, found atop the phone.

After you press the Power button, the phone turns itself on. You see the Droid X logo and animation, and the phone may scream "Droid" at you. Eventually, you're plopped into an unlocking screen.

The main unlocking screen is shown in Figure 2-1. To access your phone, use your finger to slide the green padlock icon to the right.

If you've added more security, you see one of two additional unlocking screens. One type uses a pattern lock, shown in Figure 2-2. Drag your finger over the dots on the screen, duplicating the pattern you've preset. Only by dragging over the dots in the proper sequence does the phone unlock.

Slide to the right to unlock the phone.

Slide to the left to silence the phone.

Figure 2-1: Unlocking the phone.

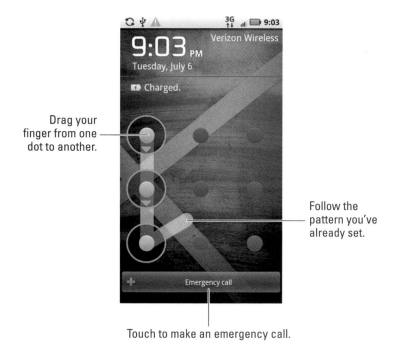

Drag your finger from one dot to another.

Follow the pattern you've already set.

Touch to make an emergency call.

Figure 2-2: Inputting the phone's security pattern.

Another type of unlocking screen uses a *PIN*, or secret number, which must be input before you're allowed access to the phone. Type the number using the keypad. Touch the check mark button to accept, as shown in Figure 2-3.

Back up and erase

Touch to accept.

Touch to make an emergency call.

Figure 2-3: Typing the phone's PIN.

Eventually you see the Home screen, which is where you control the phone and run applications and do all sorts of other interesting things. The Home screen is covered in Chapter 3.

- After unlocking the phone, you may hear some alerts or see notifications. These messages inform you of various events going on in the phone, such as new email, scheduled appointments, updates, and more. See Chapter 3 for information on notifications.

- The screen lock (refer to Figure 2-1) can be disabled. Refer to Chapter 21.

- The security screens (refer to Figures 2-2 and 2-3) add an extra level of protection in case the phone is ever lost or stolen. You can choose the pattern lock, a PIN, or opt not to have a security screen. See Chapter 21 for information on setting up extra security for your Droid X.

- Even if the phone has a security pattern, you can still make emergency calls: Touch the Emergency Call button.

- For information on turning off the phone, see the section "Turning off the phone," later in this chapter.

TECHNICAL STUFF

There's an android in your phone

You might see or hear the term *android* used in association with your phone. That's because your phone, like your computer, has an *operating system,* the main program in charge of a computer's hardware. The operating system controls everything. On the Droid X, the operating system is Android.

The Android operating system was developed by Google. Well, actually, it was developed by another company, which Google gobbled. Anyway: Android is based on the popular Linux operating system, used to power desktop computers and larger, more expensive computers all over the world. Android offers a version of Linux customized for mobile devices, such as the Droid X but also Google's own Nexus One phone as well as many other phones I can't think of right now.

Because the Droid X uses the Android operating system, your phone has access to thousands of software programs. The process of putting these programs on your phone is covered in Chapter 19.

Waking the phone

Most of the time, you don't turn off your phone. Instead, the phone does the electronic equivalent of falling asleep. Either it falls asleep on its own (after you've ignored it for a while) or you put it to sleep by singing it a lullaby or following the information in the section "Snoozing the phone," later in this chapter.

In Sleep mode, the phone is still on and can still receive calls (as well as email and other notifications), but the touchscreen is turned off.

The phone wakes itself when it receives a call; you see the unlock screen, similar to the one shown earlier, in Figure 2-1, though information about the caller appears on the touchscreen: Slide the unlock tab to the right to unlock and answer the phone.

When the phone isn't ringing, you can wake it up at any time by pressing the Power button. A simple, short press is all that's needed. The phone wakes up, yawns, and turns on the touchscreen display, and you can then unlock the phone, as described in the preceding section.

- Touching the touchscreen when it's off doesn't wake the phone.
- Pressing the camera shutter button while the phone is sleeping doesn't wake the phone.

✔ Pressing the Home soft button (shown in the margin) wakes the phone, though none of the other soft buttons wakes the phone.

✔ The camera shutter button doesn't wake the phone.

✔ Loud noises don't wake the phone.

✔ The phone doesn't snore while it's sleeping.

✔ See the section "Snoozing the phone," later in this chapter, for information on manually putting the phone to sleep.

✔ When the Droid X is playing music, which it can do while it's sleeping, information about the song appears on the unlocking screen (not shown in Figure 2-1). You also find controls to play and pause or to skip to the next or previous song. See Chapter 17 for more information on using the Droid X to play music.

Account and Synchronization Setup

After initially turning on your phone and getting things configured, you're ready to go. Well, unless you opted to skip the account synchronization step or you just didn't have a chance to synchronize the proper accounts. Don't fret! The Droid X welcomes your ability to procrastinate, by providing more account synchronization options, as described in this section.

Opening a Google account

It really, *really,* helps to have a Google account to get the most from your Droid X phone. If you don't have a Google account, run — don't walk or mince — to a computer and follow these steps to create your own Google account.

1. **Open the computer's Web browser program.**

2. **Visit the main Google page at `www.google.com`.**

   Type **www.google.com** on the Web browser's address bar.

3. **Click the Sign In link.**

   Another page opens, where you can log in to your Google account. You don't have a Google account, so:

4. **Click the link to create a new account.**

   The link is typically found beneath the text boxes where you would log in to your Google account. As I write this chapter, the link is labeled Create an Account Now.

5. **Continue heeding the directions until you've created your own Google account.**

Eventually, your account is set up and configured. I recommend that you log off and then log back in to Google, just to ensure that you did everything properly. Also, create a bookmark for your account's Google page: Pressing Ctrl+D or Command+D does that job in just about any Web browser.

Continue reading in the next section for information on synchronizing your new Google account with the Droid X.

> ✔ A Google account gives you access to a wide array of free services and online programs. They include Gmail for electronic messaging, Calendar for scheduling and appointments, the online picture-sharing program Picasa, an account on YouTube, Google Finance, blogs, Google Buzz, and other features that are instantly shared with your phone.
>
> ✔ Information on using the various Google programs on your phone is covered throughout this book; specifically, in Part IV.

Setting up a Google account on your phone

The only time you need to set up a Google account for your Droid X is when you neglect to initially set up the account when you first buy the phone, when you postpone setup, or when you add a second Google account to the one you already have. If you have the Google account already set up, great: Work through the steps in this section.

If you haven't yet configured a Google account, follow the steps in the preceding section and then continue with these steps:

1. **Go to the Home screen.**

   The Home screen is the Droid X main screen. Get there by pressing the Home soft button, found at the bottom of the touchscreen.

2. **Press the Menu soft button.**

   The Menu soft button is found below the touchscreen; its icon is shown in the margin.

3. **Touch Settings.**

   The Settings window is where you configure many of the Droid X features and program options.

4. **Choose Accounts.**

5. **Touch the Add Account button.**

6. **Choose Google.**

7. **Read the screen and touch the Next button.**

8. **If you've already read the preceding section and have created your Google account on a computer, touch the Sign In button.**

   Yes, it's possible to create a Google account using your phone and not a computer. It's just easier to use a computer. Trust me.

9. **Touch the Username text box.**

   The onscreen keyboard appears.

10. **Input your Google account username.**

11. **Touch the Password text box.**

12. **Input your Google account password.**

    Refer to the suggestions in Step 10 in the earlier section "Turning on the Droid X for the first time" for help on inputting your Google password.

13. **Touch the Sign In button.**

    If you need to, click the Done button on the onscreen keyboard so that you can see and touch the Sign In button.

    Wait while Google contacts your account and synchronizes any information. It takes longer when you have more information for Google to synchronize.

    And you're done.

After you touch the Sign In button, you return to the main Setup Accounts window. You can press the Home soft button to return to the Home screen. You're done setting up the Droid X for synchronization with your Google account.

   ✔ See Chapter 3 for more information about the Home screen.

   ✔ You can also add other accounts for synchronizing, such as Facebook, Twitter, and Skype Mobile. Other chapters in this book cover the specifics.

Changing your Google password

Experts say that you should change your computer passwords often. How often? Well, I know of some government agencies where the password changes every 90 seconds. You don't need to be that severe with your Google account password.

When you change your Google password, do so on your computer first. Then you have to inform the Droid X. If you don't, your phone complains that it cannot access Google to update and synchronize information. Follow these steps to reset your Google password:

1. **On your desktop computer, direct the Web browser to the Google main page: Type** www.google.com.

2. **From the top of the page, click the Settings link.**

   As I write this chapter, the link is found in the upper right part of the page.

3. **Choose Google Account Settings from the Settings link menu.**

4. **By the Security heading, click the Change Password link.**

5. **Obey the directions on the screen for setting a new password.**

   Now that the password is reset, you need to update the Droid X with that information. If you don't, the phone pesters you incessantly. Continue with these steps:

6. **Wake up or turn on your Droid X.**

   In a few moments, your phone generates a notification. You see an Alert icon appear on top of the phone's display, in the notification area.

7. **Slide down the notification area by swiping it with your finger.**

   The specifics for performing this action are covered in Chapter 3.

8. **From the list of notifications, choose Sign-In Error.**

   The text *Sign-In Error* is followed by the name of your Google account.

9. **Type the new Google password into the box that appears on the touch-screen display.**

   Refer to information in the earlier sections "Turning on the Droid X for the first time" and "Setting up a Google account on your phone" for more information on typing your Google account password.

10. **Touch the Sign In button.**

After you enter the new password, the phone instantly becomes happy and continues to sync the Google account information.

Press the Home soft button to return to the Home screen.

Configuring the Droid X for corporate use

To access your various work accounts, you need to set up your Droid X for synchronizing with your corporate Exchange Server account. Syncing puts the phone on speaking terms with your corporate email and calendar programs and other information sources. Obviously, this process is something that mere individuals need not bother with; only the suits need to pay attention.

First of all, if your company is *really* big, you probably have someone do all the account setup for you. In fact, they might even apply special restrictions to the Droid X, prohibiting you from doing innocent, diversionary things, such as play games or visit online casinos. Regardless, those digital martinets will probably do the setup for you, or have instructions ready. Defy them at your own peril.

To set up the Droid X on your own, follow these steps:

1. **From the Home screen, touch the Menu soft button.**

2. **Touch the Settings icon to open the Settings screen.**

3. **Choose Accounts.**

4. **Touch the Add Account button at the bottom of the screen.**

5. **Choose Corporate Sync.**

6. **If prompted, agree to the service terms.**

    After agreeing to the terms, you see a screen full of text boxes into which you type all sorts of interesting information. The information is supplied to you from your organization's IT or IS department. Bug them for details.

7. **Fill in the various text fields with information about your corporate sync account.**

8. **Touch the Next button.**

    Continue as the Droid X attempts to contact your organization's mother ship.

9. **Touch the Finish button.**

You're done. Of course, other things may or may not happen at this point, depending on the information shared on your corporate network and how you use the Droid X to access that information.

You can press the Home soft button to return to the Home screen, from whence you may do other interesting things with your Droid X.

Goodbye, Phone

There are three ways to dismiss your Droid X from existence. The first way is to put the phone to sleep — to *snooze* it. The second is to turn off the phone. The third involves an elephant wearing electric cheese graters for boots and, because of space constraints and unreasonable elephant rental fees, isn't covered in this edition of the book.

Snoozing the phone

To snooze the phone, press and release the Power button. No matter what you're doing, the phone's display turns off. The phone itself isn't off, but the touchscreen display is dark. The phone enters a low-power state to save battery life, and also to relax.

- You can snooze the phone while you're making a call. Simply press and release the Power button. The phone stays connected, but the display is turned off.

- Your Droid X will probably spend most of its time in Snooze mode.

- Snoozing doesn't turn off the phone; you can still receive calls while it's asleep.

- Snooze mode allows you to keep talking on the phone while you put it in your pocket. In Snooze mode, there's no danger that your pocket will accidentally hang up or mute the phone in the middle of a call.

- Any timers or alarms you set still activate when the phone is snoozing. See Chapter 18 for information on setting timers and alarms.

- To wake up the phone, press and release the Power button. See the section "Waking the phone," earlier in this chapter.

- Snoozing the phone doesn't stop any music from playing. See Chapter 17 for more information on using the Droid X as a portable music player.

Controlling snooze options

There's no need to manually snooze your Droid X. That's because it has a built-in timeout: After a period of inactivity, or boredom, the phone snoozes itself automatically — just like Uncle Bob after Thanksgiving dinner.

You have control over the snooze timeout value, which can be set anywhere from 15 seconds to 30 minutes. Obey these steps:

1. **While viewing the Home screen, press the Menu soft button.**

2. **Choose Settings from the menu.**

3. **Choose Display.**

   If your Droid X hasn't yet been updated to the Android 2.2 operating system, choose the Sound & Display item instead.

4. **Scroll down the list and choose Screen Timeout.**

5. **Choose a timeout value from the list provided.**

   The standard value is 1 minute.

6. **Press the Home soft button to return to the Home screen.**

When you don't touch the screen or use the phone for a while, the sleep timer starts ticking. About ten seconds before the timeout value you set (refer to Step 5), the touchscreen dims. Then it goes to sleep. If you touch the screen before then, the sleep timer is reset.

Turning off the phone

To turn off your phone, follow these steps:

1. **Press and hold the Power button.**

   Eventually, you see the Phone Options menu, shown in Figure 2-4.

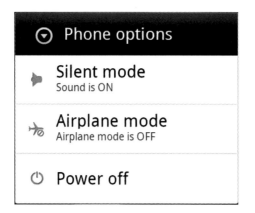

Figure 2-4: The Phone Options menu.

2. **Choose the Power Off item.**

3. **Touch the OK button to confirm.**

   Off goes the phone, crying out "Droid" as it goes.

The phone doesn't receive calls when it's turned off. Those calls go instead to voice mail: either the voice mail you set up with your cellular service or Visual Voicemail. See Chapter 7 for more information on voice mail.

If you change your mind and don't want to shut down the phone, press the Back soft button to cancel. (After Step 1, above.)

3

The Basic Droid X Tour

In This Chapter

▶ Working the touchscreen

▶ Changing the phone's volume

▶ Entering Vibration mode or Silence mode

▶ Using the phone horizontally

▶ Checking notifications

▶ Running applications and working widgets

▶ Finding applications

▶ Accessing recently used apps

*P*erhaps in the future, when robots are more popular than cellphones, a *Droid X tour* would take place when you first unpacked your new robot. It would introduce its various parts and functions, and be oh-so-very helpful and cheery — that is, before all the robots turn on humanity and enslave us for our own good. That's scary, but at least setting up the robots initially wouldn't be frustrating.

Your cellphone isn't science fiction, and therefore it lacks the inherent dangers of a race of zealous robots. As something new, however, it can pose some frustrations. To help ease you on your way, I'm offering this chapter as your beginning Droid X orientation and guide. Here, you'll read about your phone's interface, how it works, and how to get the most from your new phone experience.

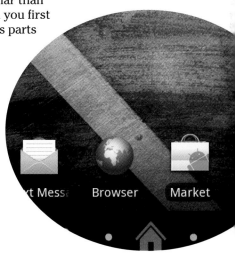

Basic Droid X Operations

The Droid X is most likely different from any other phone you've owned. As such, you should familiarize yourself with certain operations — basic things the phone does that you may not be aware of.

Using the soft buttons

Below the touchscreen are four buttons labeled with four icons. These *soft buttons* perform specific functions no matter what you're doing with the phone. Table 3-1 lists the soft-button functions.

Table 3-1		Droid X Soft-Button Functions		
Button	**Name**	**Press Once**	**Press Twice**	**Press and Hold**
▣	Menu	Display menu	Dismiss menu	Nothing
🏠	Home	Go to Home screen, display applications, or wake the phone	Voice command	Recent applications
↰	Back	Go back, close, dismiss keyboard	Nothing	Nothing
🔍	Search	Open phone and Web search	Nothing	Search-by-voice function

Not every soft button always performs the actions listed in Table 3-1. For example, if there's no menu to open, pressing the Menu soft button does nothing.

Pressing the Home soft button always takes you to the main Home screen (the center one) — unless you're viewing the main Home screen, in which case pressing the Home soft button displays the Application Tray. See the later section "The Applications Tray" for more information.

✔ Various sections throughout this book give examples of using the soft buttons.

✔ You can configure what happens on your Droid X when you press the Home soft button twice. Refer to Chapter 21 for more information.

Manipulating the touchscreen

The touchscreen works in combination with one or two of your fingers. You can choose which fingers to use, or whether to be adventurous and try using the tip of your nose, but touch the touchscreen you must. Choose from several techniques:

Touch: In this simple operation, you touch the screen. Generally, you're touching an object, such as a program icon or a button, or a control, such as a gizmo you use to slide something around.

Double-tap: Touch the screen in the same location twice. Double-tapping can be used to zoom in on an image or a map, but it can also zoom out. Because of the double-tap's dual nature, I recommend using the pinch or spread operation instead.

The long press: Touch and hold part of the screen. Some operations on the Droid X, such as moving an icon on the Home screen, begin with a long press.

Swipe: When you swipe, you start with your finger in one spot and then drag it to another spot. Usually, swipes are up, down, left, or right, which moves material displayed in the direction you swipe your finger. Swipes can be fast, flick-like actions, or they can be slow. This operation is also known as a *flick*.

Pinch: A pinch involves two fingers, which start out separated and then are brought together. The effect is used to enlarge or reduce an image or a map. The pinch is used to zoom out.

Spread: In the opposite of a pinch, you start out with your fingers together and then spread them. The spread is used to zoom in.

You cannot use the touchscreen while wearing gloves, unless they're gloves specially designed for using an electronic touchscreen.

Setting the volume

The phone's volume controls are found on the right side of the phone as it's facing you. Press the top part of the button to set the volume higher. Press the bottom part of the button to lower the volume.

The volume controls work for whatever noise the phone is making at the time: When you're on the phone, the volume controls set the level of the incoming phone call. When you're listening to music or watching a video, the volume controls set that media volume.

Volume can be preset for the phone, media, and notifications. See Chapter 21 for information.

"Silence your phone!"

You can't be a citizen of the 21st century and not have heard the admonition "Please silence your cellphones." Here's how to obey that command with your Droid X phone:

1. **Wake up the phone.**

   Obviously, if the phone is turned off, there's no need to turn it on just to make it silent. So, assuming that your phone is snoozing, press the Power button to see the main screen (refer to Figure 2-1, in Chapter 2).

2. **Slide the Silencer button to the left.**

   You're good.

When you're using the phone and someone demands that you silence it, press and hold the Power button until you see the Phone Options menu. From that menu, choose Silent Mode.

- You can also silence the Droid X by setting the volume all the way down to zero: After you press the Volume Down button one more time, the phone automatically enters Vibration mode.

- When the phone is in Vibration mode, the Vibration Mode status icon appears on the status bar, as shown in the margin.

- To make the phone noisy again, repeat the steps in this section but slide the Silencer button to the right.

- If you're concerned about missing a call, activate the phone's Vibration mode. For details, see the section about setting incoming call signals in Chapter 5.

- When the phone is silenced, the Ringer Is Silenced icon appears on the status bar.

- Also see Chapter 21, which covers all the options for silencing the Droid X, including the double-tap and face-down features.

Going horizontal

The Droid X features an *accelerometer* gizmo. It's used by various programs in the phone to determine in which direction the phone is pointed or whether you've reoriented the phone from an upright to a horizontal position.

The easiest way to see how the vertical-horizontal orientation feature works is to view a Web page on your Droid X. Obey these steps:

1. **Touch the Browser application on the Home screen.**

   The Droid X launches its Web browser program, venturing out to the Internet. Eventually, the browser's first page, its *home* page, appears on the touchscreen.

2. **Tilt the Droid X to the left.**

   As shown in Figure 3-1, the Web page reorients itself to the new, horizontal way of looking at the Web. For some applications, this method is truly the best way to see things.

Landscape orientation

Portrait orientation

Figure 3-1: Vertical and horizontal orientations.

3. Tilt the phone upright again.

The Web page redisplays itself in its original, upright mode.

Unless you haven't updated the software on your Droid X, landscape orientation works only when the phone is tilted to the left (refer to Figure 3-1). Future releases of the Android operating system allow the phone to be tilted to the left or right for Landscape mode.

Oh, and don't bother turning the phone upside down and expect the image to flip that way, though some applications may delight you by supporting that feature.

- ✔ See Chapter 11 for more information on using your phone to browse the Web.

- ✔ Some applications switch their view from portrait to landscape orientation whenever you tilt the phone. Most applications, however, are fixed to portrait orientation.

- ✔ Some applications present themselves only in Landscape view, such as the YouTube application when playing a video.

 ✔ A great application for demonstrating the Droid X accelerometer is the game *Labyrinth*. You can purchase it at the Android Market or download the free version, *Labyrinth Lite*. See Chapter 19 for more information on the Android Market.

There's No Screen Like Home

The first thing you see after you unlock your Droid X is the *Home* screen, illustrated in Figure 3-2. The Home screen is also the location you go to whenever you end a call or quit an application.

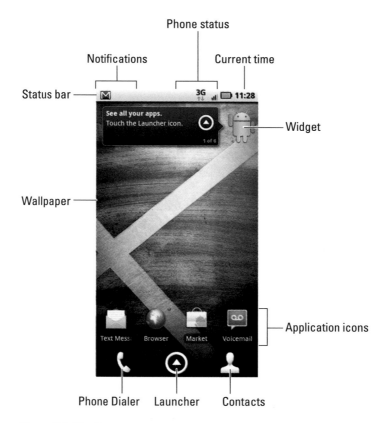

Figure 3-2: The Home screen.

Here are the key items to notice on the Home screen (refer to Figure 3-2):

Status bar: The top of the Home screen is a thin, informative strip I call the *status bar.* It contains notification icons and status icons, plus the current time.

Notification icons: These icons come and go, depending on what happens in your digital life. For example, a new icon appears whenever you receive a new email message or have a pending appointment. The section "Reviewing notifications," later in this chapter, describes how to deal with notifications.

Status icons: These icons represent the phone's current condition, such as the type of network it's connected to, its signal strength, and its battery status, as well as whether the speaker has been muted or a Wi-Fi network is connected.

Widgets: A *widget* is a teensy program that can display information, let you control the phone, access features, or do something purely amusing. You can read more about widgets in Chapter 21.

Application icons: The meat of the meal on the Home screen plate is the collection of application icons. Touching an icon runs the program.

Launcher: Touching the Launcher button icon displays the Applications Tray, a scrolling list of all applications installed on your phone. The section "The Applications Tray," later in this chapter, describes how it works.

And now, the secret: The Home screen is seven times wider than what you see on the front of your Droid X. It has left and right wings to the Home screen, as illustrated in Figure 3-3.

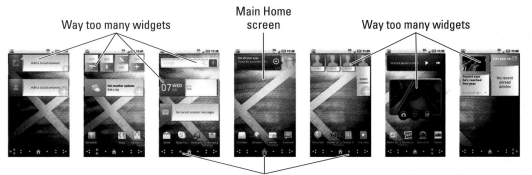

Figure 3-3: All the Home screens.

To view the left and right sides of the Home screen, swipe your finger left or right across the touchscreen display. The Home screen slides over one page in each direction every time you swipe.

The wider Home screen gives you more opportunities to place applications and widgets. As shown in Figure 3-3, the Droid X Home screens hold a lot of widgets. Refer to Chapter 21 for information about deleting widgets you don't need and for other information about customizing the Home screen.

> ✏ Touching part of the Home screen that doesn't feature an icon or a control doesn't do anything — unless you're using the *Live Wallpaper* feature. In that case, touching the screen changes the wallpaper in some

way, depending on the selected wallpaper. You can read more about Live Wallpaper in Chapter 21.

✔ The variety of notification and status icons is broad. You see the icons referenced in appropriate sections throughout this book.

✔ No matter which part of the Home screen you're viewing, the top part of the touchscreen stays the same — the status bar always displays notification and status icons and the time.

✔ To return to the Home screen at any time, press the Home soft button.

I've Been Working on the Home Screen

I recommend getting to know three basic Home screen operations: reviewing notifications, starting applications, and accessing widgets.

Reviewing notifications

Notifications appear as icons at the top of the Home screen, as illustrated earlier, in Figure 3-2. To see the actual notifications, peel down the top part of the screen, as shown in Figure 3-4.

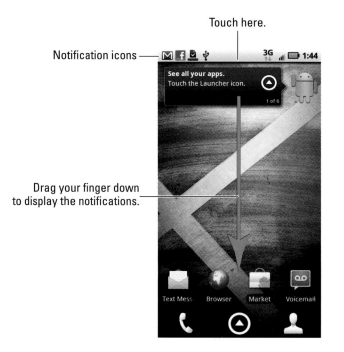

Touch here.

Notification icons

Drag your finger down to display the notifications.

Figure 3-4: Accessing notifications.

The operation works like this:

1. **Touch the notification icons at the top of the touchscreen.**

2. **Swipe your finger all the way down the front of the touchscreen.**

   This action works like controlling a roll-down blind: You grab the top part of the touchscreen and drag it downward all the way. The notifications panel appears, as shown in Figure 3-5.

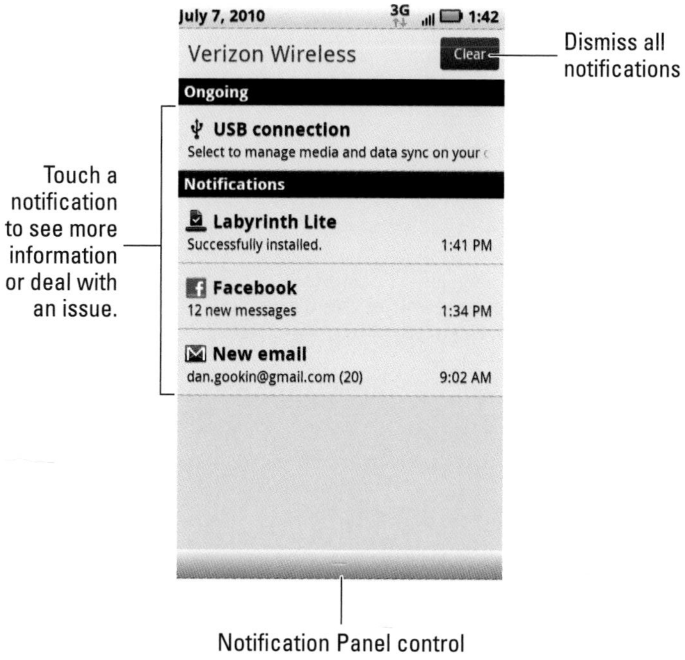

July 7, 2010   3G ⬆⬇ ▯▯▯ ▭ 1:42 — Dismiss all notifications

Verizon Wireless   Clear

Ongoing

Ψ **USB connection**
Select to manage media and data sync on your

Notifications

Touch a notification to see more information or deal with an issue. —

🖥 **Labyrinth Lite**
Successfully installed.   1:41 PM

📘 **Facebook**
12 new messages   1:34 PM

✉ **New email**
dan.gookin@gmail.com (20)   9:02 AM

Notification Panel control

Figure 3-5: The notifications panel.

You may need to drag the notification panel all the way to the bottom of the touchscreen to prevent it from rolling back up again. Use the notification panel control to pull it all the way down (refer to Figure 3-5).

3. **Touch a notification to see what's up.**

Touching a notification switches you to the program that generated the icon. For example, touching a Gmail notification displays a new message or your inbox.

If you choose not to touch a notification, you can "roll up" the notification list by sliding the notification panel control back to the top of the touchscreen.

✔ The notification icons don't disappear until you've chosen each one — and sometimes those icons can stack up!

✔ To dismiss all notification icons, touch the Clear button (refer to Figure 3-5).

✔ When more notifications are present than can be shown on the status bar, you see the More Notifications icon displayed, as shown in the margin. The number on the icon indicates how many additional notifications are available.

✔ Dismissing notifications doesn't prevent them from appearing again in the future. For example, notifications to update your programs continue to appear, as do calendar reminders.

✔ Some programs, such as Facebook and the various Twitter apps, don't display notifications unless they're running. See Chapter 12.

✔ When new notifications are available, the Droid X notification light flashes. Refer to Chapter 1 for information on locating the notification light.

✔ See Chapter 18 for information on dismissing calendar reminders.

✔ Notification icons appear on the screen when the phone is locked. Remember that you must unlock the phone before you can drag down the status bar to display notifications.

Starting an application

Running an application on the Home screen is cinchy: Touch its icon. The application starts.

✔ Not all applications appear on the Home screen, but all of them appear when you display the Applications Tray. See the section "The Applications Tray," later in this chapter.

✔ When an application closes or you quit that application, you return to the Home screen.

✔ *Application* is often abbreviated as *app*.

Accessing a widget

A *widget* is a teensy program that floats over the Home screen (refer to Figure 3-3). To use a widget, simply touch it. What happens after that depends on the widget.

For example, touching the Calendar widget displays a list of today's appointments in the Calendar app. Touching the Google widget displays the onscreen keyboard and lets you type, or dictate, something to search for on the Internet. The Power Control widget turns various phone features off or on.

Information on these and other widgets appears elsewhere in this book. See Chapter 21 for information on working with widgets.

Using Car Home

The Droid X features an alternative Home screen, provided for the scary proposition of using your phone while driving an automobile. The Car Home screen (refer to Figure 1-5, in Chapter 1) is designed to be easy to see at a glance and to offer you access to the phone's more popular features without distracting you much from the priority of piloting your car.

The Car Home screen appears automatically whenever your Droid X is nestled into the Car Adapter accessory, discussed in Chapter 1. To see the Car Home manually, you start the Car Dock app: Touch the Launcher button on the Home screen, scroll the list of applications, and touch the Car Dock icon.

The Applications Tray

The place where you find all applications installed on your Droid X is the *Applications Tray*. Though you may find shortcuts to applications (apps) on the Home screen, the Applications Tray is where you go to find *everything*.

Discovering all apps on your phone

To start a program — an *app* — on the Droid X, heed these steps:

1. **Touch the Launcher button on the Home screen.**

   The Launcher is the center button, with a triangle in a circle.

   After touching the Launcher button, you see the Applications Tray, shown in Figure 3-6.

2. **Scroll the list of app icons by swiping your finger up or down.**

3. **Touch an icon to start that app.**

The app that starts takes over the screen and then does whatever good thing it's supposed to do.

The terms *program*, *application*, and *app* all mean the same thing.

Finding lost apps

You'll probably accumulate lots and lots of apps on your Droid X. Eventually, the list that the Applications Tray displays might grow quite long. In fact, you may not even remember the name of the program you're looking for. Either way, it's no problem because you can easily search your phone for any app. Follow these steps:

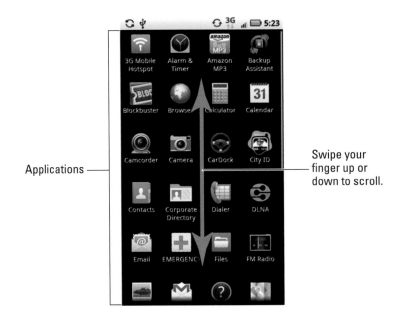

Applications

Swipe your finger up or down to scroll.

Figure 3-6: The Applications tab shows your phone's apps.

1. Press the Search soft button.

The Search screen appears. A search text box appears atop the screen, and the phone's onscreen keyboard appears at the bottom.

2. Use your finger to type all or part of the app's name.

See Chapter 4 for more information on using the onscreen keyboard.

As you type, items matching the text you've typed appear in the list. The items include applications, music, contacts, and even locations on the Internet. When you're looking for a program, you see the text *Application* appear beneath the program name.

3. Scroll the list to explore the apps that have been found.

Use your finger to swipe the list up and down.

4. Touch the name of the app you're looking for.

The app starts.

Searching for apps is a small part of searching for all kinds of information on the Droid X, such as contact information, appointments, and email. Various chapters throughout this book describe other ways you can use the Droid X search function.

See Chapter 19 for information on how to shop the Android Market to find more apps for your phone.

Reviewing your most recently used apps

If you're like me, you probably use the same apps repeatedly, on both your computer and your phone. You can easily access the list of recent programs on the Droid X by pressing and holding the Home soft button. When you do, you see the six most recently accessed programs, similar to the ones shown in Figure 3-7.

Figure 3-7: Recently used apps.

For programs you use all the time, consider creating shortcuts on the Home screen. Chapter 21 describes how to create shortcuts for apps and create shortcuts to people and shortcuts for instant messaging and all sorts of fun stuff.

Future releases of the Android operating system may present more than just six recently-used apps when you press and hold the Home button.

4

Human–Droid Interaction

I would guess that the first droid humanity became familiar with was C-3PO, from the film *Star Wars*. The protocol droid has a shiny, gold body and a tiresome manner. In the film, one of the first things a human said to him was, "Okay, shut up." That doesn't bode well for the beginning of all human–droid interaction.

The Droid X phone you own is the ultimate communications device, kind of like C-3PO but without legs or an annoying personality. Communications takes place not only between you and others on the phone but also between you and the phone itself. This chapter covers that human–phone interaction — specifically, how you can get text into the phone by using the onscreen keyboard or dictation.

Keyboard Mania

To input text information on your phone, you use the *onscreen keyboard*. It looks similar to the keyboard on your computer — or, if you remember seeing Ed Sullivan on live TV, it looks like a typewriter keyboard.

You operate the onscreen keyboard by touching its keys with your finger. That's simple enough, yet I wrote this section to explain the finer points of using the onscreen keyboard.

> ✔ The Droid X also lets you dictate text into your phone. See the section "Voice Input," later in this chapter.
>
> ✔ You can also use the Swype method to type text. See the later section "Take a Swype at the Old Hunt-and-Peck."

Displaying the onscreen keyboard

The *onscreen keyboard* shows up any time the phone demands text as input, such as when you're composing email, typing a text message, or using any application where text is required.

Normally, the onscreen keyboard just pops up — for example, when you touch a text field or an input box on a Web page. Then you start typing with your finger or — if you're good — your thumbs.

The alphabetic version of the onscreen keyboard is shown in Figure 4-1. The keys A through Z (lowercase) are there, plus a Shift/Caps Lock key, Delete key, comma, space, and period.

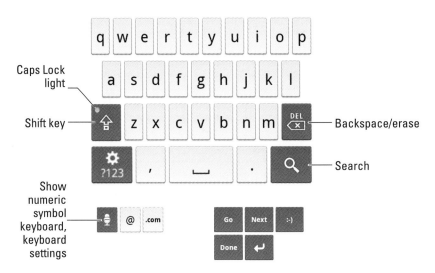

Figure 4-1: The onscreen keyboard.

The Search key changes its look depending on the application. The key's variations are described in Table 4-1.

Table 4-1	Special Keyboard Buttons
Symbol	**What It Does**
🔍	The Search key appears when you're typing text in a Search box or directing the Droid X to find something.
Go	The Go key appears when you're typing text into a single field or text box. This key tells the application that you're done typing and want to proceed as though you pressed the Enter key.
Next	The Next key is used when filling in multiple fields in a form. You can move to the next field, and it comes in handy when you can't see the next field on the touch screen.
Done	The Done key is used to tell the Droid X that you're finished typing and want the keyboard to go away.
↵	The Return key serves the same function as the Return or Enter key on a computer keyboard.
:-)	The :-) key is used when typing text messages to insert a smile (an *emoticon*) into your missive.

The comma key is replaced by the Voice Input button when voice input is available as an alternative to typing text.

The comma key might also be replaced by two keys: the @ symbol key and a key that generates the text .com. Those keys usually show up when you're typing an email address.

Touch the ?123 key to see the number keys as well as the standard punctuation symbols that share those keys on a computer keyboard. That keyboard variation is shown in Figure 4-2.

Pressing the Alt key on the number-and-symbol keyboard displays special symbols, as shown in Figure 4-3. When the Alt key has been pressed, its light turns on, as shown in the figure.

To return to the standard *alpha keyboard* (refer to Figure 4-1), touch the ABC key.

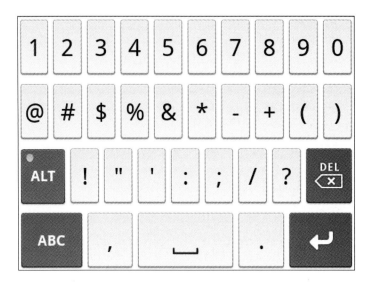

Figure 4-2: The number-and-symbol keyboard.

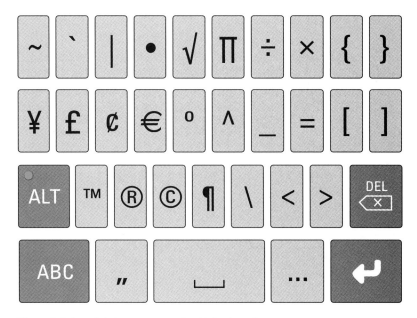

Figure 4-3: Special characters on the Alt keyboard.

✔ Type with your finger first, and then eventually you become good enough to type with your thumbs. Or perhaps not; I still can't thumb-type well.

✔ Some applications show the onscreen keyboard when the phone is in landscape orientation. If so, the keyboard displays the same keys but offers more room for your stump-like fingers to type.

✔ Not every application features a horizontal keyboard, however, so you might be stuck using the narrower version of the keyboard.

✔ See Chapter 21 for information on how to adjust the onscreen keyboard.

Typing on your Droid X

Using the Droid X multitouch keyboard works just as you'd expect: Touch the key you want and that character appears in the program you're using. It's magic! A blinking cursor on the touchscreen shows where new text appears, which is similar to how text input works on your computer.

As you type on the onscreen keyboard, the button you touch appears enlarged on the screen, as shown in Figure 4-4. That's how you can confirm that your fingers are touching the character that you intend to type.

Figure 4-4: Typing the d key.

The characters you type appear in whichever application accepts text input; you see what you type as you type it, just like on a computer. Also, similar to a computer, when you type a password on your phone, the character you type appears briefly on the screen and is then replaced by a black dot.

- When you make a mistake, press the Del key to back up and erase.

- Above all, it helps to *type slowly* until you get used to the keyboard.

- To set the Caps Lock, press the Shift key twice. The little light comes on (refer to Figure 4-1), indicating that Caps Lock is on.

- You can insert an automatic period at the end of a sentence by pressing the space key twice. In fact, pressing the space key twice at any time changes the first space you typed into a period. As a bonus, the next character you type automatically appears in uppercase to start a new sentence.

- People generally accept that typing on a phone isn't perfect. Don't sweat it if you make a few mistakes as you type instant messages or email, though you should expect some curious replies about unintended typos.

- The key that shows both a period and comma produces both characters: Touch the key once to get a period, touch the key twice quickly to get a comma.

- See the later section "Choosing a word as you type" to find out how to deal with automatic typo and spell correction.

- See the later section "Text Editing" for more details on editing your text.

- When you tire of typing, you can always touch the microphone button on the keyboard and enter Dictation mode. See the section "Voice Input," later in this chapter.

- You can also choose to use the Swype input method, which is faster than typing with your fingers — or even your thumbs. See the later section "Take a Swype at the Old Hunt-and-Peck" for details.

Accessing special characters

You can type more characters on your phone than are shown on all three variations of the onscreen keyboard (refer to Figures 4-1 through 4-3). To access those characters, you press and hold a specific key to see a pop-up palette of options.

So, don't think you're getting gypped when you don't see the key you want on the Droid X's multitouch keyboard.

Onscreen keyboard special characters

On the onscreen keyboard, you access special characters by pressing and holding a specific key. When you do, a pop-up palette of options appears, from which you choose a special character.

To determine which keys on the onscreen keyboard sport extra characters, note the ellipsis that appears when you press the key, as shown in the margin. When you press and hold that key (a *long press*), you see the pop-up palette of options, as shown in Figure 4-5. Choose the character you want from that palette or touch the X button to cancel.

Extra characters are available in uppercase as well; press the Shift key before you long-press on the onscreen keyboard.

Certain symbol keys on the onscreen keyboard also sport extra characters. For example, various currency symbols are available when you long-press the $ key. You'll find a host of emoticons available on the Smile key.

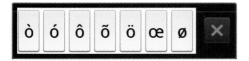

Figure 4-5: Optional characters on the O key.

Choosing a word as you type

As a *smart*phone, the Droid X makes a guess at the words you're typing as you type them. A list of suggestions appears, as shown in Figure 4-6. You can choose a suggestion by touching it with your finger; the word instantly appears on the screen, saving you time (and potentially fixing your terrible spelling or typing, or both).

You can press the space key to automatically choose the word suggestion highlighted in orange (refer to Figure 4-6). That's a good way to save on typing but also the source of miscommunication when the phone guesses wrong on the right word.

Text you've typed   The phone's best guess

Suggestions

More suggestions

Figure 4-6: Suggestions for your lousy typing.

To fix an incorrectly chosen word, use the Del key to back up and erase. Type slower next time.

Take a Swype at the Old Hunt-and-Peck

The Swype utility is designed to let you type like greased lightning on a touchscreen. The secret is that Swype allows you to type without lifting your finger from the keyboard; you literally swipe your finger over the touchscreen to rapidly type words.

Though Swype is an amazing tool, it's not for everyone. It appeals most to the younger crowd, who send text messages like crazy. Still, Swype is a worthy alternative to using the normal onscreen keyboard: Even when you're new and slow with Swype, you'll probably create text faster than doing the old touchscreen hunt-and-peck.

✔ Though Swype may be fast, it's not as fast as using dictation. See the later section "Voice Input."

✔ Don't confuse Swype with Skype, which is a utility you can use to place free phone calls and send instant text messages over the Internet. See Chapter 20 for details on Skype Mobile.

Activating Swype

You can turn on Swype any time you see the onscreen keyboard. Follow these steps:

1. **Press and hold the ?123 button to summon the Multi-Touch Keyboard menu.**

   Refer to Figure 4-1 for the key's location on the keyboard.

2. **Choose Input Method.**

3. **Choose Swype.**

   You may be given the option to view a Swype tutorial; do so, if you're prompted.

After switching to the Swype input method, you see a new keyboard, as shown in Figure 4-7. You're now ready to start using Swype for typing text. Or, rather, for *swyping* text.

Even though Swype is active, you can continue to use your finger (or thumbs) to touch-type on the keyboard. And, as shown in Figure 4-7, you can still use dictation when the Swype keyboard is active.

  ✔ To view the Swype tutorial, press the Swype button on the keyboard (refer to Figure 4-7) and then touch the Tutorial button.

  ✔ See the section "Deactivating Swype" for when you want to return to the standard Droid X onscreen keyboard.

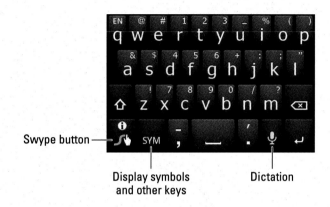

Swype button

Display symbols and other keys

Dictation

Figure 4-7: The Swype keyboard.

Using Swype to create text

The key to using Swype is to not lift your finger from the keyboard. The secret to learning to use Swype is to start slowly; don't worry that the teenager sitting next to you is swyping so fast it looks like he's drawing Chinese characters on the phone.

Your first task in Swype is to learn how to type simple, short words: Keep your finger on the touchscreen and drag it over the letters in the word, such as the word *howdy,* shown in Figure 4-8. Lift your finger when you've completed the word, and the word appears in whichever app you're using.

Capital letters are typed by dragging your finger above the keyboard after touching the letter, as shown in Figure 4-9, where *Idaho* is typed.

Figure 4-8: Swype the word *howdy*.

Figure 4-9: Swyping a capital letter.

To create a double letter, such as the *oo* in *book*, you do a little loop on that key. In Figure 4-10, the word *Hello* is typed, which uses both the capital letter trick and the double-letter trick.

When Swype is confused about the characters you type, a pop-up window appears with word suggestions in it, as shown in Figure 4-11.

Rise above the keyboard
to get a capital letter.

Drag a loop
on a letter
for double
letters.

Figure 4-10: Swyping double letters.

Dismiss
suggestions

View
additional
suggestions

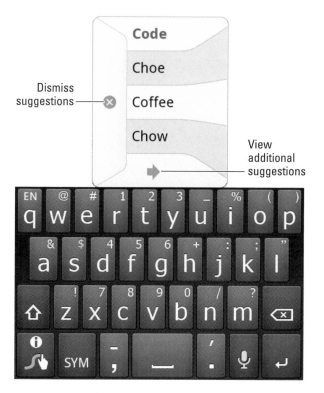

Figure 4-11: Choose the right word.

Choose a suggestion from the list or switch to the alternative suggestions, as illustrated in Figure 4-11.

For more information on Swype typing tips, refer to the tutorial found by touching the Swype button on the keyboard (refer to Figure 4-7).

- ✒ The Swype software interprets your intent as much as it interprets your accuracy. Even being *close to* the target letter is good enough; as long as you create the correct pattern over the keyboard, Swype usually displays the right word.

- ✒ Slow down and you'll get the hang of it.

Deactivating Swype

To return to the normal, onscreen keyboard and disable Swype, follow these steps:

1. **From the Home screen, touch the Launcher button.**

   Up pops the list of applications on your phone.

2. **Choose the Settings icon.**

3. **Choose Language & Keyboard.**

4. **Choose Input Method.**

5. **Choose Multi-Touch Keyboard**

   The onscreen keyboard is activated.

You can press the Home soft button to return to the Home screen when you're done with the Language & Keyboard Settings window.

Text Editing

Editing is the part of writing where you admit that nothing <ahem> reads good the first time. Though you may not be editing on your cellphone for content reasons, you'll probably want to fix the typos and ensure that the automatic word selection thing did its job properly. Happily, editing on the Droid X works well.

Moving the cursor

The first task in editing text is to move the *cursor,* that blinking vertical line where text appears, to the right spot. To move the cursor, simply touch that part of the text where you want the cursor to blink. This method works, but because your finger is probably fatter than the spot where you want the cursor, it's not quite effective.

To better position the cursor, touch the screen quickly. A target icon appears where the cursor is located, as shown in the margin. While that icon is visible, touch the screen again right on the icon and keep your finger down. A pop-up magnification bubble appears, which lets you better position the cursor.

If a pop-up menu appears instead of the target option, try again: Press the Back soft button to dismiss the pop-up menu and try again.

Selecting text

If you're familiar with selecting text in a word processor, selecting text on the Droid X works the same. Well, *theoretically,* it works the same: Selected text appears highlighted on the touchscreen. You can then delete, cut, or copy that block of selected text. It's the method of selecting text on a phone that's different.

Start selecting text by pressing and holding — a *long press* — any part of a text screen or input box. When you do, the Edit Text menu appears, as shown in Figure 4-12.

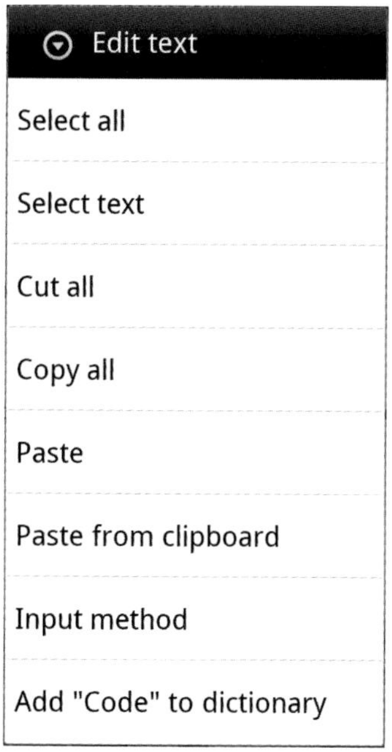

⊙ Edit text
Select all
Select text
Cut all
Copy all
Paste
Paste from clipboard
Input method
Add "Code" to dictionary

Figure 4-12: The Edit Text menu.

The first two options on the Edit Text menu (refer to Figure 4-12) deal with selecting text:

Select All: Choose this option to select all text, either in an input box or whatever text you've been entering or editing in the current application.

Select Text: Choose this option to select a block of text starting at the cursor's location. Use the pointers at the start and end of the text, shown in Figure 4-13, to select the starting and ending point of a block of text. As you drag the pointers, a magnifying bubble appears, which allows you to be more precise.

Drag to set   Drag to set
block starts.   block ends.

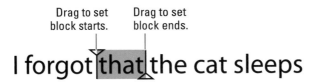

I forgot that the cat sleeps

Figure 4-13: Selecting a block of text.

After the text is selected, you can do four things with it: Delete it, replace it, copy it, or cut it. Delete text by touching the Del key on the keyboard. You replace text by typing something new while the text is selected. The next section describes how to cut or copy the text.

  ✔ To dismiss the Edit Text menu, press the Back soft button.

  ✔ By summoning the Edit Text menu, you select the word in which the cursor is blinking.

  ✔ You can cancel a text selection by tapping the text.

  ✔ Quickly select a single word by touching it twice with your finger.

Selecting text on a Web page

When you're browsing the Web on your Droid X, text is selected by summoning a special menu item. Obey these steps:

  1. **Press the Menu soft button to summon the Web browser's menu.**

  2. **Choose the More command.**

  3. **Choose Select Text.**

  4. **Drag your finger over the text on the Web page you want to copy.**

  5. **Lift your finger to complete selecting the text.**

When you're finished selecting, the text is instantly copied. You can then paste the text into any application on your phone that accepts text input. See the next section.

Refer to Chapter 11 for more information on surfing the Web with your phone.

Cutting, copying, and pasting text

After selecting a chunk of text — or all the text — on the screen, you can then cut or copy that text and paste it elsewhere. Copying or cutting and then pasting text works just like it does on your computer.

Follow these steps to cut or copy text on your phone:

1. **Select the text you want to cut or copy.**

   Selecting text is covered earlier in this chapter.

2. **Long-press the selected text.**

   Touch the text on the touchscreen and keep your finger down. You see the Edit Text menu, similar to the one shown in Figure 4-14.

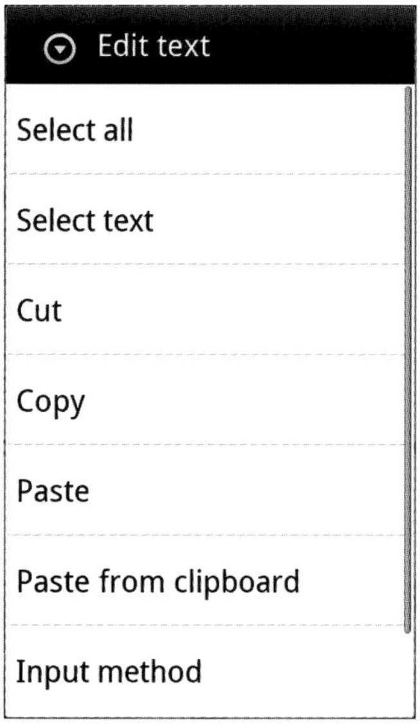

⊙ Edit text
Select all
Select text
Cut
Copy
Paste
Paste from clipboard
Input method

Figure 4-14: The Edit Text cut-and-copy menu.

3. **Choose Cut or Copy on the menu to cut or copy the text.**

   When you choose Cut, the text is removed; the cut-and-paste operation moves text.

4. **If necessary, start the application you want to paste text into.**

5. **Choose the input box or text area where you want to paste the copied or cut text.**

6. **Move the cursor to the exact spot where the text is to be pasted.**

7. **Long-press the text box or area.**

8. **Choose the Paste command from the Edit Text menu (refer to Figure 4-14).**

   The text you cut or copied appears where the cursor was blinking.

The text you paste can be pasted again and again. Until you cut or copy additional text, you can use the Paste command to your heart's content.

✔ You can paste text only into locations where text is allowed. Odds are good that if you can type, or whenever you see the onscreen keyboard, you can paste text.

✔ The Paste from Clipboard command allows you to choose a previously cut or copied chunk of text for pasting. After choosing Paste from Clipboard, you see a list of text blocks. Touch one to paste that chunk-o-text into an app.

✔ When you initially select text, the menu that opens (refer to Figure 4-12) contains two commands you can use to select *and* cut or copy text: Choose Cut All to cut all text in a box or text area. Choose Copy All to copy all text. You can then use the Paste command, described in this section, to paste that chunk of text.

✔ Cutting and copying text works best with text you've input yourself. There are many times you won't be able to select, cut, or copy text on the Droid X, for example, when reading email.

Voice Input

One of the most amazing things about the Droid X is its uncanny ability to interpret your dictation as text. Yes, it's almost as good as Mr. Spock talking to the computer on *Star Trek*. In fact, it should amaze you — which I admit is impressive for a cellphone.

Voice input is available anytime you see the Microphone icon, similar to the one shown in the margin. To begin voice input, touch the icon. A voice input screen appears, as shown in Figure 4-15.

Figure 4-15: The Voice Input program.

When you see the text *Speak now,* speak directly into the phone.

As you speak, the Microphone icon (refer to Figure 4-15) flashes green. The green flash doesn't mean that the phone is envious of what you're saying. No, the green flash merely indicates that the phone is listening.

After you stop talking, the phone digests what you said. You see your voice input appear as a wave-like pattern on the screen. Eventually, the text you spoke — or a close approximation — appears on the screen. It's magical, and sometimes comical.

- ✒ The first time you try voice input, you might see a description displayed. Touch the OK button to continue.

- ✒ See Chapter 5 for information on dialing the phone using your voice.

- ✒ A Microphone icon shows up on the onscreen keyboard variations. (Refer to Figures 4-1 through 4-7.) Touch that Microphone button to dictate, rather than type, to your phone.

- ✒ The Microphone icon appears only when voice input is allowed. Not every application features voice input as an option.

- ✒ The better your diction, the better the result. Also, try to speak in short sentences.

- ✒ You can edit your voice input just as you edit any text. See the section "Text Editing," earlier in this chapter.

- ✒ You have to speak any punctuation in your text. For example, you would need to say, "I'm sorry comma Belinda" to have the phone produce the text I'm sorry, Belinda (or similar wording).

- ✒ Common punctuation marks you can dictate includes the comma, period, exclamation point, question mark, and colon.

- ✒ Pause your speech before and after speaking punctuation.

✔ The Voice Command app, found in the Applications Tray, can be used to blast out vocal orders to your Droid X. Start the app and wait a second to see a list of potential commands. Try a few of them, though I admit that this feature is a bit rough around the edges, especially compared with the Droid X dictation capabilities.

✔ The Droid X features a voice censor, which replaces any naughty words you might utter with a series of pound (#) symbols. The phone knows a lot of blue terms, including the famous "Seven Words You Can Never Say On Television," but apparently the terms *crap* and *damn* are fine. Don't ask me how much time I spent researching this topic.

Part II
Your Basic Phone

Sam Clemens

Mobile 573-555-1130

Hannibal, MO

*T*he most complex Swiss Army Knife is called the *Giant*. It has 85 devices for 110 functions. The Giant is 9-inches wide, weighs 2 pounds, and costs about $1400. Despite all that, it remains at its core a knife. In fact, just about any fancy do-it-all gizmo tends to have a core function that can be traced back to its origins. The same holds true for your Droid X.

At its most basic, the Droid X is a phone. It's used to make and receive phone calls. All the other features — the fancy stuff covered in Parts III and IV of this book — are really extras and bonus goodies. Take them away and you're left with using the Droid X as a phone, which is the subject of this part of the book.

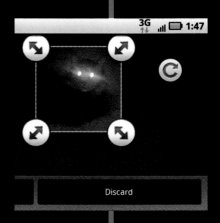

5

The Telephone Thing

In This Chapter

▶ Calling someone

▶ Connecting with a contact

▶ Trying out voice dialing

▶ Getting a call

▶ Checking into a missed call

▶ Perusing the call log

*O*nce upon a time, all a cellphone could do was place and receive phone calls. No Internet. No music. No camera. Possibly even no list of contacts. It was a simple task, but a necessary one: The owner of a cellphone in the 1980s lugged around a 20-pound device the size of a brick that had a one-hour battery life and cost a dollar a minute to use, just for the luxury of making a cellular call. The Droid X offers you the same luxury, albeit lighter, cheaper, and occasionally easier to use.

Home 202-456-1111

Washington, DC

Reach Out and Touch Someone

Email may have killed off the personal letter, but nothing replaces a phone call. It's personal. It's good to hear someone's voice. Making phone calls on the Droid X is cinchy, if you've mulled through the information in this section.

Making a phone call

To place a call on your phone, heed these steps:

1. **Touch the phone icon, found on the Home screen just to the left of the Launcher button.**

   You see the Phone dialpad, similar to the one shown in Figure 5-1.

Signal strength

Phone number

Delete

Dialpad

Dial voice mail

Voice dial

Connect

Figure 5-1: Dialing a phone number.

2. **Input the number to call.**

Touch the keys on the dialpad to input the number. If you make a mistake, use the Delete key (refer to Figure 5-1) to back up and erase.

As you dial, you may hear the traditional touch-tone sound as you input the number. The phone may also vibrate as you touch the numbers. These sound and vibration settings can be changed; see Chapter 21.

3. **Touch the green phone button to make the call.**

The phone doesn't make the call until you touch the green button.

As the phone attempts to make the connection, two things happen:

- First, the Call in Progress notification icon appears on the status bar. The icon is a big clue that the phone is making a call or is actively connected.

- Second, the screen changes to show the number that was dialed, similar to the one shown in Figure 5-2. When the recipient is on your Contacts list, the name appears as shown in the figure. Further, if a picture is part of the person's contact information, the picture appears, as shown in the figure.

Even though the touchscreen is pretty, at this point you need to listen to the phone: Put it to your ear or listen on earphones or a Bluetooth headset.

4. When the person answers the phone, talk.

What you say is up to you, though I can recommend from experience that it's a bad idea to coldly open your conversation with a neighbor about the fact that you just accidentally killed their cat.

Use the phone's volume buttons (on the side of the Droid X) to adjust the speaker volume during the call.

5. To end the call, touch the red End button.

The phone disconnects. The phone call in-progress notification goes away.

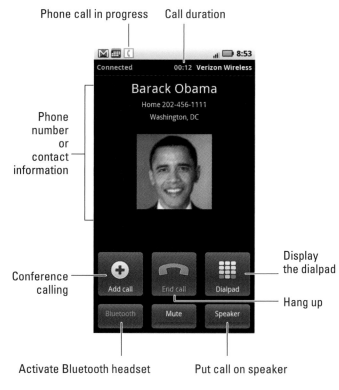

Figure 5-2: Your call has gone through!

Signal strength and network information you don't have to read

Two technical status icons appear to the left of the current time and battery status at the top of the Droid X screen. These icons represent the network the phone is connected to as well as the signal strength.

The signal-strength icon displays the familiar bars, rising from left to right. The more bars you see, the better the signal. A lack of a signal is shown by zero bars, often with an X over the bars.

When the phone is out of its service area but still receiving a signal, you see a Roaming icon, where an *R* appears near the bars. See Chapter 20 for more information on roaming.

To the left of the signal bar icon is the network icon. No icon means that no network is available, which happens when the network is down or you're out of range. Otherwise, you see an icon representing one of the different types of cellular data networks to which the Droid X can connect:

✔ A GPRS icon appears when the Droid X is connected to a 2G network using the General Packet Radio Service (GPRS) protocol.

✔ An EDGE icon shows up when the Droid X is connected to an EDGE 2G digital network. EDGE stands for *Enhanced Data Rates for GSM Evolution*, just in case you do crossword puzzles.

✔ A 3G icon appears when the Droid X is connected to a 3G network.

The network icons animate when a signal is being transmitted.

See Chapter 13 for more information on the network connection and how it plays a role in your phone's Internet access.

You can do other things while you're making a call on the Droid X. Just press the Home button to run an application, browse the Internet, check an appointment time, or do whatever. These activities don't disconnect you, though your cellular carrier may not allow you to do other things with the phone while you're on a call.

You can also listen to music while you're making a call, though I don't recommend it, because the music volume and call volume cannot be set separately.

To return to the call after doing something else, swipe down the notifications at the top of the screen and touch the notification for the current call. You return to the call screen, similar to the one shown earlier, in Figure 5-2. Continue yapping. (See Chapter 3 for information on reviewing notifications.)

✔ You can connect or remove the earphones at any time during the call. The call is neither disconnected nor interrupted by doing so.

✔ If you're using the earphones, you can press the phone's Power button during the call to turn off the display and lock the phone. I recommend turning off the display so that you don't accidentally touch the Mute or End button during the call.

✔ You can't accidentally mute or end a call when the phone is pressed against your face; a proximity sensor in the phone detects when it's close to something and the touchscreen is automatically disabled.

✔ Don't worry about holding the phone too far away from your mouth; it picks up your voice just fine.

✔ To mute the call, touch the Mute button (refer to Figure 5-2). A Mute icon, shown in the margin, appears as the phone's status (atop the touchscreen).

✔ Touching the Speaker button lets you hold the phone at a distance to listen and talk, which allows you to let others listen and share in the conversation. The Speaker icon appears as the phone's status when the speaker is active.

✔ Don't hold the phone to your ear when the speaker is active.

✔ If you're wading through one of those nasty voice mail systems, touch the dialpad button (refer to Figure 5-2) so that you can "Press 1 for English" when necessary.

✔ See Chapter 6 for information on using the Add Call button.

✔ The contact picture (refer to Figure 5-2) appears if you've assigned a picture to the contact, or the picture may be pulled from one of your social networking sites — if you've set up those sites on the Droid X. See Chapter 12.

✔ If you've logged into your social networking sites and the person you're calling is one of your friends or followers, that person's recent social networking status appears below the contact icon. For example, in Figure 5-2, President Obama's Facebook status would appear, if you were logged into Facebook when the call was made and President Obama were one of your Facebook friends.

✔ When using a Bluetooth headset, connect the headset *before* you make the call.

✔ If you need to dial an international number, press and hold the 0 (zero) key until the plus-sign (+) character appears. Then input the rest of the international number. Refer to Chapter 20 for more information on making international calls.

✔ You hear a beep when the call is dropped or if the other party hangs up on you. You can confirm the disconnection by looking at the phone, which shows that the call has ended.

✔ You cannot place a phone call when your phone has no service; check its signal strength (refer to Figure 5-1). Also see the nearby sidebar, "Signal strength and network information you don't have to read."

✔ You cannot place a phone call when the phone is in Airplane mode. See Chapter 20 for information.

✔ The phone call in-progress notification icon (refer to Figure 5-2) is a useful indicator. When you see the notification, it means that the phone is connected to another party. To return to the phone screen, swipe down the status bar and touch the phone call's notification. You can then press the End button to disconnect or just put the phone to your face to see who's on the line.

Dialing a contact

Because your Droid X is also your digital Little Black Book, an easy method for placing a phone call is to simply dial one of the folks on your Contacts list. Follow these steps:

1. **On the Home screen, touch the Phone icon, found to the left of the Launcher button.**

2. **Choose Contacts from the icons shown at the top of the window.**

   See Figure 5-3 for the location of the Contacts button.

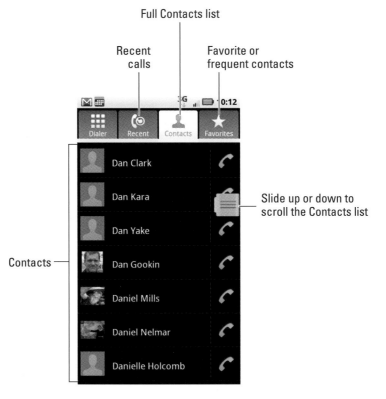

Figure 5-3: Choosing a contact to dial!

3. **Scroll the list of contacts to find the person you want to call.**

   To rapidly scroll, you can swipe the list with your finger or use the tab that appears on the right side of the list (refer to Figure 5-3): Drag the tab around by using your finger.

4. **Touch the green phone button by the contact you want to call.**

   The contact is dialed immediately. Or, if the contact has multiple phone numbers, you see a menu from which you can choose a number to dial.

At this point, dialing proceeds as described earlier in this chapter.

   ✏ If you touch the contact's name in Step 4, you can see a list of phone numbers to choose from, which may be a better option if your contact has multiple phone numbers.

   ✏ You can also call a contact by accessing a shortcut icon on the Home screen: Touch the icon to display the contact's information. Choose a phone number to dial.

   ✏ See Chapter 8 for more information about the Contacts list.

   ✏ See Chapter 21 for information on placing shortcut icons on the Home screen.

Phoning someone you call often

As sort of a computer, the Droid X keeps track of your phone calls. Also, you can flag certain people whose numbers you want to keep handy as your favorites. You can take advantage of these two features to quickly call the numbers you phone most often, or to redial a number.

To use the call log to return a call, or to call someone right back, follow these steps:

1. **Touch the Phone icon on the Home screen.**

2. **Touch the Recent button, found at the top of the window.**

   Refer to Figure 5-3.

   You see a list of recent calls you've made or calls that came in. You can choose an item to see more information; to call someone back, though, it's just quicker to move to Step 3.

3. **Touch the Phone button by the entry.**

   The Droid X dials the contact.

People you call frequently, or contacts you've added to your Favorites list, can be accessed by touching the Favorites button (refer to Figure 5-3). Scroll the list to find a favorite contact, and then touch the green phone button to dial.

Where is that call coming from?

The Droid X can display the location for both incoming and outgoing calls, similar to the ones shown in Figures 5-2 and 5-4. That feature works courtesy of the City ID app.

City ID is a subscription service, though you get a free 15-day trial with your Droid X. After

that, you have to sign up to pay for the service. Though it may not help you identify callers you know, it is a handy tool for gleaning information about unknown incoming calls.

Open the City ID app in the Applications Tray to learn more information about City ID.

Refer to Chapter 8 for information on how to make one of your contacts a favorite.

Using the Voice Dialer

The Droid X understands your speech, which means that you can not only dictate to the phone but also dial the phone using your voice and not your finger.

The quick-and-dirty way to dial the phone with your voice is to follow these steps:

1. **Press and hold the Search soft button.**

2. **Say the word** Call, **followed by the contact's name, or you can speak the phone number.**

When the contact is recognized, the number is dialed immediately. Otherwise, you see a list of names to choose from — though that's not really in the spirit of voice dialing.

You can also access the Voice Dialer by touching the Voice Dialer button found at the bottom of the phone keypad (refer to Figure 5-1). Also, a Voice Dial shortcut icon appears on the first Home screen to the right of the main Home screen.

> ✒ You have to be pretty dang fast to touch that Cancel button if the phone chooses the wrong contact to dial. I recommend that you not try this trick unless you can see the phone to confirm that it's dialing the proper number.

> ✒ Be precise! If the contact is named William Johnson, the Droid X may not dial it when you say *Bill Johnson*.

> ✒ The number that's dialed is the default, or main, number that was set up when you added the contact. See Chapter 8 for information on how to set the main number for a contact.

> ✒ See Chapter 4 for additional information on using the voice input ability of the Droid X.

It's the Phone!

A while back, when phones known as *landlines* were all the rage, getting a phone call was quite an exciting event. Heck, you didn't even know who was calling you until you picked the thing up and eagerly said "Hello!" You may not be as excited to receive a phone call these days, what with the popularity of cellphones, but it's still exciting to know that someone out there cares enough to call — even when it's a bill collector.

Well, maybe not when it's a bill collector, but you get the idea.

Receiving a call

Several things can happen when you receive a phone call on your Droid X:

- ✓ The phone rings or makes a noise signaling you to an incoming call.
- ✓ The phone may vibrate.
- ✓ The touchscreen display turns on (refer to Figure 5-4).
- ✓ The car in front of you explodes and your crazy passenger starts screaming in an incoherent yet comical manner.

Only the last item happens in a Bruce Willis movie. The other three possibilities, or a combination thereof, are your signals that you have an incoming call. A simple look at the touchscreen tells you more information, as illustrated in Figure 5-4.

To answer the call, slide the green Answer button to the right. Then place the phone to your ear or use the headset, if one is attached.

To ignore the call, slide the red Decline button to the left. The phone stops ringing and the call is immediately sent to voice mail.

You can also touch the volume button (up or down) to silence the ringer.

If you're already on the phone when you receive an incoming call, you hear a tone. At that point, the touchscreen displays information about the incoming call, similar to the one shown earlier, in Figure 5-4, and you can answer or ignore the call. When you choose to answer, the current call is placed on hold; see Chapter 6 for more information on handling multiple calls.

- ✓ The contact picture, such as Mr. Clemens (refer to Figure 5-4), appears only when you've assigned a picture to that contact or the picture has been imported from your social networking sites. Otherwise, a generic silhouette icon shows up.

✓ If you're using a Bluetooth headset, you touch the control on the headset to answer your phone. See Chapter 13 for more information on using Bluetooth gizmos.

✓ The sound you hear when the phone rings is known as the *ringtone*. You can configure the Droid X to play a number of ringtones, depending on who is calling, or you can set a universal ringtone. Ringtones are covered in Chapter 6.

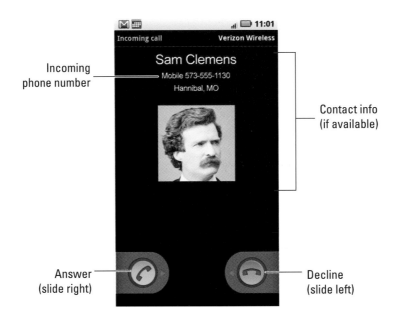

Figure 5-4: You have an incoming call.

Setting the incoming call-signal volume

Whether the phone rings, vibrates, or explodes depends on how you configure the Droid X to signal you for an incoming call. Abide by these steps to set the various options (but not explosion) for your phone:

1. **On the Home screen, touch the Launcher to view all apps on the phone.**

2. **Choose the Settings icon to open the phone's settings screen.**

3. **Choose Sound.**

   On older versions of the Android operating system, choose the Sound & Display item.

4. **Set the phone's ringer volume by touching Ringer Volume.**

5. **Manipulate the Ringer Volume slider left or right to specify how loud the phone rings for an incoming call.**

   After you release the slider, you hear an example of how loudly the phone rings.

6. **Touch OK to set the ringer volume.**

   If you'd rather just mute the phone, touch the Silent Mode option on the main Sound & Display Settings screen.

7. **To activate vibration when the phone rings, touch the option Phone Vibrate.**

   A green check mark by that option indicates that Vibration mode is active.

8. **Touch the Home button when you're done.**

When the next call comes in, the phone alerts you by using the volume setting or vibration options you've just set.

 ⨞ The vibration option is a good one to choose for those times when you need to silence the phone. See Chapter 3 for information on temporarily silencing the phone.

 ⨞ When the phone is silenced, the Ringer Is Silenced icon appears on the status bar.

 ⨞ Turning on vibration puts an extra drain on the battery. See Chapter 22 for more information on power management for your phone.

 ⨞ See Chapter 6 for information on changing the Droid X ringtone.

Who's Calling Who When?

I don't know what type of brain they put in the Droid X, but it's not my teenage son's brain. That particular brain was terrible at remembering who phoned, when they phoned, and what they said. He has since moved out of the house, and I now have a Droid X that does a *far* better job of remembering who called and when.

Dealing with a missed call

The notification icon for a missed call looming at the top of the screen means that someone called and you didn't pick up. Fortunately, the Droid X remembers all the details for you.

To deal with a missed call, follow these steps:

1. **Display the notifications.**

   See Chapter 3 for details on how to deal with notifications.

2. **Touch the Missed Call notification.**

   A list of missed calls is displayed.

3. **To return the call, touch the green phone button.**

Also see the next section for more information on the Recent call log.

Reviewing recent calls

The key to knowing who called and when is to use the Droid X Recent call log. Here's how it works:

1. **From the Home screen, touch the Phone icon.**

2. **At the top of the Phone screen, choose Recent.**

   The Recent call log is displayed in Figure 5-5. You see the list of people who have phoned you, starting with the most recent call in chronological order. Icons next to each entry describe whether the call was incoming, outgoing, or missed, as illustrated in the figure.

Each entry in the Recent call log displays information about the call, and if the call was from one of your contacts, you see contact information, as shown in Figure 5-5.

The call log can be quite long. Use your finger to scroll the list.

Using the Recent call log is a quick way to add a recent call as a contact. Simply touch the recent call and choose the command Add to Contacts from the menu. See Chapter 8 for more information about contacts.

A Recent Calls shortcut icon appears on the Home screen just to the right of the main Home screen. Touch that shortcut icon to be instantly whisked to the Recent call log, as shown in Figure 5-5.

To clear the call log, press the Menu soft button. Choose the Clear List command.

Display call log

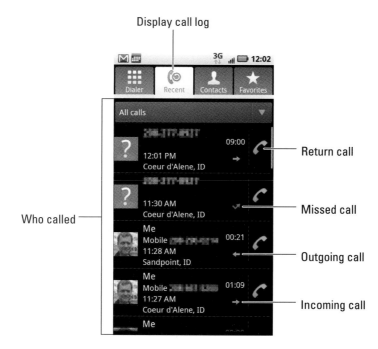

Who called

Return call

Missed call

Outgoing call

Incoming call

Figure 5-5: The Recent call log.

More Phone Stuff

In This Chapter

▶ Handling multiple incoming calls

▶ Setting up a conference call

▶ Configuring call forwarding options

▶ Banishing a contact forever to voice mail

▶ Finding a better ringtone

▶ Assigning ringtones to your contacts

▶ Using your favorite song or sound as a ringtone

A phone was a phone was a phone, until the 1980s or so — coincidentally, just after the breakup of the old Bell system. About that time, the various Phone Companies began to offer newfangled features, such as call waiting, multiline calling, and Caller ID. Customers were eager to have the new features, and more than willing to pay the outrageous fees associated with what today seem like standard features. In fact, I used to pay an extra $7.95 a month just for Caller ID.

Maximus Interrupt

Mobile 812-555-1879

Rome, IN

The features that folks paid extra for years ago are now part of the standard cellphone package. Your Droid X handles them effortlessly, if you know where those features are and how to make them useful. This chapter shows you the way.

Speed Dial

How fast can you dial a phone? Pretty fast — specifically, for ten of your friends or the folks you phone most often. The feature is *Speed Dial,* and, unlike customers of the Phone Company, you don't have to pay extra for it, at least not on your Droid X.

To set up Speed Dial, follow these steps:

1. **From the Home screen, touch the Phone button.**

   The Phone button is found to the left of the Launcher, at the bottom of the Home screen.

2. **Press the Menu soft button.**

3. **Choose Speed Dial Setup.**

   The first Speed Dial number is already configured to your carrier's voice mail. The remaining numbers, 2 through 9, are blank.

4. **Touch a blank item in the list.**

   The blank lines contain the text *Add Speed Dial.* To the left of the blank item is the Speed Dial number, 2 through 9.

5. **Choose a contact to Speed-Dial.**

6. **If presented with a menu, choose the specific phone number to Speed-Dial.**

7. **Repeat Steps 4 and 5 to add more Speed Dial numbers.**

When you're done adding numbers, press the Back or Home button to exit the Speed Dial Setup screen.

Using Speed Dial is simple: Summon the phone dialer (refer to Figure 5-1, in Chapter 5), and then press and hold *(long-press)* a number on the dialpad. When you release your finger, the Speed Dial number is dialed.

To remove a Speed Dial number, follow Steps 1 through 3 in this section. Touch the minus button to the left of the Speed Dial number to remove it. You can then add another Speed Dial number in that slot or just leave it empty.

To add a recently called number to the Speed Dial list, long-press the recent caller from the Recent call log. Choose the option Add to Speed Dial from the menu that appears. This trick works only when Speed Dial numbers are available. See Chapter 5 for more information on the Recent call log.

Multiple Call Mania

Human beings can hold only one conversation at a time. I remember hearing that theory in a psychology class lecture, but then the guy next to me started talking and I couldn't focus on what the professor was saying. So, I'll never know for certain. I do know, however, that the Droid X is capable of handling more than one call at a time. This section explains how it works.

Receiving a new call when you're on the phone

You're on the phone, chatting it up. Suddenly, someone else calls you. What happens next?

The Droid X alerts you to a new call. The phone may vibrate or make a sound. Look at the front of the phone to see what's up with the incoming call, as shown in Figure 6-1.

You're already on the phone.

Contact information (if present)

Incoming caller's number

Answer the second call.

Send the second call to voice mail.

Figure 6-1: Suddenly, you have an incoming call!

You have three options:

Answer the call. Touch the big, green Answer button to answer the incoming call just as you answer any call on your phone. The call you're on is placed on hold.

Send the call directly to voice mail. Touch the big, red Ignore button to send the incoming call directly to voice mail.

Ignore the call. Do nothing. The call eventually goes into voice mail, if you have set the option Forward When Unanswered, as described in the section "Forwarding phone calls," later in this chapter.

When you choose to answer the call and the call you're on is placed on hold, you return to the first call when you end the second call. Or, you can manage multiple calls as described in the next section.

Contact information about the incoming call (refer to Figure 6-1) appears only when that caller is on your phone's Contacts list.

Juggling two calls

After answering a second call, as described in the preceding section, your Droid X is now working with two calls at a time. You can speak with only one person at a time; juggling two calls isn't the same thing as a conference call.

To switch callers, touch the Switch Calls button. Every time you touch the Switch Calls button, you connect to the other caller.

To end a call, touch the End button, just as you normally would. It might appear as though both calls have been disconnected, but that's not the case: In a few moments, the call you didn't disconnect "rings" as though the person called you back. Actually, the person didn't call you back; the Droid X is simply returning you to that ongoing conversation.

✓ Lamentably, the screen doesn't show you which call you're on; it merely says In Call and you have to figure out on your own whom you're switching to when you touch the Switch Calls button.

✓ The number of different calls your phone can handle depends on your carrier. For most of us, that's only two calls at a time. In that case, a third person calling you either hears a busy signal or is sent directly to voice mail.

✓ If the person on hold hangs up, you may hear a sound or feel the phone vibrate when the call is dropped.

✓ The Android operating system may be updated for your Droid X in the future, in which case handling multiple calls might work differently. For example, a Swap button might be used to switch between multiple calls. Likewise, a Merge Calls button might appear, allowing you to hold a conference call. I will note on my Web page any updates or changes to the Android operating system and how they affect this book:

    www.wambooli.com/help/phone

Making a conference call

Unlike an incoming call that interrupts a conversation, a *conference call* is one that you set out to make intentionally. You make one call, and then you *add* a second call. Touch a button on the Droid X touchscreen, and then everyone is talking. Here's how it works:

1. **Phone up the first person.**

   Refer to Chapter 5 if you need to hone your Droid X phone-calling skills.

2. **After your phone connects and you complete a few pleasantries, touch the Add Call button.**

   The first person is put on hold, and you see the dialpad.

3. **Dial the second person.**

   Or, you can summon the number from the Contacts list.

   Say your pleasantries and inform the party that the call is about to be merged.

4. **Touch the Merge Calls button.**

   The two calls are now joined. Everyone you've dialed can talk to and hear each other.

5. **To end the conference call, disconnect the last person you called: Touch the End Last Call button.**

   The second person you dialed is disconnected; the call ends. You're still taking to the first person.

6. **To end the first conversation, touch the End Call button.**

   The conference call is over.

If your cell provider allows, you can connect to more than two callers for a conference call. In that case, repeat Steps 3 and 4 to connect the third person. You also need to repeat Step 5 to disconnect each caller.

When several people are in a room and want to participate in a call, you can always put the phone in Speaker mode: Touch the Speaker button.

Send a Call Elsewhere

Banishing unwanted calls on the Droid X is relatively easy. You can dismiss the phone's ring by touching the Volume button. Or, you can send the call scurrying into voice mail by sliding the red Ignore button to the left, as described in the section in Chapter 5 about receiving a call.

Other options exist for the special handling of incoming calls. They're the forwarding options, described in this section.

Forwarding phone calls

Call-forwarding is the process by which you send elsewhere a phone call coming into your Droid X. For example, you can send to your office all calls you receive when you're on vacation. You then have the luxury of having your cell-phone while still making calls but freely ignoring anyone who calls you.

The options for call forwarding on the Droid X are set by the cell carrier and not by the phone itself. In the United States, when Verizon is your cellular provider, the call forwarding options work as described in Table 6-1.

Table 6-1	Verizon Call-Forwarding Commands	
Number to Input First	**Number to Input Second**	**Result**
*71	Forwarding number	Forward unanswered incoming calls
*72	Forwarding number	Forward all incoming calls
*73	(Nothing)	Cancel call forwarding

For example, to forward all calls to (714) 555-4565, you input ***727145554565** and touch the green Dial button on the Droid X. You hear just a brief tone after dialing, and then the call ends. After that, any call coming into your phone rings at the other number.

- ✔ You must disable call forwarding for your Droid X to return to normal cellphone operations. Dial *73.

- ✔ The Droid X doesn't even ring when you forward a call using *72. Only the phone number you've chosen to forward to rings.

- ✔ You don't need to input the area code for the forwarding number when it's a local call. In other words, if you need to dial only 555-4565 to call the forwarding number, you only need to input ***725554565** to forward your calls.

- ✔ The Android operating system has Forward features that are now unavailable on the Droid X, though they might be made available in the future. If so, you can find them on the Settings screen: Choose Call Settings, and then choose Call Forwarding.

Sending a contact directly to voice mail

You can configure the Droid X to forward any of your cellphone contacts directly to voice mail. It's a great way to deal with a pest! Follow these steps:

1. **Touch the Phone icon on the Home screen.**

   The Phone icon is found on the bottom of the Home screen, just to the left of the Launcher icon.

2. **If necessary, touch the Contacts button at the top of the screen.**

   The Contacts list opens.

3. **Choose a contact.**

   Use your finger to scroll the list of contacts until you find the annoying person you want to eternally banish to voice mail.

4. **Touch the Menu soft button.**

5. **Choose Edit.**

6. **If necessary, press the Back soft button to dismiss the onscreen keyboard.**

7. **Choose Additional Info from the bottom of the list.**

   Scroll the contact information to see the gray Additional Info button.

8. **Touch the gray square next to Send Straight to Voicemail.**

   Touching the square places a green check mark in the square, which activates the Send Straight to Voicemail feature.

9. **Touch the Save button.**

   Now all incoming calls from that contact are instantly sent to voice mail.

To unbanish your contact, repeat these steps, but in Step 8 touch the square to remove the green check mark.

✔ This feature is one reason you might want to keep contact information for someone with whom you really don't ever want to have contact.

✔ See Chapter 8 for more information on contacts.

✔ Also see Chapter 7, on voice mail.

Fun with Ringtones

I confess: Ringtones can be fun. They uniquely identify your phone's ring, especially when you forget to mute your phone and you're hustling to turn the thing off because everyone in the room is annoyed by your ringtone choice of *Soul Bossa Nova.*

On the Droid X, you can choose which ringtone you want for your phone. You can create your own ringtones or use snippets from your favorite tunes. You can also assign ringtones for individual contacts. This section explains how it's done.

Choosing the phone's ringtone

To select a new ringtone for your phone, or to simply confirm which ringtone you're using already, follow these steps:

1. **From the Home screen, touch the Launcher button.**

2. **Choose Settings.**

3. **Choose Sound.**

   Older versions of the Android operating system list ringtone settings under the Sound & Display category.

4. **Choose Phone Ringtone.**

   If you have a ringtone application, you may see a menu asking you which source to use for the phone's ringtone. Choose Android System.

5. **Choose a ringtone from the list that's displayed.**

   Scroll the list. Tap a ringtone to hear a preview.

6. **Touch OK to accept the new ringtone or touch Cancel to keep the phone's ringtone as is.**

You can also specify the ringtone used for notifications: in Step 4 of the preceding list, choose Notification Ringtone instead of Phone Ringtone.

Setting a contact's ringtone

Ringtones can be assigned by contact so that when your annoying friend Larry calls, you can have your phone yelp like a whiny puppy. Here's how to set a ringtone for a contact:

1. **Touch the Phone icon on the Home screen.**

2. **Choose Contacts from the top of the window.**

3. **From the list, choose the contact to which you want to assign a ringtone.**

4. **Touch the Menu soft button.**

5. **Choose Edit.**

6. **Press the Back soft button so that the onscreen keyboard goes away.**

7. **Choose Additional Info from the bottom of the scrolling list.**

   More options for editing the contact are displayed.

8. **Choose Ringtone.**

If you see a Complete Action Using menu, choose the option Android System to select one of the phone's ringtones. Otherwise, you can use another listed application to choose a ringtone.

9. **Choose a ringtone from the list.**

   The same list is displayed for the phone's ringtones.

10. **Touch OK to assign the ringtone to that contact.**

11. **Touch the Save button to save the new settings.**

Whenever that contact calls, the Droid X rings using the ringtone you've specified.

Using music as a ringtone

You can use any tune from the Droid X music library as the phone's ringtone. The first part of the process is finding a good tune to use. Follow along with these steps:

1. **Touch the Launcher button on the Home screen to display all apps on the phone.**

2. **Touch Music to open the music player.**

3. **Choose a tune to play.**

   See Chapter 17 for specific information on how to use the Music application and use your Droid X as a portable music player.

   The song you want must appear on the screen, or it can be playing, for you to select it as a ringtone.

4. **Press the Menu soft button.**

5. **Choose Use As Ringtone.**

   The song — the entire thing — is set as the phone's ringtone. Whenever you receive a call, that song plays.

The song you've chosen is added to the list of ringtones. When you choose that ringtone, the song plays — from the beginning — whenever an incoming call comes in and until you answer the phone, send the call to voice mail, or choose to ignore the call and eventually the caller goes away and the music stops.

You can add ringtones for as many songs as you like by repeating the steps in this section. Follow the steps in the earlier section "Choosing the phone's ringtone" for information on switching between different song ringtones.

Refer to the steps in the earlier section "Setting a contact's ringtone" to assign a specific song to one of your contacts.

 A free app at the Android Market, Zedge, has oodles of free ringtones available for preview and download, all shared by Android users around the world. See Chapter 19 for information about the Android Market and how to download and install Zedge.

Creating your own ringtones

You can use any MP3 or WAV audio file as a ringtone for the Droid X, such as a personalized message, a sound you record on your computer, or an audio file you stole from the Internet. As long as the sound is in either MP3 or WAV format, it can work as a ringtone on your phone.

The secret to creating your own ringtone is to transfer the audio file from your computer to the Droid X. This topic is covered in Chapter 13, on synchronizing music between your computer and phone. After the audio file is in the phone's music library, you can choose it as a ringtone just as you can assign any music on the Droid X as a ringtone, as described in the preceding section.

Message for You!

In This Chapter

▶ Configuring basic voice mail

▶ Retrieving messages

▶ Setting up Visual Voice Mail

▶ Reviewing Visual Voice Mail messages

I like the term *voice mail.* It has a professional ring to it. Long gone are the days when folks had answering machines. The term sounds so 1970s. An answering machine had a cassette tape. Voice mail is digital and modern. You leave voice mail. You pick up voice mail. You send someone to voice mail. It's a useful thing, and apparently it's both a noun and a verb.

Your Droid X comes with voice mail provided by your cellular carrier. That type can be rather dull and tedious, when you wade through the various prompts and such. A better solution is to use Visual Voice Mail, which provides a modern, touchscreen interface for reviewing and managing messages. Both types of voice mail are covered in this chapter.

Carrier Voice Mail

Your cellphone provider most likely offers a voice mail feature. It's standard: Missed calls are picked up by the voice mail system. Your phone alerts you to the missed call, and then you phone the voice mail system, listen to your calls, and use the phone's dialpad to delete messages and repeat messages and use other features you probably don't know about because no one ever pays attention.

ail (1/3)   Last Upda

Bill Gates (M)
Today, 9:52pm

Daniel Gookin (M)
Today, 9:39pm

Steve Jobs (M)
Today, 8:55pm   0:15

The meat of voice mail on the Droid X is Visual Voice Mail, covered later in this chapter. Even so, this section covers the basics of generic-carrier voice mail, which is necessary to configure before you can use Visual Voice Mail.

Setting up carrier voice mail

If you haven't yet done it, you need to set up voice mail on your phone. Even if you believe it to be already set up and configured, consider mincing through these steps, just to be sure:

1. **From the Home screen, touch the Launcher button.**

2. **Choose Settings.**

3. **Choose Call Settings.**

4. **Choose Voicemail Service.**

5. **Choose My Carrier, if it isn't chosen already.**

   When My Carrier is already chosen, the phone is configured to use your cell service provider's voice mail. You're done. Otherwise, continue:

6. **Back on the Call Settings screen, choose Voicemail Settings.**

   The number that's shown should be the one for your carrier's voice mail service. For example, for my carrier, the number is *86. If you need to change the number, refer to the next section.

I recommend phoning your carrier voice mail after the initial setup, which completes its configuration: From the Dialer screen, touch the Voicemail button, found in the bottom left of the dialer, next to the green phone button. For the first time you call voice mail, touch the Call Voicemail button to get things set up.

After initially setting up voice mail, you can use the Call Voicemail button at any time to retrieve your messages, configure your voice mail inbox, or just sit back and wistfully listen to the cheerful Verizon robot.

Don't forget to complete setting up your voice mail box by creating a customized greeting. When you don't, you may not receive any voice mail messages, or people may believe that they've dialed the wrong number.

Changing the carrier voice-mail number

When you need to change your voice mail number, follow the Steps in the preceding section. In Step 7, use the dialpad that opens to type a new number, as shown in Figure 7-1.

Figure 7-1: Setting the carrier voice mail number.

Type a new voice mail number, if necessary, as shown in the figure. Touch OK to set that number for your phone's voice mail.

Getting your messages

When you have voice mail, you see a New Voicemail icon on the status bar. It's your clue to voice mail looming in your carrier's voice mail system.

To access your messages, pull down the notifications. Touch the New Voicemail notification. The Droid X dials the carrier voice mail.

To phone up voice mail at any time, touch the Voicemail button, found to the left of the green phone button at the bottom of the Dialer screen. On the next screen, touch the Call Voicemail button to connect with your cellular provider's voice mail system.

What happens after the voice mail system is dialed depends on your carrier. I'm using Verizon in the United States, so I have to input my password — the number I set when my carrier voice mail was originally configured. Then I listen to new messages, or I can use the dialpad to control voice mail, by reviewing older messages and doing other stuff.

Table 7-1 lists the commands that are current for Verizon voice mail service at the time this book goes to press. These commands may change later.

Table 7-1	Verizon Voice-Mail System Commands
Number or Character Dialed	*Result*
*	Go to the main menu, or, if you're already at the main menu, disconnect from voice mail
1	Listen to messages
2	Send a message to another phone number on the Verizon system
4	Review or change personal options, such as your message greeting
5	Restart the session
7	Delete the message you just heard
88	After listening to a message, call the sender
9	Save the message you just heard
#	End input

✔ You don't have to venture into carrier voice mail just to see who's called you. Instead, check your call log to review recent calls. Refer to Chapter 5 for information on reviewing the call log.

✔ Calls sent to voice mail aren't flagged as "missed" in the call log. Chapter 5 discusses reviewing the call log.

✔ See Chapter 3 for more information on reviewing notifications.

Visual Voice Mail

A better option than using carrier voice mail is to set up and use *Visual Voice Mail*. It's a feature on the Droid X that provides more flexibility than standard carrier voice mail when dealing with missed calls. For example, if you're using Visual Voice Mail, you can choose which messages to listen to and also pause and replace messages, for example.

The only drawback to Visual Voice Mail is that it costs extra. You must subscribe to the service, which runs $2.99 per month as this book goes to press.

Setting up Visual Voice Mail

To configure Visual Voice Mail to work on your Droid X, first set up carrier voice mail as covered earlier in this chapter. Visual Voice Mail is simply an interface into your existing carrier voice mail.

After you have carrier voice mail up and running, and especially after you set your password or PIN, follow these steps:

1. **Touch the Launcher button to pop up the list of all apps installed on your phone.**

2. **Choose Voicemail.**

3. **Touch the button labeled Subscribe to Visual Voice Mail.**

4. **Review the license agreement.**

5. **Scroll down and touch the Accept button.**

6. **Input your existing voice mail PIN.**

7. **Touch the Login button.**

   If it works, you're done. If not, you have more setup to do:

8. **Touch the OK button to start the provisioning process.**

   You may be asked whether you want to subscribe to Premium Voice Mail, which isn't necessary for using the basic Visual Voice Mail service.

9. **Choose Subscribe to sign up for Premium Voice Mail.**

   A nice, long, legal-sounding block of text appears. Blah, blah, blah. Scroll to the bottom of the text to find the Accept and Decline items.

10. **Touch Accept.**

11. **Press the Back soft button to exit the last setup screen.**

It may take a few moments for Visual Voice Mail to be configured. When it's ready, you see the Visual Voice Mail notification on the status bar. See the next section to find out how to deal with the notification.

The steps listed in this section may vary, depending on updates and enhancements to the Visual Voice Mail system.

Accessing your Visual Voice Mail

Visual Voice Mail serves as your access to all voice mail left on your phone. After it's configured (see the preceding section), you never need to dial carrier voice mail again. Simply pull down a Voicemail notification or start the Voicemail app, and all your messages are instantly available on the screen.

When new voice mail arrives, you see the notification icon. The number in the icon indicates how many new messages are available. To access your message, pull down the notifications and choose Voicemail. You see the Visual Voice Mail screen, shown in Figure 7-2.

Date and time the message was left
Voicemail contact info or phone number

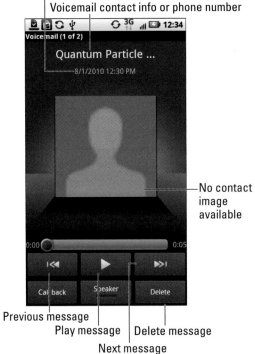

No contact image available

Previous message
Play message   Delete message
Next message

Figure 7-2: Visual Voice Mail.

Touch the Play button to listen to the message. You can pause a message as its playing by touching the Pause button (that replaces the Play button).

To call the person back, touch the Call Back button.

To delete the message, touch the Erase button. Touch the OK button to confirm.

Press the Back soft button to see a Visual Voice Mail inbox, where all your voice mail messages are listed. Choose a message from the list to listen to it, delete it, or return the call.

Visual Voice Mail uses the same greeting set as when you first configured carrier voice mail. To change the greeting, you have to dial carrier voice mail and follow the menu prompts.

Friends, Enemies, Contacts

*L*ong gone are the days when people remembered phone numbers. I once prided myself on knowing about 20 phone numbers by heart, including my close relatives and friends, and even the movie theater. Thanks to cellphones and computers, hardly anyone knows anyone else's phone number now. That's because this type of information is stored and recalled electronically. The only information you need to know about someone now is their name.

The Droid X helps perpetuate the "disconnect" between people you know and the numbers associated with them. You can use your phone, which coordinates with information stored on your Google account as well as on your social networking Web sites, to keep contact information for everyone you know and everyone you meet. It's all part of the *Contacts list*.

Some applications access or affect the Contacts list. You're alerted to them when they're installed on your phone. See Chapter 19 for more information on the Android Market.

The People You Know

Somewhere buried in your phone's bosom is a list of lots of people you know. I call them your *contacts*. I would normally write a contact lens joke here, but I just can't seem to be pithy enough, so I'll leave it at that.

Presenting the Contacts list

To peruse your phone's complete address book, touch the Phone icon, found on the Home screen. Touch the Contacts button atop the window. You see a list of all contacts on your phone, organized alphabetically by first name and similar to the one shown in Figure 8-1.

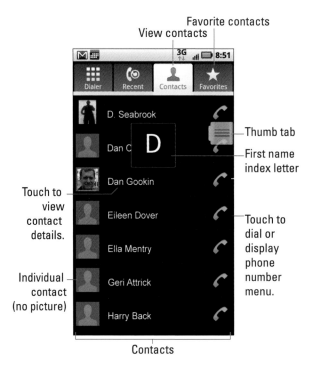

Figure 8-1: The Contacts list.

Scroll the list by swiping with your finger. You see a thumb tab (refer to Figure 8-1), which you can use to quickly navigate up and down the list. A large letter appears, telling you where you are in relation to the names in the list.

You can also access the Contacts list by touching the Contact icon, found to the right of the Launcher button at the bottom of the Home screen. The Droid X then displays your contacts in three screens: The screen on the left displays the Contact History, or those contacts you've accessed recently. The center screen shows all contacts, A to Z. The screen on the right lists the social networking status for your contacts. Use your finger to swipe left and right to see each of the contact screens.

To do anything with a contact, you first have to choose it: Touch a contact name and you see more information, as shown in Figure 8-2.

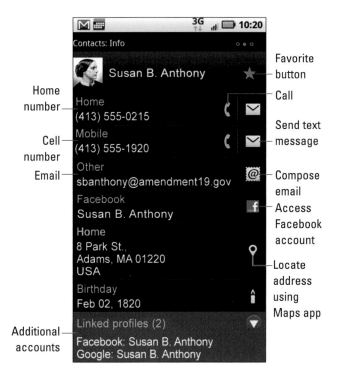

Figure 8-2: More details for a contact.

You can do a multitude of things with the contact after it's displayed, as shown in the figure:

> **Make a phone call.** To call a contact, touch one of the contact's Call entries, such as Home or Mobile. See Chapter 5.

> **Send a text message.** Touch the Text Message icon (refer to Figure 8-2) to open the Messaging app and send that contact a message. See Chapter 9 for information about text messaging on your Droid X.

Compose an email message. Touch the Email link to compose an email message to the contact. When a contact has more than one email address, you can choose to which one you want to send the message. Chapter 10 covers using email on your phone.

View social networking info. Visit the contact's Facebook or Twitter accounts by touching the appropriate social networking icon. See Chapter 12 for more information on accessing sites such as Facebook and Twitter using your Droid X.

Locate your contact on a map. When a contact has a home or business address, you can touch the little doohickey next to the address (refer to Figure 8-2) to summon the Maps application. Refer to Chapter 14 for all the fun stuff you can do with Maps.

Oh, and if you have added birthday information there, you can view it as well. Singing "Happy Birthday" is something you have to do on your own.

When you're done viewing the contact, press the Back soft button.

✔ Looking for yourself in the Contacts list? Try looking under the name *Me*.

✔ Touching the Contacts icon, found to the right of the Launcher icon on the Home screen, displays an abbreviated contacts list. To see the full list, choose the Contacts button after touching the Phone icon to the left of the Launcher icon.

✔ The information displayed as Linked Profiles (refer to Figure 8-2) is culled from other accounts you can link to your phone's address book. The easiest way to link is to set up social networking on the Droid X, as covered in Chapter 12.

Searching contacts

You can have a massive number of contacts. For example, I have 414 contacts on my phone. I started out with just 80 contacts that I imported from Gmail, with many more added as I set up social networking on the Droid X. The rest of the accounts were added as I phoned or met people. The problem: Skimming the list can take a while.

Rather than scroll the Contacts list with angst-riddled desperation, press the Search soft button. A Quick Search text box appears. Type a few letters from the contact's name and quickly you see the list of contacts narrowed to those few whose names match the letters you type. Touch a name from the search list to view the contact's information.

You can also voice-search for a contact. Touch the Microphone icon next to the Quick Search text box and then speak the contact's name when prompted to "speak now." The results display any matching contacts and, on good days, even options to call that person directly.

🖛 See Chapter 5 for information on voice dialing.

🖛 The section "A New Contact Is Born" deals with adding new contacts. It's next.

🖛 No correlation exists between the number of contacts you have and the number of bestest friends you have — none at all.

Using a Contact Quick Task widget

Motorola (or Verizon — I mean, who really knows?) preconfigured your Droid X with some Contact Quick Task widgets on the Home screen, just to the right of the main Home screen. Four are available, as shown in Figure 8-3.

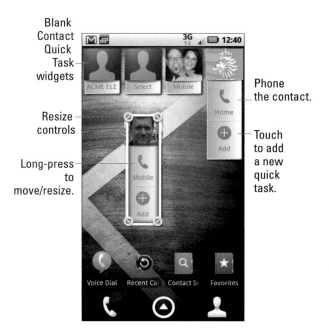

Figure 8-3: Quick Task widgets.

When you touch a blank widget (refer to Figure 8-3), the full Contacts list is displayed. Choose a contact to assign to the widget, and then touch various contact options — phone, text message, email — to place on the widget.

The first time you touch a widget that has a phone number, you're prompted to activate one-touch calling. After that, touching the widget, or the phone part of a widget, instantly calls that contact.

Contacts can have multiple quick tasks assigned to them: To create more tasks, resize the widget to allow for more buttons. Long-press the widget then re-size the corners by dragging them around with your finger. When you see the Add button, the widget is large enough to sport another quick task.

Refer to Chapter 21 for information on adding a Contact Quick Task widget. It's found in the Motorola category.

Chapter 21 also contains information on removing widgets, in case you find them crowding your Home screen.

A New Contact Is Born

You have many ways to put contact information into your phone. You can build a list of contacts from scratch, but that method is tedious. More likely, you collect contacts as you use your phone. Or, you can borrow contacts from your Gmail, Facebook, Twitter, or other contacts. In no time, you have a phone full of contact information.

Making a new contact

You can make a new contact for your Droid X phone in many ways.

Add a contact from the Recent call log

One of the quickest ways to build your Contacts list is to add people as they phone you — assuming that you've told them about your new phone number. After someone calls, you can use the call log to add the person to your Contacts list. Obey these steps:

1. **From the Home screen, touch the Phone icon to the left of the Launcher.**

2. **Choose Recent from the top of the window.**

3. **Choose the phone number you want to create a contact for.**

4. **Choose New to create a new contact, or choose Existing to add the phone number to a contact you already have.**

   The Existing option is useful for when people call you from a cell number that you know they have but refuse to give to you.

   I assume that you're creating a new contact and have chosen New in Step 4.

5. **Fill in the contact's information.**

   Fill in the blanks — as many as you know about the caller: given name and family name and other information, if you know it. If you know no additional information, that's fine; just filling in the name helps clue you in to who is calling the next time that person calls (using that number).

Use the Next button on the onscreen keyboard to hop between the various text fields for the contact.

Touch the Additional Info button to add information such as birthday, anniversary, or Web site URL and to assign a personal ringtone for the contact.

6. Touch the Save button.

You're done.

Create a new contact from scratch

Sometimes, you must create a contact when you meet another human being in the real world. In that case, you have more information to input, and the process starts like this:

1. Touch Contacts on the Home screen.

The Contacts icon is to the right of the Launcher button.

2. Press the Menu soft button.

3. Choose Add Contact.

4. Fill in the information as completely as you can.

Fill in the text fields with the information you know: given name, family name, and phone number plus perhaps an email address. That's all good, basic information for a contact.

Use the green plus-sign button to add another item, such as a second phone number or an email address.

Touch the gray button to the left of the phone number or email address to choose the location for that item, such as Home, Work, or Mobile.

Touch the Additional Info button at the bottom of the list to add *even more* information!

5. Touch the Save button to finish editing and add the new contact.

The new contact is automatically synced with your Google account on the Internet. That's the beauty of the Droid X: You don't need to duplicate your efforts; the phone automatically updates all your Google account information on both the Droid X and the Internet.

Make a contact in Gmail on the Internet

One of the easiest ways to build up your list of new contacts is to use your Gmail Contacts list on the Internet. It's easy because you're using a computer with a real keyboard and mouse to help you input the information. That method generally works better than typing with your thumbs on the Droid X.

To add a new Gmail contact, follow these steps:

1. **On a computer, browse to your Google Gmail account at `http://gmail.google.com`.**

2. **Log in, if necessary.**

3. **Choose Contacts from the links listed on the left side of the page.**

4. **Click the New Contact button.**

   The button features a single plus sign next to a generic human icon.

5. **Fill in the contact information.**

   Use the Add links to add more than one email address, phone number, or address or another type of information — for example, when a contact has both home and work addresses.

6. **Click the Save button to save the contact information.**

   You can repeat Steps 4 through 6 to create additional contacts.

Because the Droid X stays in sync with your Google account, any new contacts you create on the Internet are automatically updated on your phone.

Build up contacts from your social networking sites

After you tell your Droid X which social networking sites you use, the phone scours those sites, looking for your friends and followers for information. New contacts are built from that information and automatically placed into your phone's Contacts list. Even the avatar images associated with the accounts are saved on the Droid X Contacts list.

The key to pulling in contacts from your social networking sites is to use the Social Networking app on the Droid X. Using that app is covered in Chapter 12.

Find a new contact by using a Maps location

When you use the Maps application to locate a restaurant, an apothecary, or a shooting range, you can quickly create a contact for that location. Here's how:

1. **After searching for your location, touch the cartoon bubble that appears on the map.**

   For example, in Figure 8-4, the Syringa Japanese Cafe & Sushi Bar has been found.

   See Chapter 14 for detailed information on how to search for a location using the Maps application.

2. **Scroll to the bottom of the information summary for the business and choose the item Add As a Contact.**

The information from the Maps application is copied into the proper fields for the contact, including the address and phone number, plus other information (if available).

3. **Touch the Save button.**

   The new contact is created.

Figure 8-4: A business has been located.

Editing a contact

When information about a contact changes, or perhaps if your thumbs were a bit too big when you created the contact while riding a bus during an earthquake, you can edit the contact's information. Aside from just editing existing information or adding new items, you can do a smattering of interesting things, as covered in this section.

- ✒ See Chapter 6 for information on configuring a contact so that all their incoming calls go to voice mail.

- ✒ Also refer to Chapter 6 on how to set a contact's ringtone.

- ✒ Contact information can come from multiple sources, so editing information for a contact on your phone doesn't change the original source. That is, unless the source is your Gmail Contacts list, in which case the Droid X synchronizes your edits on the phone with the Contacts list on the Internet and vice versa.

Make basic changes

To make minor touch-ups on any contact, start by locating and displaying the contact's information. Press the Menu soft button and choose Edit. You can then add new information by touching a field and typing on the onscreen keyboard. You can edit information as well: Touch the field to edit and change whatever you want.

Chapter 4 contains information on how to edit text on the Droid X.

When you're done editing, touch the Save button.

Add a picture to a contact

Displaying a contact with a pretty picture is so much nicer than using just the standard silhouette icon. Well, unless your contact is, in fact, a two-dimensional silhouette.

To add a picture to your contact, it helps to already have the picture stored on the phone. You can transfer the picture from a computer (covered in Chapter 13) or snap a shot with the phone anytime you see the contact or a person or an object that resembles the contact.

After the contact's photo, or any other suitable image, is stored on the phone, follow these steps to update the contact's information:

1. **Locate and display the contact's information.**

2. **Press the Menu soft button.**

3. **Choose Edit.**

4. **Touch the picture icon next to the First Name field.**

5. **Choose the Take Photo command if the contact is in front of you and willing to have their picture taken, or choose the Use Existing Photo command to pull a picture from the phone's photo gallery.**

   When you choose to take the contact's photo, you use the Droid X camera. Choose Done to keep the photo, Retake to try again, or Cancel to give up. Skip to Step 7.

   When you elect to use an existing photo, you see the camera's photo gallery. Browse the Gallery for a suitable image; touch the image you want to use for the contact.

6. **Select the size and portion of the image you want to use for the contact.**

   Use Figure 8-5 as your guide. You can choose which portion of the image to use by moving the cropping box; resize the cropping box to select more or less of the image; and rotate the image.

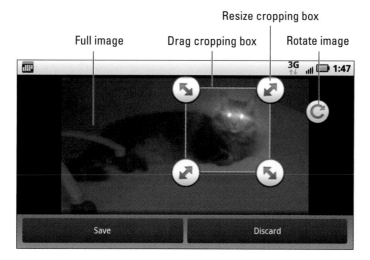

Full image | Drag cropping box | Resize cropping box | Rotate image

Figure 8-5: Choosing a contact's image.

7. **Touch Save to assign the image to the contact.**

8. **Touch the Save button to complete the editing of the contact.**

   The image is now assigned, and it appears whenever you phone the contact or they phone you.

You can add pictures to contacts on your Google account by using any computer. Just visit your Gmail Contacts list to edit a contact. You can then add to that contact any picture stored on your computer. The picture eventually gets synced with the same contact on your Droid X.

> ✔ Refer to Chapter 15 for more information on how the Droid X camera works.
>
> ✔ See Chapter 16 for more information on using the Gallery.
>
> ✔ To change an existing photograph, follow Steps 1 through 4 in this section but choose Change Icon.
>
> ✔ To remove a contact's photo, follow Steps 1 through 4 and then choose the Remove Photo command in Step 5.

Make a favorite

A *favorite* contact is someone you stay in touch with more often than others. It doesn't have to be someone you like — just someone you (perhaps unfortunately) phone often, like your bail bondsman.

When you touch the Favorites button in the Contacts list (refer to Figure 8-1), you see a list of favorites. The top part of the list shows contacts you've flagged as favorites. The bottom part of the list displays numbers you frequently call.

To add a contact to the Favorites list, display the contact's information and touch the Favorite button (the star) in the upper right corner of the Contacts screen (refer to Figure 8-2). When the star is red, as shown in the figure, the contact is one of your favorites.

To remove a favorite, touch the contact's star until it loses its color. Removing a favorite doesn't delete the contact but removes it from the Favorites list.

> ✔ Occasionally peruse the names in the bottom part of the Favorites list — the frequent callers. You might consider promoting some of them to your favorites.

> ✔ Contacts have no idea whether they're on your list of favorites, so don't believe that you're hurting their feelings by not making them favorites.

Sharing a contact

You know Bill? I know Bill, too! But you don't have his contact information? Allow me to share that with you. Here's what I do:

1. **Summon the contact you want to share from your Contacts list.**

2. **Press the Menu soft button.**

3. **Choose Share Name Card.**

4. **Choose a method to share the contact, such as Gmail or Text Messaging.**

5. **Proceed with composing an email message, typing a text message, or completing whatever action is necessary to send the contact information.**

In a few Internet moments, the message is received. It contains an attachment, which is the contact's *vCard* information. The recipient can then import that card or do whatever else with it to add it to their own Contacts list.

Removing a contact

Every so often, consider reviewing your phone's contacts. Purge those folks whom you no longer recognize or you've forgotten. It's simple:

1. **Locate the contact in your Contacts list and display the contact's information.**

2. **Press the Menu soft button.**

3. **Choose Delete.**

4. **Touch Delete to remove the contact from your phone's address books as well as from any other address books that are listed.**

Because your Contacts list is synchronized with other accounts, such as your Gmail contacts for your Google account, the contact is also removed there.

For some linked accounts, such as Facebook, deleting the account from your phone doesn't remove the human from your Facebook account. The warning paragraph just before this paragraph explains as much.

Part III
Other Forms of Communication

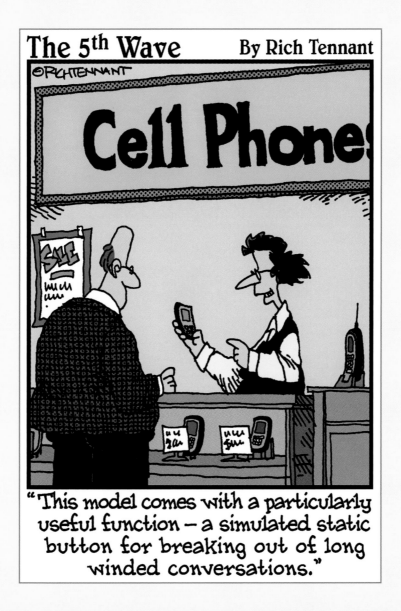

The 5th Wave   By Rich Tennant

Cell Phones

SALE

"This model comes with a particularly useful function – a simulated static button for breaking out of long winded conversations."

Predators
Inbox

⬤ **Barbara Gookin** ☆
To: Dan Gookin   Mar 20

You cannot change the laws of physics.

On Sat, Mar 20, 2010 at 7:13 PM, Dan Gookin
<dan.gookin@gmail.com> wrote:
>
> This is much too long to weight.

 Reply   Reply to all   ➡ Forward

*1*n 1844, the official message sent to open the
first telegraph line was *What hath God wrought.*
In 1876, Alexander Graham Bell said, "Mr. Watson,
come here, I want to see you" over his telephone
invention. And in 1973, the first email message
was sent between two computer scientists, the
first asking the second whether he was interested
in purchasing some low-cost Viagra.
Communications has come a long way.

You can employ your Droid X smartphone in a
variety of ways to send messages using multiple
methods. The most obvious way is the phone. And
while the Droid X lacks a telegraph feature, you
can use it to send email as well as other forms of
communications far and wide, obvious or not, as
covered in this part of the book.

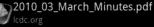

Download history

🖼 **book.gif**
www.wambooli.com
47.55KB Download complete.

⭘ **burp.wav**
www.wambooli.com
6.59KB Download complete.

2010_03_March_Minutes.pdf
lcdc.org
112KB Download complete.

🖼 **megan-fox0.jpg**
thefilmwiz.com
34.81KB Download complete.

PC Mode   ⭘

Windows Media Sync   ⭘

USB Mass Storage   ⭘

Charge Only   ⭘

OK   Cancel

9

When Your Thumbs Do the Talking

In This Chapter

▶ Creating a text message

▶ Getting a text message

▶ Texting pictures, videos, and media

▶ Managing your text messages

*T*exting is the cellphone feature that lets you choose to type, rather than talk, to exchange information. It's like turning the phone into a telegraph machine, but without the Morse code. Though that comparison may sound silly, texting is extremely popular. It's a way to communicate quickly, to exchange information without interrupting a meeting.

The process of texting need not be explained to anyone under the age of 25. Those kids text all the time. Heck, texting is a major moneymaker for the cellular companies. For the rest of us, texting is something you can do from time to time to stay in touch. It's handy. It might even be considered fun.

Where are you?

3:36 P

I'm about to be arrested

e r t y u i

Message for You!

The common term for using a cellphone to send a text message to another cellphone is *texting*. I prefer to say it as "sending a text message." The program that handles this job on your Droid X is Text Messaging.

✔ Some Android applications can affect messaging. You're alerted to whether the program affects messaging before it's installed. See Chapter 19.

✔ Your cellular service plan may charge you per message for every text message you send. Some plans feature a given number of free messages per month. Other plans, favored by teenagers (and their parents), feature unlimited texting.

✔ Though using Skype Mobile isn't exactly the same as sending a text message, you can send instant messages to folks. The person you're chatting with should have Skype installed, either on a PC or mobile phone.

✔ The nerdy term for texting is *SMS*, which stands for Short Message Service.

Composing a new text message to a contact

Because most cellphones sport a text messaging feature, you can send a text message to just about any mobile number. It works like this:

1. **Open the Contacts icon on the Home screen.**

2. **Choose a contact, someone to whom you want to send a text message.**

   You can choose a contact from the Contacts list or your favorites.

3. **Touch the Message icon next to the contact's mobile number.**

   The Message icon looks like an envelope (refer to Figure 8-2, in Chapter 8).

   A message composition window appears, which also tracks your text conversation, similar to the one shown in Figure 9-1.

Figure 9-1: Typing a text message.

4. **Type the message text.**

   Be brief. A text message has a 160-character limit. See the later sidebar "Common text-message abbreviations," for some common and useful text message shortcuts and acronyms.

5. **Touch the Send button.**

   The message is sent instantly. Whether the contact replies instantly depends. When the person replies, you see the message displayed (refer to Figure 9-1).

6. **Read the reply.**

7. **Repeat Steps 4 through 6 as needed — or eternally, whichever comes first.**

There's no need to continually look at the phone, waiting for a text message. Whenever your contact chooses to reply, you see the message recorded as part of an ongoing conversation. See the later section "Receiving a text message."

   ✔ You can send text messages only to cellphones. Grandma cannot receive text messages on her landline that she's had since the 1960s.

   ✔ See Chapter 4 for information on using the Droid X keyboard.

   ✔ You can press and hold the :-) button on the onscreen keyboard to see a whole range of smiles and other symbols *(emoticons)* that you can instantly insert into your messages.

   ✔ Yes, using Swype to type is much faster than using the standard onscreen keyboard. See Chapter 4.

   ✔ You can also dictate text messages by clicking the Microphone button on the onscreen keyboard. See Chapter 4 for more information on voice input.

   ✔ Add a subject to your message by touching the Menu soft button and choosing Add Subject.

   ✔ Phone numbers and email addresses sent in text messages become links. You can touch a link to call that number or visit the Web page.

   ✔ You cannot put the Enter (new line) key in the middle of a text message. In other words, a text message cannot appear with a break between two lines. To break a line between two messages, send two messages.

   ✔ Press the Back soft button to dismiss the onscreen keyboard, which can be useful when the keyboard obscures all or part of a message.

   ✔ Continue a conversation at any time: Open the Text Messaging application, peruse the list of existing conversations, and touch one to review what has been said or to pick up the conversation.

   ✔ Do not text and drive. Do not text and drive. Do not text and drive.

Common text-message abbreviations

Texting isn't about proper English. Indeed, many of the abbreviations and shortcuts used in texting are slowly becoming part of the English language, such as LOL and BRB.

The weird news is that these acronyms weren't invented by teenagers. Sure, the kids use them, but the acronyms find their roots in the Internet chat rooms of yesteryear. Regardless of their source, you might find them handy for typing messages quickly. Or, maybe you can use this reference for deciphering an acronym's meaning. You can type acronyms in either upper- or lowercase.

2	To, also		NP	No problem
411	Information		OMG	Oh my goodness!
BRB	Be right back		PIR	People in room (watching)
BTW	By the way		POS	Person over shoulder (watching)
CYA	See you		QT	Cutie
FWIW	For what it's worth		ROFL	Rolling on the floor, laughing
FYI	For your information		SOS	Someone over shoulder (watching)
GB	Goodbye		TC	Take care
GJ	Good job		THX	Thanks
GR8	Great		TIA	Thanks in advance
GTG	Got to go		TMI	Too much information
HOAS	Hold on a second		TTFN	Ta-ta for now (goodbye)
IC	I see		TTYL	Talk to you later
IDK	I don't know		TY	Thank you
IMO	In my opinion		U2	You, too
JK	Just kidding		UR	Your, you are
K	Okay		VM	Voice mail
L8R	Later		W8	Wait
LMAO	Laughing my [rear] off		XOXO	Hugs and kisses
LMK	Let me know		Y	Why?
LOL	Laugh out loud		YW	You're welcome
NC	No comment		ZZZ	Sleeping

Sending a text message when you know only the phone number

I recommend that you create a contact for anyone you plan to message. It just saves time to have the contact there, with — at minimum — a name and phone number. When you don't want to first create a contact, send any cellphone a text message by following these steps:

1. **Open the Text Messaging app.**

   The Text Messaging app, like all apps installed on the Droid X, can be found on the Applications Tray: Touch the Launcher button on the Home screen.

   You see a list of current conversations (if any), organized by contact name or phone number.

2. **Choose New Text Message, found at the top of the touchscreen.**

3. **Input a cellphone number in the To field.**

   The onscreen keyboard automatically appears, though you have to touch the ?123 key to see the number keys.

   When the number you type matches one or more existing contacts, you see those contacts displayed. Choose one to send a message to that person; otherwise, continue typing the phone number.

4. **Touch the Enter Message Here text box.**

5. **Type your text message.**

6. **Touch the Send button to send the message.**

The message is sent instantly. You can wait for a reply or do something else with the phone, such as snooze it or choose to talk with a real person, face to face. Or, you can always get back to work.

Receiving a text message

Whenever a new text message comes in, you see a message appear at the top of the Droid X touchscreen. The message goes away quickly, and then you see the New Text Message notification, shown in the margin.

To view the message, pull down the notifications, as described in Chapter 3. Touch the messaging notification and that conversation window immediately opens.

Whether to send a text message or an email?

The concept of sending a text message is similar to sending an email message. Both methods of communication have advantages and disadvantages.

Text messages are short and to the point. They're informal, more like quick chats. Indeed, the speed of reply is often what makes text messaging useful. But, like email, sending a text message doesn't guarantee a reply.

An email message can be longer than a text message. You can receive email on any computer or device that accesses the Internet. Email message attachments are handled better, and more consistently, than text message (MMS) media. Though email isn't considered formal communication, not like a paper letter or a phone call, it ranks a bit higher in importance than text messaging.

Multimedia Messages

When a text message contains a bit of audio or video or a picture, it ceases becoming a mere text message and transforms into — *ta-da!* — a multimedia message. This type of message even has its own acronym, MMS, which supposedly stands for Multimedia Messaging Service.

- You can send pictures, video, and audio using multimedia messaging.

- There's no need to run a separate program or do anything fancy to send media in a text message; the same Messaging app is used on the Droid X for sending both text and media messages. Just follow the advice in this section.

- Not every mobile phone has the ability to receive MMS messages. Rather than get the media, the recipient is directed to a Web page where the media can be viewed on the Internet.

Composing a multimedia message

One of the easiest ways to send a multimedia message is to start with the source, such as a picture or video stored on your phone. You can then choose to use MMS to share that media item, by heeding these directions:

1. **Locate in the Gallery the image or video you want to share.**

   You have to be viewing the image or video, so if it appears in a folder or an album, open the album and then touch the image to view it.

   See Chapter 16 for more information on how the Gallery works.

 2. **Press the Menu soft button.**

3. Choose Share.

It's found on the bottom of the screen.

4. Choose Text Messaging from the pop-up menu.

When the image or video is too large to send as a text message, you see a warning message. Dismiss the warning and try again with a smaller image or video.

5. Type a contact name or phone number into the To text field.

Type only the first part of a contact name, and then choose the proper contact from the list that appears.

6. Type a message in the Enter Message Here text box.

7. Touch the Send button to send the multimedia message.

Unlike sending a text message, sending the multimedia message takes some time.

After the message is sent, you see a copy of the image or video in the message history.

Attaching media to a message

You don't need to go hunting for already created multimedia to send in a message; you can attach media directly to any message or ongoing conversation. It works like this:

1. Compose a text message as you normally do.

Refer to the directions earlier in this chapter, in the section "Composing a new text message to a contact."

2. Press the Menu soft button.

3. Choose Insert.

A pop-up menu appears, shown in Figure 9-2, and lists various media items you can attach to a text message.

Here's a summary:

Take Picture: Take a picture right now and send it in a text message.

Picture: Choose an image stored in the phone's Gallery.

Audio: Attach a song from the music library.

Record Audio: Record an audio clip, such as your voice, and then send it.

Video: Choose a video you've taken with the phone and stored in the Gallery.

Record Video: Record a video and then send it as media in a text message.

Slideshow: Create a collection of photos to send together.

Name card: Attach contact information in the form of a vCard.

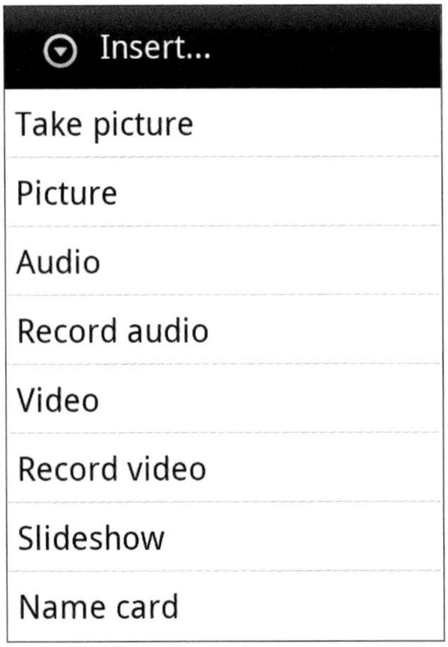

⊙ Insert...
Take picture
Picture
Audio
Record audio
Video
Record video
Slideshow
Name card

Figure 9-2: Various items to stick into a text message.

More options may appear on the menu, depending on which apps you have installed on your Droid X.

4. Choose a media attachment from the pop-up menu.

What happens next depends on the attachment you've selected.

For the Pictures and Video attachments, you choose from among media stored on your phone.

For Take Picture, Record Video, and Record Audio, you create the media and then send it.

The Slideshow option presents a second screen, where you collect pictures from the Gallery. Use the icons on top of that screen to add pictures from the Gallery. Use the Preview button to examine the slideshow.

The Name Card option displays the phone's address book. Choose a contact and that contact's information is then translated into a vCard file and attached to your text message.

5. **Optionally, compose a message to go with the media attachment.**

6. **Touch the Send button to send your media text message.**

In just a few, short, cellular moments, the receiving party will enjoy your multimedia text message.

✒ Not every phone is capable of receiving multimedia messages.

✒ Be aware of the size limit on the amount of media you can send; try to keep your video and audio attachments brief.

✒ A *vCard* is a contact-information file format, commonly used by email programs and contact management software. Whether the recipient can do anything with a vCard in a multimedia text message is up to the recipient's phone software.

Receiving a multimedia message

Multimedia attachments come into your Droid X just like any other text message does, but you see a thumbnail preview of whatever media was sent, such as an image, a still from a video, or a Play button to listen to audio. To preview the attachment, touch it. To do more with the multimedia attachment, long-press it. Choose how to deal with the attachment by selecting an option from the menu that's displayed.

For example, to save an image attachment in a text message, long-press the image thumbnail and choose the Save Picture command.

Some types of attachments, such as audio, cannot be saved.

Clean Up Your Conversations

Even though I'm a stickler for deleting email after I read it, I don't bother deleting my text message threads. That might be because I get far more email than text messages. Anyway, were I to delete a text message conversation, I would follow these exact steps:

1. **Open the conversation you want to remove.**

   Choose the conversation from the main Messaging screen.

2. **Touch the Menu soft button.**

3. **Choose Delete.**

4. **Touch the Yes button to confirm.**

   The conversation is gone.

It's an emergency alert!

Another type of message you can receive on your Droid X is the emergency alert. To peruse your options, open the Applications Tray and open the EMERGENCY app. On the main screen, you see any pending alerts, such as evacuation alerts for your area or even AMBER Alerts.

To configure emergency alerts, press the Menu soft button when viewing the main Emergency Alert screen. Choose the command Emergency Alert Settings. You can review the types of available alerts by choosing the Receive Alerts menu command.

Press the Home soft button to exit the EMERGENCY app.

If I wanted to delete every dang doodle conversation shown on the main Messaging screen, I'd follow these steps:

1. **Touch the Menu soft button.**

2. **Choose Select Multiple.**

3. **Touch the box next to each conversation you want to zap.**

   Obviously, if you want to keep one, don't touch its box; touch all boxes to delete all conversations.

   A green check mark appears by conversations slated for execution.

4. **Touch the Delete button.**

The selected messages are gone.

10

The Electronic Missive

In This Chapter

▶ Understanding email on the Droid X

▶ Receiving a new message

▶ Finding messages and email text

▶ Creating and sending email

▶ Working with email attachments

▶ Configuring a new email account

▶ Making an email signature

▶ Changing various email options and settings

*I*t's been said that the number-one reason for most people to use the Internet is email. I suppose that it makes sense: People across great distances, such as from the living room to the kitchen, have traditionally wanted to communicate. Messengers provided the delivery service for centuries before the electronic age began. Then came the telegraph, telephone, radio and, finally, email.

As a communications device, your Droid X is more than capable of sending and receiving email. In fact, because it's a Google phone, you instantly receive updates of your Gmail on the Droid X. You can also configure the phone to access your non-Gmail email, making your electronic missives conveniently available wherever you go.

Mail Call!

Electronic mail is handled on the Droid X by two apps: Gmail and Email.

The Gmail app hooks directly into the Gmail account associated with your Google account. In fact, they're exact echoes of each other: The Gmail you receive on your computer is also received on your phone.

You can also use the Email app on your phone to connect to non-Gmail electronic mail, such as the standard mail service provided by your ISP.

Regardless of the app, electronic mail on your phone works just like it does on your computer: You can receive mail, create new messages, forward email, send messages to a group of contacts, work with attachments, and so on. As long as your phone has a data connection, email works just peachy.

- ✔ You can run the Gmail and Email apps by touching the Launcher on the Home screen and then locating the apps on the Applications Tray.

- ✔ Adding the Gmail or Email app icon to the Home screen is easy: See Chapter 21.

- ✔ A Gmail account was created for you when you signed up for a Google account. See Chapter 2 for more information about setting up a Google account.

- ✔ The Email program can be configured to handle multiple email accounts, as discussed later in this chapter.

- ✔ Though you can use your phone's Web browser to visit the Gmail Web site, you should use the Gmail app to pick up your Gmail.

- ✔ If you forget your Gmail password, visit this Web address:

    www.google.com/accounts/ForgotPasswd

- ✔ Refer to Chapter 13 for information on the Droid X data connection.

You've Got Mail

The Droid X works flawlessly with Gmail. In fact, if Gmail is already set up to be your main email address, you'll enjoy having access to your messages all the time by using your phone.

Regular email, handled by the Email program, must be set up before it can be used. See the later section "Email Configuration" for details. After completing that quick and relatively painless setup, you can receive email on your phone just as you can on a computer.

Getting a new message

You're alerted to the arrival of a new email message in your phone by a notification icon. The icon differs between a new Gmail message and an Email message.

 For a new Gmail message, you see the New Gmail notification, shown in the margin, appear at the top of the touchscreen.

For a new email message, you see the New Email notification.

To deal with the new-message notification, drag down the notifications and choose the appropriate one. You're taken right to your inbox to read the new message.

> ✔ See the later section "Setting email options" to set up how the phone reacts when you get a new email message.

> ✔ Refer to Chapter 3 for information on notifications and how to peruse them.

Checking the inbox

To peruse the mail you have, start your email program — Gmail for your Google mail or Email for other mail you have configured to work with the Droid X — and open your electronic inbox.

To check your Gmail inbox, start the Gmail app. It can be found on the Applications Tray, or it might dwell on the Home screen just to the left of the main Home screen. The Gmail inbox is shown in Figure 10-1.

 To get to the inbox screen when you're reading a message, touch the Menu soft button and choose the command Back to Inbox.

Figure 10-1: The Gmail inbox.

To check your Email inbox, open the Email app. You're taken to the inbox for your primary email account, though when you have multiple email accounts on your Droid X, you should use the Messaging app, covered in the next section.

> ✓ Gmail is organized using *labels*, not folders. To see your Gmail labels from the inbox, touch the Menu soft button and choose View Labels.

> ✓ Email messages that appear on your Droid X aren't deleted from the mail server. That way, you can read the same email messages later, using a computer. Most computer email programs, however, are configured to delete messages from the mail server. When they do, those messages may no longer show up on the Droid X.

Visiting your universal inbox

There is an app in the Applications Tray called Messaging. It's the home plate for every account on your Droid X that receives messages. It includes your email accounts, both Gmail and Email, as well as social networking sites and even text messaging.

To view all your messages, open the Messaging app. You see the main screen, shown in Figure 10-2. There you find icons for all accounts on your Droid X, including mail, social networking, and text messaging.

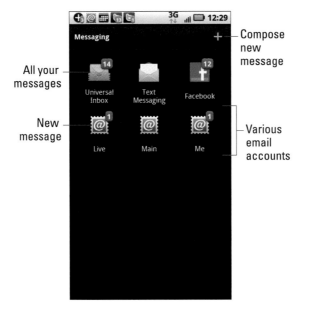

Figure 10-2: All your messages in one place.

New messages for an account are noted by a number shown in a red rectangle (refer to Figure 10-2.)

To view all messages — from email to Facebook updates — touch the Universal Inbox icon.

Composing a new message is done by touching the green plus-sign button (refer to Figure 10-2). Choose an account or a method for creating the new message from the menu that appears. You're then taken to the appropriate program (Email, Facebook, Text Messaging) to craft the new message.

Notice that your Gmail inbox is missing from the Messaging window. Gmail is its own program on the Droid X; your Gmail messages don't show up in the universal inbox. This situation may change in future Droid X software updates.

Reading an email message

As mail comes in, you can read it by choosing the New Email notification, described earlier in this chapter. You can also choose new email by viewing the inbox. The message appears on the screen, as shown in Figure 10-3. Reading and working with the message operate much the same as in any email program you've used.

Figure 10-3: Reading a Gmail message on your phone.

In Gmail, to read other messages in the inbox, touch the Older button (refer to Figure 10-3). To read newer messages in the inbox, press the Menu soft button and choose the Newer command.

In the Email or Messaging program, you browse the messages in your inbox by touching the up or down buttons, found at the bottom of the message window.

Here are some things you can do with an email message you read on your Droid X:

✔ To reply to the message, touch the Reply button.

✔ Touch the Reply to All or Reply All button to send a response to every-one in the original message's To and CC fields.

✔ Use Reply All only when everyone else *must* get a copy of your reply. Because most people find endless Reply All email threads annoying, use the Reply All option judiciously.

✔ Type or dictate your message reply; refer to Chapter 4 for information on typing and talking, if you're unfamiliar with either.

✔ Touch the Send button to send the reply message.

✔ Touch Cancel to cancel your reply, and then touch the Yes button to confirm.

✔ To forward a Gmail message, touch the Forward button.

✔ Refer to the later section "Composing a new electronic message" for information on (surprisingly) composing a new electronic message, which also applies when you forward or reply to an email.

✔ When you touch the Star icon in a Gmail message, you're flagging the message. Those starred messages can be viewed or searched separately, making them easier to locate later.

✔ To delete a message, touch the Delete button. I see no reason to delete messages in the Email program, because they're deleted when your computer's email program picks them up later.

✔ I find it easier to delete (and manage) Gmail using a computer.

✔ Future releases of the Android operating system change the look of the Gmail program (refer to Figure 10-3). Primarily, two buttons replace the single Older button: a < button for newer messages and a > button for older messages.

Searching Gmail

You can use the Search soft button to search Gmail on your phone, just as you can search for anything else. The key is to use the Search soft button while you're in the Gmail program. Here's how:

1. **Open the Gmail inbox.**

2. **Touch the Search soft button.**

3. **Type the text to find.**

   You can also dictate the text by first pressing the Microphone button on the onscreen keyboard and then speaking what you're trying to find.

4. **Touch the Search button to begin the search.**

   Peruse the results.

The search results are limited to text in those program's messages. To perform a wider search throughout the entire phone, touch the Search soft button when viewing the Home screen.

Make Your Own Mail

Every so often, someone comes up to me and says, "Dan, you're a computer freak. You probably get a lot of email." I generally nod and smile. Then they say, "How can I get more email?" The answer is simple: To get mail, you have to send mail. Or, you can just be a jerk on a blog and leave your email address there. That works too, though I don't recommend it.

Composing a new electronic message

Crafting an email epistle on your Droid X works exactly like creating one on your computer. Figure 10-4 shows the basic setup.

Here's how to get there:

1. **Start an email program, either Gmail or Email, or use the Messaging app.**

2. **Press the Menu soft button.**

3. **Choose Compose.**

   You need to be viewing the inbox, not a specific message, for the Compose command to be available.

   In the Messaging app, choose an account. You use this account to send the message.

   A new message screen appears, looking similar to Figure 10-4 but with none of the fields filled in.

4. **If necessary, touch the To field to select it.**

5. **Type the first few letters of a contact name, and then choose a matching contact from the list that's displayed.**

You can also send to any valid email address not found in your Contacts list, by typing that address. Notice that the onscreen keyboard changes to add the @ (at-sign) and .com keys, which makes typing email addresses easier.

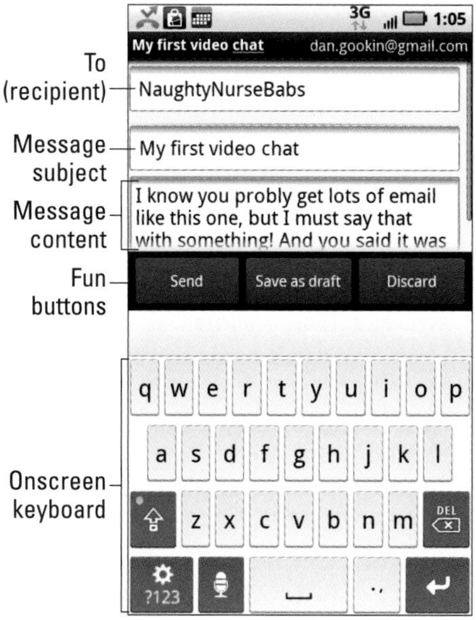

Figure 10-4: Writing a new email message.

6. **Type a subject.**

   Touch the Subject field and use the onscreen keyboard to type a subject. Or, you can dictate the subject using voice input, as described in Chapter 4.

7. **Type the message.**

   Touch the Compose Mail field and use your best thumb-typing skills to compose your letter. Or, you can dictate the message.

8. **Touch the Send button to whisk your missive to the Internet for immediate delivery.**

   Or, you can touch either the Discard or Cancel button to trash the message. If prompted, touch OK or Yes to confirm its deletion.

   In Gmail, when you touch the Save As Draft button, the message is stored in the Drafts folder. You can open this folder to re-edit the message. Touch Send to send it.

Copies of the messages you send in the Email program are stored in the Sent mailbox. If you're using Gmail, copies are saved in your Gmail account, which is accessed both from your phone or from any computer connected to the Internet.

- Refer to Chapter 8 for more information on the Contacts list.

- Chapter 4 covers typing, voice input, and message editing.

- To summon the CC field in Gmail, press the Menu soft button and choose the command Add Cc/Bcc; in the Email program, press the Menu soft button and choose the button Add CC.

Starting a new message from a contact

A quick and easy way to compose a new message is to find a contact and then create a message using that contact's information. Heed these steps:

1. **Open the Contacts list.**

   Touch the Phone button to the left of the Launcher on the Home screen, and then choose Contacts from the top of the list.

2. **Locate the contact to whom you want to send an electronic message.**

   Review Chapter 8 for ways to hunt down contacts in a long list.

3. **Touch the icon next to the contact's email address.**

4. **Choose Compose to use Gmail to send the message or choose Email to send an email message using your main email account.**

   At this point, creating the message works as described in the preceding section; refer to it for additional information.

Message Attachments

You can send and receive email attachments by using your Droid X. Though that feature is nice, an email attachment is more of a computer thing, not something that's wholly useful on a cellphone.

For receiving attachments, the Droid X lets you view the attachment, to see its contents. Not every attachment is viewable, however. It all depends on the type of file attached to the message.

Email messages with attachments are flagged in the inbox with paper clip icons, which seems to be the standard I-have-an-attachment icon for most email programs. When you open one of these files, you may see the attachment name appear, as shown in Figure 10-5. Touch the Preview button to witness the attachment on your phone.

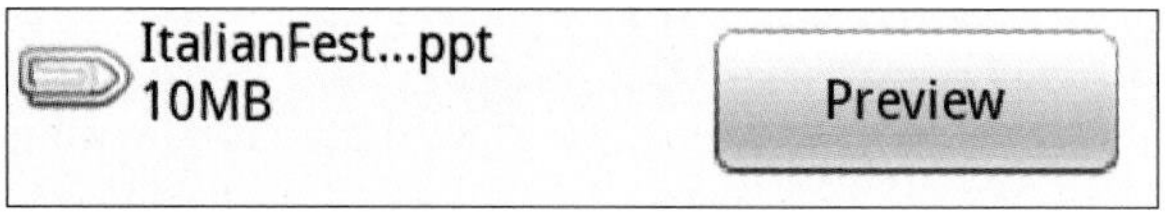

ItalianFest...ppt
10MB

Preview

Figure 10-5: An email attachment.

What happens after you touch the Preview button depends on the type of attachment. Sometimes, you see a list of apps from which you can choose one to open the attachment. Many Microsoft Office documents are opened by the QuickOffice app.

Some attachments cannot be opened. In those cases, use a computer to fetch the message and attempt to open the attachment. Or, you can reply to the message and inform the sender that you cannot open the attachment on your phone.

- ✔ Sometimes, pictures included in an email message aren't displayed. You find a Show Pictures button in the message, which you can choose to display the pictures.

- ✔ You cannot save certain email attachments on your phone. Wait until you retrieve these messages on your computer to save the attachments.

- ✔ You can add an attachment to an email message you create, though attachments are limited to photos and videos: Touch the Menu soft button and choose either the Attach or Attach Files command. You can then choose what to attach.

- ✔ You can browse the Gallery and choose a photo or video to email: Long-press the photo and choose the Share command from the bottom of the screen. Choose Email or Gmail from the pop-up menu to begin a new message with that photo or video attached.

- ✔ See Chapter 16 for more information on the Gallery.

Email Configuration

There are a few things you can do to customize the email experience on your Droid X. You can add one or more of your Internet email accounts so that you can receive email on your phone at any time. You can customize an email signature, plus set other options, some of which are boring, so I don't discuss them in this section.

Setting up an email account

When you have and use non–Gmail email accounts, you can configure the phone's Email program to work with each of them. Here's how it's done:

1. **Start the My Accounts app.**

   The My Accounts app is found in the Applications Tray, which you access by touching the Launcher button at the bottom of the Home screen.

2. **Touch the Add Account button.**

3. **Choose the Email icon to add your Internet email account.**

   If prompted, touch the I Agree check mark and then the Next button to agree to the Motorola Service Agreement.

   The Droid X needs to know information about your email account — those techy tidbits typically supplied by your ISP or whatever outfit provides your email service.

4. **Input the email address you use for the account.**

5. **Input the password for that account.**

6. **Remove the check mark by the option Automatically Configure Account.**

   Though the Droid X is good, it's not good enough to guess how to configure a standard Internet email account without some additional information.

   If you're configuring a Web-based email account, such as Windows Live or Mobile Me, you can keep the check mark and touch the Next button. In many cases, the Droid X can automatically configure those accounts. If so, you see a Success message; touch the Done button and you're ready to use the account on the Droid X.

7. **Touch the Next button.**

8. **Choose General Settings.**

9. **Fill in the information for account name, real name, and email address.**

   For the Account Name field, type a name to recognize the account, such as Comcast Email or AOL Email or whatever name helps you recognize the account.

   In the Real Name field, type your name, screen name, or whatever name you want to appear in the From field of your outgoing email messages.

   The Email Address field is the address your recipients use when replying to your messages.

10. **Touch the OK button.**

11. **Choose Incoming Server.**

12. **Fill in the fields per the information provided by your Internet service provider (ISP).**

    For most ISP email, the server type is POP.

    The Server field contains the name of the ISP's POP server.

    The Port is 110 for a POP server, so you can leave that field as is.

    The username is the name you use to log in to your ISP to retrieve email.

    The password is your ISP email password.

13. **Touch the OK button.**

14. **Choose Outgoing Server.**

15. **Fill in the fields.**

    Fill in the SMTP Server name as provided by your ISP.

    The Port is 25 for SMTP servers.

    As you did in Step 11, fill in your username and password for your ISP's email.

16. **Touch the OK button.**

17. **Choose Other Settings.**

18. **Ensure that Never Delete Messages is chosen from the list.**

    By selecting Never Delete Messages, you ensure that email you receive on your Droid X can be picked up later when you use your computer.

19. **Touch OK.**

20. **Touch OK again to create the email account.**

The account is now listed in the My Accounts screen, along with Google and Facebook and whatever other accounts you're accessing from your Droid X.

You can set up a ton of email accounts on the Droid X, one for each email account you have. They all appear in a list in the Messaging program, as shown earlier, in Figure 10-2.

Not every Web-based email account can be accessed by the Droid X. When doubt exists, you see an appropriate warning message. In most cases, the warning message also explains how to properly configure the Web-based email account to work with your phone.

Creating a signature

I highly recommend that you create a custom email signature for sending messages from your phone. Here's my signature:

```
DAN

This was sent from my Droid X.
Please forgive the typos.
```

To create a signature for Gmail, obey these directions:

1. **Start Gmail.**
2. **Press the Menu soft button.**
3. **Choose Settings.**

   If you see no settings, choose Back to Inbox and repeat Steps 2 and 3.

4. **Choose Signature.**
5. **Type or dictate your signature.**
6. **Touch OK.**

You can obey these same steps to change your signature; the existing signature shows up after Step 4.

To set a signature for the Email program, heed these steps:

1. **Start a new message.**
2. **Press the Menu soft button.**
3. **Choose More and then choose Email Settings.**
4. **Choose Compose Options.**
5. **Edit the Email Signature area to reflect your new signature.**

   The preset signature is *Sent via DROID on Verizon Wireless.* Feel free to edit it at your whim.

6. **Touch the Done button.**
7. **Press the Back button to return to the message, where you can touch Cancel to stop composing a new message.**

The signature you set appears in all outgoing messages.

Setting email options

A smattering of interesting email settings are worth looking into. To reach the Settings screen in Gmail, follow Steps 1 through 3 in the first set of steps from the preceding section; for Email, follow Steps 1 through 4 in the second set of steps.

Here are some items worthy of note:

- To specify how frequently the Email program checks for new messages, choose Email Delivery on the Email settings screen. Put a check mark by Data Push and then set the check frequency by choosing the Fetch Schedule item.

- Choose Email Notifications in Gmail, or Notifications in Email, to have the phone alert you to new messages.

- Choose a specific ringtone for the account by touching Select Ringtone, beneath Notifications for Gmail. In the Email program, choose Email Notifications and then Select Ringtone.

- Specify whether the phone vibrates upon the receipt of new email by choosing Vibrate.

- The ringtone and vibration options are available only when Email Notifications is selected.

Out on the Web

I doubt that when the World Wide Web was created anyone envisioned someone browsing the Web on a cellphone. That was back in the early 1990s. Cellphones back then had text screens, not the LCD screens of today. Those phones didn't talk with the Internet, let alone browse the Web.

Where you were once limited to wasting time on the Web with your computer, you're now free to waste time on the Internet anywhere you go with your Droid X. The screen may be smaller than a computer monitor, but if you're comfortable using the Web already, you'll find refreshing familiarity in using it on your cellphone. If you don't, this chapter can serve as your handy guide.

✔ If possible, activate the Droid X Wi-Fi connection before you venture out on the Web. Though you can use the phone's cellular data connection, the Wi-Fi connection is *far* faster. See Chapter 13 for more information.

✔ The Droid X has apps for Gmail, Facebook, Twitter, and YouTube and potentially other popular locations or activities on the Web. I highly recommend using those applications on the phone, as opposed to visiting the Web sites using the phone's browser.

Behold the Web Page

The World Wide Web should be familiar to you. Using the World Wide Web on a cellphone, however, may not be. Don't worry. Consider this section your quick orientation.

Looking at the Web

Begin your venture out on the Internet by starting the Browser app. You might find it on the main Home screen, or you can locate it on the Applications Tray. The Browser app is your phone's Web browser. Figure 11-1 shows how it looks.

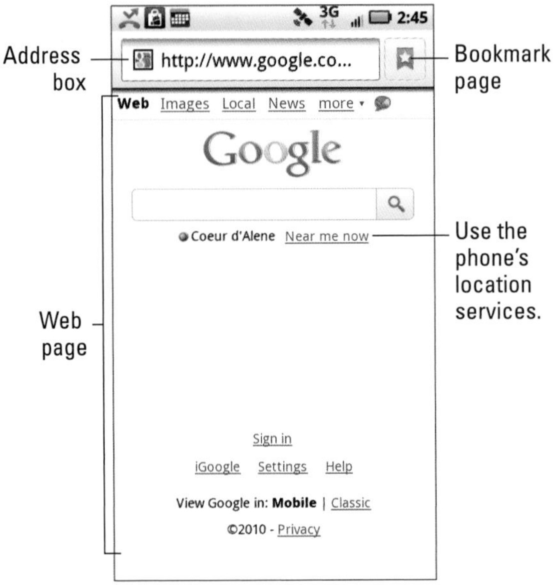

Figure 11-1: The Browser.

Because the Droid X screen isn't a full desktop screen, not every Web page looks good on it. Here are a few tricks you can use:

- Pan the Web page by dragging your finger across the touchscreen. You can pan up, down, left, and right.
- Double-touch the screen to zoom in or zoom out.
- Pinch the screen to zoom out, or spread two fingers to zoom in.

✔ Tilt the phone to its side to read a Web page in Landscape mode. Then you can spread or double-tap the touch screen to make teensy text more readable.

Visiting a Web page

To visit a Web page, type its address into the Address box (refer to Figure 11-1). You can also type a search word, if you don't know the exact address of a Web page. You can touch the Go button to search the Web or visit a specific Web page.

If you don't see the Address box, swipe your finger so that you can see the top of the Web page, where the Address box lurks.

You click links on a page by using your finger on the touchscreen.

✔ To reload a Web page, press the Menu soft button and choose the Refresh command. Refreshing updates Web sites that change often, and the command can also be used to reload a Web page that may not have completely loaded the first time.

✔ To stop a Web page from loading, touch the X button that appears to the right of the Address box. (The X button replaces the Bookmarks button — refer to Figure 11-1.)

Browsing back and forth

To return to a previous Web page, press the Back soft button. It works just like clicking the Back button on a computer's Web browser.

The Forward button also exists in the Browser program: Press the Menu soft button and choose the Forward command.

To review the long-term history of your Web browsing adventures, follow these steps:

1. **Press the Menu soft button.**
2. **Choose Bookmarks.**
3. **At the top of the Bookmarks page, choose History.**

To view a page you visited weeks or months ago, you can choose a Web page from the History list.

To clear the History list, press the Menu soft button while viewing the History list and choose the Clear History command.

Using bookmarks

Bookmarks are those electronic breadcrumbs you can drop as you wander the Web. Need to revisit a Web site? Just look up its bookmark. This advice assumes, of course, that you bother to create (I prefer *drop*) a bookmark when you first visit the site. Here's how it works:

1. **Visit the Web page you want to bookmark.**

2. **Touch the Bookmark button, found at the top of the Browser window.**

   Refer to Figure 11-1 to see the location of the Bookmark button. After pressing the button, you see the Bookmarks screen, shown in Figure 11-2. The screen lists your bookmarks, showing Web site thumbnail previews.

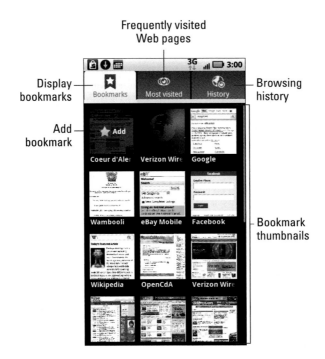

Figure 11-2: Adding a bookmark.

3. **Touch the Add button.**

   The Add button appears in the upper left square on the Bookmarks screen (refer to Figure 11-2). It has the name of the site or page you're bookmarking just below the square.

4. **If necessary, edit the bookmark name.**

   The bookmark is given the Web page name, which might be kind of long. I usually edit the name to something shorter that can fit into the thumbnail squares.

5. **Touch OK.**

After the bookmark is set, it appears in the list of bookmarks, usually at the end. You can swipe the list downward to see the bookmarks and all their fun thumbnails.

Another way to add a bookmark is to touch the Most Visited tab at the top of the Bookmarks screen (refer to Figure 11-2). That screen lists Web pages you visit most often. To add one of those pages, long-press the thumbnail and choose the command Add Bookmark.

✔ To visit a bookmark, press the Menu soft button and choose the Bookmarks command. Touch a bookmark thumbnail to visit that site.

✔ Remove a bookmark by long-pressing its thumbnail on the Bookmarks screen. Choose the command Delete Bookmark. Touch the OK button to confirm.

✔ Bookmarked Web sites can also be placed on the Home screen: Long-press the bookmark thumbnail and choose the command Add Shortcut to Home.

✔ You can switch between Thumbnail and List views for your bookmarks: When viewing the Bookmarks screen, press the Menu soft button and choose the List View command to switch to List view. To return to Thumbnail view, press the Menu soft button and choose Thumbnail View.

✔ You can obtain the MyBookmarks app at the Android Market. The app can import your Internet Explorer, Firefox, and Chrome bookmarks from your Windows computer into the Droid X. See Chapter 19 for more information on the Android Market.

✔ Refer to Chapter 4 for information on editing text on the Droid X.

Managing multiple Web page windows

Because the Browser app sports more than one window, you can have multiple Web pages open at a time on your Droid X. You have several ways to summon another browser window:

✔ *To open a link in another window,* press and hold that link by using your finger. Choose the command Open in New Window from the menu that appears.

> ✔ *To open a bookmark in a new window,* long-press the bookmark and choose the command Open in New Window.
>
> ✔ *To open a blank browser window,* press the Menu soft button and choose New Window.

You switch between windows by pressing the Menu soft button and choosing the Windows command. All open Browser windows are displayed on the screen; switch to a window by choosing it from the list. Or, you can close a window by touching the X button to the right of the window's name.

New windows open using the home page that's set for the Browser application. See the section "Setting a home page," later in this chapter, for information.

Searching the Web

The handiest way to find things on the Web is to use the Google widget, often found floating on the first Home screen to the left of the main Home screen, and shown in Figure 11-3. Use the Google widget to type something to search for, or touch the Microphone button to dictate what you want to find on the Internet.

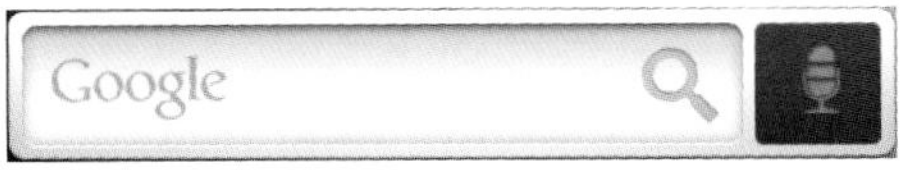

Figure 11-3: The Google widget.

To search for something any time you're viewing a Web page in the Browser app, press the Search soft button. Type the search term into the box. You can choose from a suggestions list, shown in Figure 11-4, or touch the Go button to complete the search using the Google search engine.

To find text on the Web page you're looking at, as opposed to searching the entire Internet, follow these steps:

1. **Visit the Web page where you want to find a specific tidbit o' text.**

2. **Press the Menu soft button.**

3. **Choose the More command.**

4. **Choose Find on Page.**

5. **Type the text you're searching for.**

6. **Use the left- or right-arrow button to locate that text on the page —
backward or forward, respectively.**

The found text appears highlighted in green.

7. **Touch the X button when you're done searching.**

When the text isn't found, nothing is highlighted on the page; you see 0
matches displayed beneath the search text box.

See Chapter 21 for more information on widgets, such as the Google widget.

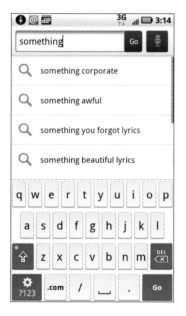

Figure 11-4: Searching for things on the Internet.

Sharing a page

The Android operating system lets you easily share information you find on
your phone. With regard to the Web pages you visit, you can easily share
links and bookmarks. Follow these steps:

1. **Long-press the link or bookmark you want to share.**

2. **Choose the command Share Link.**

A pop-up menu of places to share appears, looking similar to Figure 11-5.
The variety and number of items on the Share Via menu depends on the
applications installed on your phone.

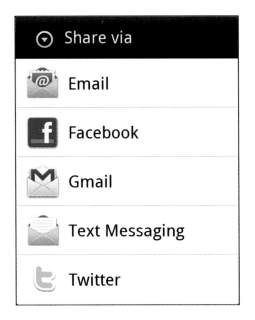

Figure 11-5: Options for sharing a Web page.

3. Choose a method to share the link.

For example, choose Email to send the link by mail, or Text Messaging to share via a text message.

4. Do whatever happens next.

Whatever happens next depends on how you're sharing the link.

Most likely, whatever happens next opens another application, where you can complete the process. Refer to various parts of this book for the specifics.

The Perils and Joys of Downloading

One of the most abused words in all computerdom is *download*. People don't understand what it means. It's definitely not a synonym for *transfer* or *copy*, though that's how I hear it used most often.

For the sake of the Droid X, a *download* is a transfer of information from another location to your phone. When you send something from the phone, you're *uploading* it. There. Now the nerd in me feels much better.

You can download information from a Web page into your phone. It doesn't work exactly like downloading does for a computer, which is why I wrote this section.

- ✔ There's no need to download program files to your Droid X. If you want new software, you can obtain it from the Android Market, covered in Chapter 19.

- ✔ When the phone is downloading information, you see the Downloading notification.

Grabbing an image from a Web page

The simplest thing to download is an image from a Web page. It's cinchy: Long-press the image. You see a pop-up menu appear, from which you choose the command Save Image.

- ✔ The image is copied and stored on your Droid X — specifically, in the Gallery in a special folder named Download.

- ✔ Refer to Chapter 16 for information on the Gallery.

- ✔ Technically, the image is stored on the phone's MicroSD card. You can read about storage on the MicroSD card in Chapter 13.

Downloading a file

When a link opens a document on a Web page, such as a Microsoft Word document or a PDF (Adobe Acrobat) file, you can download that information to your phone. Simply long-press the download link and choose the command Save Link from the menu that appears.

You can view the link by referring to the Download History screen. This screen appears after the download is complete. See the next section.

Reviewing your downloads

You can then view downloaded information by perusing the Download History screen, shown in Figure 11-6. That screen normally appears right after you download anything, or you can summon it at any time while using the Browser app, by pressing the Menu soft button, choosing the More command, and then choosing Downloads.

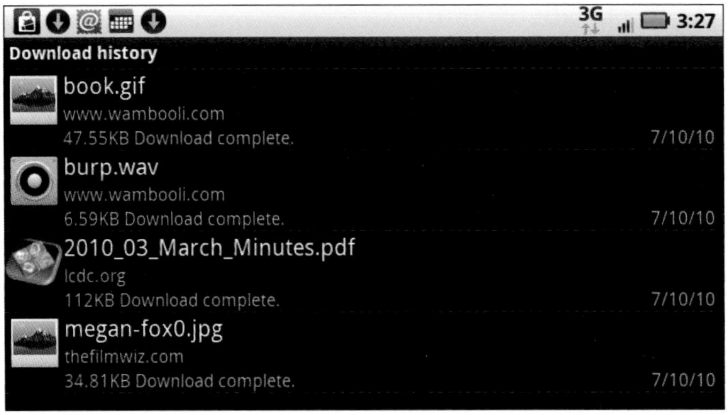

Figure 11-6: The Download History screen.

The stuff you download is viewed by using special apps on your phone, such as the QuickOffice app, which can view Microsoft Office files as well as PDF documents. Don't fret the process: Simply choose the item you download from the Download History screen and you can then see it on your phone.

- ✓ Well, of course, there are some things you can download that you cannot view. When that happens, you see an appropriately rude error message.

- ✓ You can quickly review any download by choosing the Download notification.

Web Controls and Settings

More options and settings and controls exist for the Browser program than just about every other program I've used on the Droid X. It's complex. Rather than bore you with every dang doodle detail, I thought I'd present just a few of the options worthy of your attention.

Setting a home page

The *home page* is the first page you see when you start the Browser application, and it's the first page that's loaded when you fire up a blank window. To set your home page, heed these directions:

1. **Browse to the page you want to set as the home page.**

2. **Press the Menu soft button.**

3. **Choose More.**

4. **Choose Settings.**

   A massive list of options and settings appears.

5. **Choose Set Home Page.**

   It's way down the list, so swipe the list downward as necessary.

   After choosing the Set Home Page command, you see a Set Home Page box, where you can type the home page address. Because you obeyed Step 1, you don't need to type that address right now.

6. **Touch OK.**

   The home page is set.

Unless you've already set a new home page, the Droid X comes configured with the Google search page as your home page.

If you want your home page to be blank (not set to any particular Web page), set the name of the home page (refer to Step 5) to about:blank. That's the word *about,* a colon, and then the word *blank,* with no period at the end and no spaces in the middle. I prefer a blank home page because it's the fastest Web page to load. It's also the Web page with the most accurate information.

Changing the way the Web looks

You can do a few things to improve the way the Web looks on your phone. First and foremost, don't forget that you can orient the phone horizontally to see a wide view on any Web page.

From the Settings screen, you can also adjust the text size used to display a Web page. Heed these steps:

1. **Press the Menu soft button.**

2. **Choose More.**

3. **Choose Settings.**

4. **Choose Text Size.**

5. **Select a better size from the menu.**

   For example, try Large or Huge.

6. **Press the Back soft button to return to the Web page screen.**

I don't make any age-related comments about text size at this time, and especially at this point in my life.

Setting privacy and security options

With regard to security, my advice is always to be smart and think before doing anything questionable on the Web. Use common sense. One of the most effective ways that the Bad Guys win is by using *human engineering* to try to trick you into doing something you normally wouldn't do, such as click a link to see a cute animation or a racy picture of a celebrity or politician. As long as you use your noggin, you should be safe.

As far as the phone's settings go, most of the security options are already enabled for you, including the blocking of pop-up windows (which normally spew ads).

If Web page cookies concern you, you can clear them from the Settings window. Follow Steps 1 through 3 in the preceding section and choose the option Clear All Cookie Data.

You can also choose the command Clear Form Data and remove the check mark from Remember Forum Data. These two settings prevent any characters you've input into a text field from being summoned automatically by someone who may steal your phone.

You might be concerned about various warnings regarding location data. What they mean is that the phone can take advantage of your location on planet earth (using the Droid X GPS or satellite position system) to help locate businesses and people near you. I see no security problem in leaving that feature on, though you can disable location services from the Browser's Settings screen: Remove the check mark by Enable Location. You can also choose the item Clear Location Access to wipe out any information saved in the phone and used by certain Web pages.

See the earlier section "Browsing back and forth" for steps on clearing your Web browsing history.

A Social Networking Butterfly

In This Chapter

▶ Accessing Facebook on your phone

▶ Updating your Facebook status

▶ Sharing photos on Facebook

▶ Finding a Twitter client

▶ Sending a tweet

▶ Accessing other social networking sites

They said that the Internet would isolate people and keep us alone in our homes and away from human contact. Boy, were they wrong! The Internet is now the most social hub the world has seen since the Tower of Babel. Thanks to social networking sites on the Web, you can stay in touch with friends and relatives flung far and wide, including people you've never even met, who can suddenly become your new best friends. That connection can also be made on your phone, so now you can lead an incredible social life all by yourself, all alone, wherever you go.

Tweets (22)

Lists

Mentions (13)

Retwee

Your Life on Facebook

The most popular of all social networking sites is Facebook. At this Internet destination, you can offer your thoughts, say what you're doing, share photos and videos, play games, and enjoy other diversions. To get started, you need a Facebook account, if you don't have one already. Then you can use either the Facebook or social networking apps on your Droid X to keep up with your busy online social life.

·ages

M·

- ✔ Though you can access Facebook on the Web by using the Browser app, I highly recommend that you use the Facebook app that comes with the Droid X.

- ✔ You can also use the Social Networking app to view or set Facebook status updates, though it's not as useful as the Facebook app.

- ✔ Facebook is one of the most popular sites on the Internet as the time this book goes to press. On some days, it sees more Internet traffic than Google.

Creating a Facebook account

To use Facebook on your Droid X, you must have a Facebook account. The easiest way to do that is to visit www.facebook.com on your computer and register for a new account. Remember your login name and password.

You confirm your Facebook account by replying to an email message. After you do that, Facebook is ready for your thoughts and photos and other personal details. Also, after confirming your Facebook account, you can set it up on your phone by following these steps:

1. **From the Home screen, touch the Launcher button to display the Applications Tray.**

2. **Open the Settings icon.**

3. **Choose Accounts.**

   If you see a Facebook account listed, you're done. Otherwise:

4. **Touch the Add Account button.**

5. **Choose Facebook.**

6. **Touch the Email text box.**

7. **Type the email address you used to sign up for Facebook.**

   See Chapter 4 for help using the onscreen keyboard.

8. **Touch the Password text box.**

9. **Type your Facebook password.**

   The characters you type turn into big dots so that no one looking at the phone can see your password.

10. **Touch the Next button.**

    The Droid X signs in to your Facebook account.

11. **If prompted, touch the OK button to dismiss the Picture Source message.**

12. **Touch the Done button.**

    You're done.

You can now use the Social Networking app on your Droid X to review status updates and messages from your Facebook friends.

Visiting Facebook

To visit your Facebook account on the Droid, open the Facebook app. It's found in the Applications Tray. If you can't find a copy of the app, you can _____ Facebook for Android app by visiting the Android Market. See

_____ ebook screen is shown in Figure 12-1. It's a rather simplistic _____ it's the spot where you can check most of the things you do on _____ luding upload a photo or keep your status up-to-date wherever _____ ur Droid.

_____ se an item from the main Facebook screen, another screen _____ e information:

_____ status updates, newly added photos, and other information _____ ook friends.

_____ of all your Facebook friends, search for friends, or touch a _____ e their status and other information.

_____ ur Facebook photo albums.

Figure 12-1: Facebook on your phone.

Inbox: Read your Facebook messages, updates, and any messages you've sent.

Profile: Review your personal Facebook page, your status updates, and whatever else you're wasting your time doing on Facebook.

Notifications: Peruse a list of all comments made on your status and photo as well as any notifications or invites you've received.

 To return to the main Facebook screen from another area, press the Back soft button.

- ✔ Facebook widgets on the Home screen let you view status updates. The Facebook widgets are preinstalled on the leftmost Home screen.

- ✔ When things happen on Facebook, you see a Facebook notification icon. When you receive lots of Facebook notices or updates, a number in a red circle appears on the icon, indicating the number of new Facebook updates.

- ✔ Sometimes, choosing a Facebook notification opens the Facebook app, and sometimes it opens the Browser to visit Facebook on the Web.

- ✔ Review Chapter 3 to see how to deal with notifications.

- ✔ See Chapter 21 for information on placing the Facebook app icon on the Home screen.

- ✔ To sign out of Facebook on your phone, touch the Menu soft button when viewing the main Facebook screen and choose the Logout command. Touch the Yes button to confirm.

Setting your Facebook status

With Facebook on your phone, you can add a new status, such as "Waiting in line at Starbucks and trying not to be angry with the indecisive person at the head of the line," when you're actually waiting in line at Starbucks. I'm sure all your Facebook friends live for such moments.

To update your Facebook status on the Droid X, follow these steps:

1. **From the main Facebook screen, choose either News Feed or Profile.**

2. **Type or dictate your status in the What's On Your Mind text box.**

Your Facebook friends see your status update instantly, plus they see the tiny Mobile icon appear next to your status update, as shown in Figure 12-2.

Dan Gookin To my kids: Being dirty tells everyone else that you've actually been outside.
17 seconds ago via DROID · Comment · Like

Figure 12-2: A mobile Facebook update.

The mobile phone icon tells your pals that the update was made by using your cellphone.

Sending a picture to Facebook

One of the handiest reasons to use Facebook on a cellphone is that you can take a picture and instantly upload it to Facebook. This feature lets you easily capture and share various intimate and private moments of your life with everyone in the known universe.

To share a picture with Facebook, you can either take a picture using the Facebook app or you can upload an image you've already taken with your Droid X.

To take a picture with the Facebook app, follow these steps:

1. **Touch the Camera icon.**

   The icon is found to the left of the text box where you type your status updates. By touching the Camera icon, you switch the Droid X over to camera mode, where you can snap a picture.

2. **After taking the picture, touch the Done button.**

   Or you can touch Retake or Cancel if you're unhappy with the results.

3. **Add a caption to the image.**

   You may have to scroll the window down a bit to see the text box where you type in a caption.

4. **Touch the Upload button to send the picture you just took to Facebook.**

   In a few moments, the image is uploaded to Facebook.

Because you used Facebook to take the picture, the image is formatted properly for uploading. There is no need to make additional camera settings, unless you're adding an effect or using other Droid X camera features, described in Chapter 15.

You can also upload an existing image from your phone to Facebook. To do so, you need to use the Gallery app as discussed in Chapter 16.

Changing various Facebook settings

The commands that control Facebook are stored on the Settings screen, which you access by touching the Menu soft button while viewing the main Facebook screen and choosing the Settings command.

Most settings are self explanatory: You simply choose which Facebook events you want the Droid X to monitor. Two items you might want to set are the refresh interval and the way the phone alerts you to new Facebook activities.

Choose Refresh Interval to specify how often the Droid X checks for new Facebook activities. You might find the one-hour value to be too long for your active Facebook social life, so choose something quicker. Or, to disable Facebook notifications, choose Never.

Three options determine how the Droid X reacts to Facebook updates:

Vibrate: Vibrates the phone

Phone LED: Flashes the notification lamp on the front of the Droid X

Notification Ringtone: Plays a specific ringtone

For the notification ringtone, choose the Silent option when you want the phone not to make noise upon encountering a Facebook update.

Become Famous with Twitter

The Twitter social networking site proves the hypothesis that everyone will be famous on the Internet for 140 words or fewer.

Like Facebook, Twitter is used to share your existence with others or simply to follow what others are up to or thinking. It sates some people's craving for attention and provides the bricks that pave the road to fame — or so I believe. I'm not a big Twitter fan, but your phone is capable of letting you *tweet* from wherever you are.

 ✔ They say that of all the people who have accounts on Twitter, only a small portion of them actively use the service.

 ✔ A message posted on Twitter is a *tweet*.

 ✔ You can post messages on Twitter or follow others who post messages.

Setting up Twitter on the Droid X

My advice is to set up an account on Twitter using a computer, not your phone. Visit `http://twitter.com` on a computer and follow the directions there for creating a new account.

After creating a Twitter account, you use the Twitter app on your phone to view Twitter updates or to make tweets, which is described in the next section.

 ✔ The Twitter app I recommend, named Twitter, was developed by the Twitter people themselves. Twitter is free and available at the Android Market.

 ✔ Refer to Chapter 19 for information on the Android Market.

Tweeting to other twits

The Twitter application provides an excellent interface to many Twitter tasks, as shown in Figure 12-3. The two most basic tasks, however, are reading and writing tweets.

To read tweets, choose the Tweets item (refer to Figure 12-3). Recent tweets are displayed in a list, with the most recent information at the top. Scroll the list by swiping it with your finger.

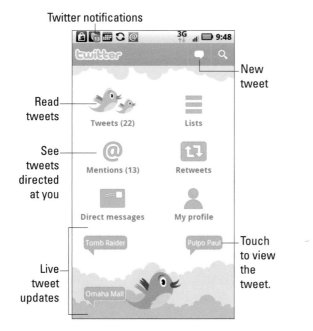

Figure 12-3: The Twitter app.

To tweet, touch the New Tweet icon (refer to Figure 12-3). You see the Create Tweet screen, shown in Figure 12-4. You can use this screen to send text, upload an image from the Gallery, or take a new picture.

Figure 12-4: Creating a tweet.

Other Social Networking Opportunities

The Web seems to see a new social networking phenomenon just about every week. The field isn't limited to Facebook and Twitter, though they capture a lot of media attention and both are extremely popular.

Other common social networking sites include

- Google Buzz
- LinkedIn
- Meebo
- MySpace

These sites may have special Android apps you can install on your Droid X, such as the MySpace Mobile app for MySpace.

As with Facebook and Twitter, you should always configure an account using a computer and then set up options on your phone.

After adding some social networking apps, you may see them appear on various Share menus on the Droid X. Use the Share menus to help you share media files with your online social networking pals.

The Droid X Connection

In This Chapter

▶ Getting the phone and the computer to talk

▶ Mounting the phone as computer storage

▶ Synchronizing media

▶ Replacing the MicroSD card

▶ Using Wi-Fi on the Droid X

▶ Connecting to a Wi-Fi network

▶ Adding a Bluetooth headset

*W*hen I think about the power and potential that are packed into the Droid X, one question comes to the forefront of my mind: Are the other devices in my life seething with jealousy over my cell-phone? Seriously: The Droid X packs more power than a typical computer from 20 years ago. Even the graphics are better. And, if other devices in my office are jealous of the Droid X, can they ever be on speaking terms?

Well, of course the Droid X is on speaking terms, with not only your computer but also a myriad of other gizmos you may have. Your phone is a congenial device. It talks with your computer, with a Wi-Fi network, with the Internet, and perhaps even with your toaster oven — if the toaster oven features Bluetooth communications.

Phone-to-Computer Sharing

Having the Droid X share information with your computer is a must. The main reason is the transfer of information: You can update your phone with information on the computer, such as music, photos, videos, and contacts. You can also update the information on your computer from the Droid X. It's all explained in this section.

The computer accesses the Droid X *MicroSD* memory card, which is where the phone stores your photos, videos, Contacts list, music, and other goodies.

Connecting the phone to the computer

Communication between your computer and the Droid X works best when both devices are physically connected. That connection happens by using the USB cable that came with the phone. Like nearly every computer cable in the Third Dimension, the USB cable has two ends:

- The A end of the USB cable plugs into the computer.
- The micro–USB end of the cable plugs into the left flank of the Droid X.

Follow these steps to connect the phone to the computer and put the two devices on speaking terms:

1. **Plug the USB cable into one of the computer's USB ports.**

2. **Plug the USB cable into the phone.**

    If the phone is turned on, an alert may sound. If you can see the screen, you see an alert notification: USB Connected. The USB notification icon (shown in the margin) appears.

   At this point, you can choose to do nothing; to make the phone and the computer start talking, however, you have to deal with the USB notification.

3. **Pull down the notifications.**

   Refer to Chapter 3 for specific instructions on pulling down notifications.

4. **Choose USB Connection.**

   You see four methods for using the USB connection to your computer, as shown in Figure 13-1.

   You can use any of the first three options — PC Mode, Windows Media Sync, and USB Mass Storage — for sharing and synchronizing between the Droid X and your computer. Each one is subtly different. For example, Windows Media Sync simply tells the computer that the Droid X is a media device, which lets you more easily share music, photos, and videos.

   The fourth option, Charge Only, uses the USB cable to recharge the battery; the phone isn't recognized by the computer as a storage device.

Figure 13-1: USB connection options.

5. **Select an option and touch the OK button.**

   The phone's main storage device, the MicroSD card, is mounted on your computer's storage system.

The first time you connect the Droid X to a PC, you see the AutoPlay dialog box appear in Windows. Choose the option Install Motorola Driver and follow the directions on the screen to proceed with installation. The Motorola Driver is required by Windows so that your computer and the phone can properly communicate.

The joys and perils of MotoConnect

When you connect the Droid X to a Windows computer, you may experience the effects of the MotoConnect program. Specifically, after connecting the Droid X, you may see a Web page open and urge you to download the V CAST Media Manager program, which is covered elsewhere in this chapter.

To manage MotoConnect, you use its icon in the notification area, usually found on the far right end of the taskbar on the bottom of the computer screen. To disable MotoConnect, right-click the Motorola icon and choose When Phone Connections, Launch⇨Nothing.

After the phone is connected, you use your computer to access the phone's MicroSD card. The card appears as a storage device mounted to your computer, just like a media card or thumb drive. In Windows, the MicroSD card can be accessed from the Computer window. On a Macintosh, the phone's MicroSD card appears as an icon on the desktop. The later section "Accessing information on the MicroSD card" has more information.

✐ When in doubt about which USB connection mode to choose, I recommend selecting the USB Mass Storage option.

✐ On a Macintosh, use either the Charge Only or USB Mass Storage option for connecting the phone. The Mac may not recognize the Droid X PC Mode or Windows Media Sync settings.

✐ When you're done accessing information on the Droid X, you should properly unmount the phone from your computer system. See the next section.

✐ The Droid X remains connected to the computer even when the touchscreen turns off (the phone "sleeps").

✐ Even after choosing Charge Only mode, you may still see the MotoConnect feature become activated and a Web page appear on the computer screen after you connect the Droid X. See the later sidebar "The joys and perils of MotoConnect" for information on halting this rude behavior.

✐ If you don't have a USB cable for your phone, you can buy one at any computer- or office-supply store. Get a USB-A-male-to-micro–USB cable.

✐ Another advantage of connecting your phone to your computer is that the phone charges itself as long as it's plugged in. It charges even when it's turned off, but the computer must be on for the phone to charge.

✐ You cannot access the phone's MicroSD card while the Droid X is mounted into a computer storage system. Items such as your music and photos are unavailable until you disconnect the phone from the computer; you see a message saying that the SD card is busy, unmounted, or unavailable. See the next section.

✐ Future releases of the Android operating system software may change the way the Droid X handles the USB connection. Specifically, you may see a full-screen USB connection window when the phone is connected to, or mounted on, the computer's storage system.

Disconnecting the phone from the computer

After transferring information between the computer and phone, you should properly unmount the MicroSD card from the computer's storage system. Heed these steps:

1. **Pull down the notifications.**

   Refer to Chapter 3 if you need more help accessing your phone's notifications.

2. **Choose USB Connection.**

3. **Choose Charge Only.**

4. **Touch the OK button to confirm.**

   The MicroSD card is unmounted and can no longer be accessed from your computer. The phone's icon disappears from the Computer window or desktop.

5. **If necessary, unplug the USB cable.**

If you choose to keep the phone connected to the computer, the phone continues to charge. (Only when the computer is off does the phone not charge.) Otherwise, the computer and phone have ended their little *tête-à-tête* and you and the phone are free again to wander the earth.

   ✔ On a Macintosh, drag the Droid X storage icon to the Trash before you disconnect the phone.

   ✔ Do not unplug the Droid X when the USB cable is connected and the MicroSD card is mounted. Doing so may damage the MicroSD card and render invalid *all* information stored on your phone. It's a Bad Thing.

   ✔ You can leave the A end of the USB cable plugged into the computer, if you find it convenient. I do. That makes it easier to reconnect the phone later.

Accessing information on the MicroSD card

Information stored on your phone (pictures, videos, music) is kept on the MicroSD card. The card works like a storage device in your computer, keeping your phone's information stored in files and organized using folders. It's all complex computer stuff, and you're free to merrily skip it all — unless you're curious about how things are stored on the phone or you need to exchange information between the phone and your computer.

To view the information on your phone, stored on the MicroSD card, follow these steps:

1. **Connect the phone to the computer.**

2. **Mount the phone's MicroSD card on the computer's storage system.**

   See specific directions in the section "Connecting the phone to the computer," earlier in this chapter. My recommendation is to choose the USB connection option USB Mass Storage.

3a. In Windows, open the Computer window.

You can choose Computer from the Start menu or press the Win+E key combination to see the Computer window. The icon representing the phone looks a typical Windows hard drive icon. The only puzzle is figuring out which drive letter icon represents the phone.

To know for certain which icon represents the Droid X MicroSD card, unmount the phone (follow the directions in the earlier section "Disconnecting the phone from the computer") and then remount it. The icon that disappears and then reappears in the Computer window represents your phone. Generally, it should be assigned the same drive letter every time you mount it.

3b. On a Macintosh, open the new drive icon that appears on the desktop.

Macs line up storage icons on the right edge of their screens, from top to bottom. The Droid X MicroSD card appears as a generic drive icon and has the name NO NAME, unless you were clever and renamed the MicroSD card.

After you mount the Droid X MicroSD card to your computer, you can access the information stored there. The information is made available just as though your phone were a thumb drive or another form of external computer storage, which in fact is what it is when the Droid X is connected to your computer.

- ✔ To transfer a file to your phone, such as a ringtone or contact, simply drag the file's icon from wherever it dwells on your computer to the MicroSD icon. This action copies the file, creating a duplicate on the phone.

- ✔ I wouldn't bother trying to organize files and folders on the MicroSD card. Sure, you can try, but the Droid X manages those folders. Anything you do is pointless, unless you're one of those obsessive people who feels compelled to organize everything.

- ✔ The best way to transfer music, photos, and videos between the phone and your PC is to use the doubleTwist program, covered in the next section.

- ✔ There's no need to synchronize information such as dates, contacts, and email between the Droid X and your computer. All that information is synchronized automatically and wirelessly between the phone and your Google account.

- ✔ When you're done accessing the MicroSD card from your computer, unmount it by following the directions in the earlier section "Disconnecting the phone from the computer."

- ✔ You don't need to use a computer to access files on your Droid X. The Files app, found in the Applications Tray, can be used to browse files and folders found on the phone. Apps are also available at the Android Market for managing the files and folders on your Droid X. Two that I can recommend are Astro and Linda. Both are free and available from the Android Market. See Chapter 19.

Synchronizing with doubleTwist

One of the most popular ways to move information from your Android phone into a computer — and vice versa — is to use the third-party utility doubleTwist. This amazing program is free, and it's available at www. doubletwist.com.

doubleTwist isn't an Android app. You use it on your computer. It lets you easily synchronize picture, music, videos, and Web page subscriptions between your computer and is media libraries and any portable device, such as the Droid X. Additionally, doubleTwist gives you the ability to search the Android Market and obtain new apps for your phone.

To use doubleTwist, connect your phone to your computer as described elsewhere in this chapter. Ensure that USB sharing is on; *mount* the MicroSD card as a USB mass storage device. The doubleTwist program often starts automatically as soon as you connect the Droid X. If it doesn't, start it manually. The simple doubleTwist interface is illustrated in Figure 13-2.

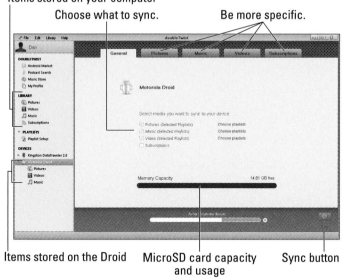

Figure 13-2: The doubleTwist synchronization utility.

To best use doubleTwist is to first ensure that the Motorola Droid X (recognized as *Droid* in Figure 13-2) is chosen from the list of media storage locations on the left side of the window. Then select all items on the General tab (refer to Figure 13-2). Click the Sync button and all your music, photos, and videos are then synchronized between the phone and your PC.

The DLNA thing

The Droid X is compliant with the Digital Living Networking Alliance, known as DLNA. These devices are configured so that they can easily share information — specifically, media files such as pictures, videos, and music. When two DLNA gizmos are connected, either directly or wirelessly, the warmth from the sharing fills the room.

Seriously, on the Droid, DLNA makes it easier for your phone to share information with DLNA-compliant computers, game consoles, televisions, and other gizmos. You must first connect the devices, directly or wirelessly, and then run either the DLNA or Media Share apps, both of which can be found on the Applications Tray.

Of course, if you have a lot of photos or videos or music on the computer, you may want to be more selective: The phone's MicroSD card can hold only so much stuff. In that case, click each tab (refer to Figure 13-2) and choose the music, pictures, videos, and subscriptions you want to synchronize between the phone and the computer. Then click the Sync button to transfer the information.

- ✔ Versions of doubleTwist are available for both the PC and the Mac.

- ✔ Refer to a handy computer book for information on installing new software, such as doubleTwist.

- ✔ doubleTwist doesn't synchronize contact information. The Droid X automatically synchronizes your phone's Contacts list with Google.

- ✔ You can use many programs on your desktop computer to store photos, videos, and music. On the PC, all three types of media are stored using the Windows Media Player. On the Mac, photos can be stored using iPhoto, and iTunes is the main music program. You have to use those programs, or similar ones, to move the media to your computer before you can use doubleTwist to synchronize that media to your phone.

- ✔ Even though you can use other programs to organize media on your computer, doubleTwist still searches everywhere on the computer to look for photos, video, and music.

- ✔ A doubleTwist app is available from the Android Market. It's a media-playing program, not one used for synchronizing files between your Droid X and a computer.

- ✔ *Subscriptions* are podcasts or RSS feeds or other types of updated Internet content that can be delivered automatically to your computer.

Unmounting, removing, and replacing the MicroSD card

Most of the time, the MicroSD card dwells contently inside your Droid X. Rarely, if ever, do you need to remove it. If you decide to remove it, you must unmount it first. This type of unmounting is different from unmounting the phone when it's connected to the computer. (Well, it's similar, but not the same.)

If you plan to remove the MicroSD card, follow these steps to ensure that none of your important data gets screwed up:

1. **Ensure that the phone isn't connected to a computer by a USB cable.**

   Free the phone from the computer, as described earlier in this chapter.

2. **From the Applications Tray, choose Settings.**

3. **Choose SD Card & Phone Storage.**

4. **Choose Unmount SD Card.**

   You should hear an alert, after which you can turn off the phone and remove its MicroSD card.

After the MicroSD card has been unmounted by following these steps, you have no access to the information stored there: The Droid X doesn't show your photos or music or other types of information.

- ✔ To reaccess the MicroSD card after unmounting it, turn the phone on again.

- ✔ You can get a second or larger-capacity MicroSD card for use with your phone at any computer- or office-supply store. You have to format the MicroSD card when you insert it into the Droid X.

- ✔ To format a new MicroSD card, follow the steps in this section. After (or in place of) Step 4, choose the command Format SD Card.

- ✔ See Chapter 1 for information on removing the MicroSD card from the phone.

The V CAST Media Manager

One thing that the MotoConnect software does is display a Web page where you can download the V CAST Media Manager. Do so. The V CAST Media Manager is a program for coordinating media — music, videos, pictures — between your PC and the Droid X.

After downloading and installing the V CAST Media Manager, connect the Droid X to your Windows computer and activate the USB connection as described earlier in this chapter. You can then use the V CAST Media Manager to view and synchronize media between the phone and the PC.

The VCAST Media Manager is a nice program, but I still prefer doubleTwist to synchronize media between a computer and a Droid X.

Wireless Network Access

Though you can't see it, wireless communications is going on all around. No need to duck — the wireless signals are intercepted only by items such as cellphones and laptop computers. The Droid X uses those signals to let you talk on the phone and communicate over the Internet and other networks.

Using the digital network

The Droid X uses the cellular network to not only send and receive phone calls but also communicate with the Internet. The phone can access several types of cellular digital network:

3G: The *third generation* of wide-area data networks is several times faster than the previous generation of data networks. 3G networks also provide for talking and sending data at the same time.

EDGE: The best of the second generation of cellular technologies allows for wide-area communications with the Internet, but not at the same time as when using voice communications.

GPRS: This second-generation (2G) network is for sending data, thought it isn't as fast as EDGE.

Your phone always uses the best network available. So, if the 3G network is within reach, it's the network the Droid X uses for Internet communications. Otherwise, the 2G (GPRS or EDGE) network is chosen.

A notification icon for the network used by the phone appears in the status area, right next to the signal strength icon. When digital information is being transmitted, the arrows in the network icon become animated, indicating that data is being sent or received or both.

As the time this book goes to press, 4G networks are starting to appear. These new networks sport speeds as much as ten times faster than 3G networks. Hopefully, soon the Droid X hardware and cellular service will be updated to handle the new 4G networks.

Creating a 3G mobile hotspot

You can configure the Droid X to share its cellular data network connection with as many as eight other devices. Those devices connect wireless with your phone, accessing a shared 3G network just like a laptop computer or other mobile device accesses a Wi-Fi network. In this process, a mobile wireless *hotspot* is created and the Droid X is one of the few smartphones that's up to the task.

To set up a 3G mobile hotspot with your Droid X, heed these steps:

1. **From the Applications Tray, open the 3G Mobile Hotspot icon.**

   You may see text describing the process. If so, dismiss the text.

2. **Touch the box to place a green check mark by 3G Mobile Hotspot.**

   A warning message appears, recommending that you plug your Droid X into a power source because the 3G mobile hotspot feature sucks down a lot of battery juice.

3. **Touch the OK button to dismiss the warning.**

   If you've not yet set up a 3G mobile hotspot, you need to supply some information.

4. **Input a password for your Droid X hotspot.**

   The password must be applied, and it must be at least eight characters long.

   I recommend placing a check mark by the Show Password option; you don't get a second chance to confirm the password, and if you mistype something using the onscreen keyboard, you'll never know what you did wrong.

5. **Touch the OK or Save button to save your settings and set up the hotspot.**

   You're done.

When the 3G hotspot is active, you see a Mobile Hotspot Service status icon appear, as shown in the margin. You can then access the hotspot using any computer or mobile device that has Wi-Fi capabilities.

To turn off the 3G hotspot, open the 3G Mobile Hotspot app and remove the green check mark.

  ✒ You cannot activate 3G network sharing and use a Wi-Fi connection at the same time on the Droid X.

  ✒ Whether your Droid X allows for 3G data sharing depends on your cellular carrier. Some carriers may limit that ability, and others may charge extra.

✔ To change the hotspot settings, press the Menu soft button when using the 3G Mobile Hotspot app. (You have to stop the service first.) Choose the Advanced button and then choose Wifi AP Mode. You can change the device name, security, password, and channel. Touch the Save button to confirm the new settings.

Turning on Wi-Fi

The cellular network's data connection is handy, mostly because it's available (almost) all over. For faster network communications, you can set up your Droid X to communicate with a wireless computer network, or Wi-Fi. It's the same method used by desktop computers and laptops for hooking up to the Internet.

To turn on the Droid X Wi-Fi network, follow these steps:

1. **From the Applications Tray, choose Settings.**

2. **Choose Wireless & Networks.**

3. **Choose Wi-Fi.**

   A green check mark appears by the Wi-Fi option, indicating that the phone's Wi-Fi abilities are now activated. If you've configured the phone to automatically connect to a nearby wireless network, the network name appears on the screen.

A helpful shortcut for turning on Wi-Fi is to use the Power Control widget, shown in Figure 13-3. The Power Control widget is preinstalled on the second Home screen to the left of the main Home screen. Touch the Wi-Fi button and the Droid X turns on its Wi-Fi abilities.

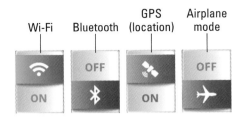

Figure 13-3: The Power Control widget.

To turn off Wi-Fi, repeat the steps in this section. Doing so turns off the phone's Wi-Fi access, disconnecting you from any networks.

See the next section for information on accessing a Wi-Fi network.

  ✔ Turning on Wi-Fi places an extra drain on the battery. So:

  ✔ Don't forget to turn off Wi-Fi when you're out of range or just out and about. That way, you save battery power.

  ✔ The Power Control widget (refer to Figure 13-3) is a collection of four individual Motorola widgets. A second Power Control widget, available under the Android Widgets category, also features a button for adjusting screen brightness.

  ✔ To turn off the 3G Mobile Hotspot, start the Mobile 3G Hotspot app (or pull down its notification on the Status Bar) and remove the green checkmark.

  ✔ Also see Chapter 22 for information on prolonging battery life.

Accessing a Wi-Fi network

Turning on the phone's Wi-Fi access is only the first part of connecting to a wireless network. The next step is joining the network. Just as you would do on a computer, you need to hunt down the wireless network by name and, optionally, input a password. Here's how it works:

1. **Choose the Settings icon from the Applications Tray.**

2. **Choose Wireless & Networks.**

3. **Ensure that Wi-Fi is on.**

   A green check mark must appear next to the Wi-Fi option.

4. **Choose Wi-Fi Settings.**

   You see a list of Wi-Fi networks displayed, as shown in Figure 13-4. If no wireless network is displayed, you're sort of out of luck regarding wireless access from your current location.

5. **Choose a wireless network from the list.**

   In Figure 13-4, I chose the Imperial Wambooli network, which is my office network.

6. **Optionally, type the network password.**

   Touch the Password text box to see the onscreen keyboard.

   Touch the Show Password check box so that you can see what you're typing; some of those network passwords can be *long*.

7. **Touch the Connect button.**

   You should be immediately connected to the network. If not, try the password again.

The phone's Wi-Fi is on.

You're alerted to nearby Wi-Fi networks.

Available networks

Manually add a Wi-Fi network

The network's signal strength

Network is password-protected.

Figure 13-4: Hunting down a wireless network.

After your phone is connected, you see the Wi-Fi status icon appear atop the touch screen. It means that the phone's Wi-Fi is on and that it's connected and communicating with a Wi-Fi network.

The VPN connection

Honestly, if you don't know what a VPN is, you don't need to bother with the VPN connection. But when you're at an organization that uses a virtual private network, you can use the Droid X to access information on that network from your phone.

After opening the Settings icon, choose Wireless & Networks, VPN Settings, and then Add VPN. Type the name of your VPN and then fill in the complex instructions that were

provided to you by the VPN manager at your organization. Or, just feign frustration and have someone else configure the phone. When you're done, press the Menu soft button and choose the Save command.

To connect with a VPN, choose Wireless & Networks from the Settings screen and then choose VPN Settings. Choose the VPN you've already set up and then touch the Connect button.

Some wireless networks don't broadcast their names, which adds security but also makes accessing them more difficult. In those cases, choose the Add Wi-Fi Network command (refer to Figure 13-4) to manually add the network. You need to input the network name, or *SSID,* and the type of security. You also need the password, if one is used. You can obtain this information from the guy with the pierced nose who sold you coffee, or from whoever is in charge of the wireless network at your location.

- Not every network has a password.

- Some public networks are open to anyone, but you have to use the Browser to find a login page that lets you access the network: Simply browse to any page on the Internet and the login page shows up.

- The phone automatically remembers any Wi-Fi network it's connected to as well as that network password.

- To change a Wi-Fi network password, touch the Wi-Fi network's name (refer to Figure 13-4) and choose the command Change Password from the pop-up menu.

- To disconnect from a Wi-Fi network, simply turn off Wi-Fi on the phone. See the preceding section.

- A Wi-Fi network is faster than a cellular data network, so it makes sense to connect with Wi-Fi whenever you can.

- Unlike a cellular data network, a Wi-Fi network's broadcast signal goes only so far. My advice is to use Wi-Fi when you plan to remain in one location for a while. If you wander too far away, your phone loses the signal and is disconnected.

Bluetooth Gizmos

One type of computer network you can confuse yourself with is Bluetooth. It has nothing to do with the color blue or any dental problems. *Bluetooth* is simply a wireless protocol for communication between two or more gizmos.

The primary way Bluetooth is used on a cellphone is by using one of those wireless earphones you see stuck on people's heads. Those people must think they're being all high-tech and cool, but they look like they have tiny staplers stuck to their earlobes. They also look like they're talking with invisible people, so stay clear!

Activating Bluetooth

You must turn on the phone's Bluetooth networking before you can use one of those Borg-earpiece implants and join the ranks of walking nerds. Here's how to turn on Bluetooth for the Droid X:

1. **From the Applications Tray, choose Settings.**

2. **Choose Wireless & Networks.**

3. **Choose Bluetooth.**

   Or, if a little green check mark already appears by the Bluetooth option, Bluetooth is already on.

You can also turn on Bluetooth by using the Power Control widget (refer to Figure 13-3). Just touch the Bluetooth button to turn it on.

To turn off Bluetooth, repeat the steps in this section.

✔ When Bluetooth is on, the Bluetooth status icon appears, as shown in the margin.

✔ Activating Bluetooth on the Droid X can quickly drain the battery. Be mindful to use Bluetooth only when necessary, and remember to turn it off when you're done.

Using a Bluetooth device

To make the Bluetooth connection between the Droid X and a set of those "I'm so cool" earphones, you need to *pair* the devices. That way, the Droid X picks up only your earphone and not anyone else's.

To pair the phone with a headset, follow these steps:

1. **Ensure that Bluetooth is on.**

2. **Turn on the Bluetooth headset.**

3. **Choose Settings from the Applications Tray.**

4. **Choose Wireless & Networks.**

5. **Choose Bluetooth Settings.**

6. **Ensure that a check mark appears by Discoverable.**

7. **Choose Scan for Devices.**

8. **If necessary, press the main button on the Bluetooth gizmo.**

   The main button is the one you use to answer the phone. You may have to press and hold the button.

   Eventually, the device should appear on the screen,

9. **Choose the device.**

10. **If necessary, input the device's passcode.**

    It's usually a four-digit number, and quite often it's simply 1234.

And now, the device is connected. You can stick it in your ear and press its main answer button when the phone rings.

By the way, when a Bluetooth device is on and paired with the phone, the notification light (on the front of the Droid X) flashes blue for an incoming call.

After you've answered the call (by pressing the main answer button on the earphone), you can chat away. The Call-in-Progress notification icon is blue for a Bluetooth call, as shown in the margin.

If you tire of using the Bluetooth headset, you can touch the Bluetooth button on the touch screen to use the Droid X speaker and microphone. (Refer to Figure 5-2, in Chapter 5, for the location of the Bluetooth button.)

- You can turn the Bluetooth earphone on or off after it's been paired. As long as Bluetooth is on, the Droid X instantly recognizes the earphone when you turn it on.

- The Bluetooth status icon changes when a device is paired. The new icon is shown in the margin.

- You can unpair a device by long-pressing the Bluetooth headset on the main Bluetooth screen. Choose the Unpair command.

- Don't forget to turn off the earpiece when you're done with it. The earpiece has a battery, and it continues to drain when you forget to turn the thing off.

Part IV
O What Your Phone Can Do!

The 5th Wave · By Rich Tennant

@RICHTENNANT

"You can do a lot with a Droid, and I guess dressing one up in G.I. Joe clothes and calling it your little desk commander is okay, too."

1 suppose this part of the book would be a lot thinner if I could only list those things that the Droid X can't do. For example, the Droid X makes a terrible Frisbee. I've tried using the Droid X as a spatula and it's just doesn't work, despite the phone's wedge-like shape. And forget about combing your hair with the Droid X. No, it's better that I just give in and write about all the amazing things your phone can do in this part of the book, specifically the non-phone things the Droid X does.

Fun with Maps and Navigation

*L*et me tell you a secret: Apparently, the Droid X was on Christopher Columbus' first voyage across the Atlantic. Hidden from history, the device was used deftly by the ship's navigator to guide Columbus from Spain to Hispaniola. Not only that, within minutes of landing, the crew was able to find an Arby's.

Of course, history didn't really happen that way, but the Droid X is definitely capable. It not only serves as your map but can also find your location, give directions, and show you which interesting places are nearby. And, if there are any Arby's in Hispaniola, the Droid X can find them.

Basic Map

I would guess that the biggest blessing from the amazing Droid X Maps app is that you no longer have to hang your head in shame over not being able to refold a map. Yep — the Maps app involves no folding whatsoever. Instead, it charts the entire country, including freeways, highways, roads, streets, avenues, drives, bike paths, addresses, businesses, and points of interest. The Maps app is incredible.

Using the Maps app

You start the Maps app by choosing Maps from the Applications Tray. If you're starting the app for the first time, you can read its What's New screen; touch the OK button to continue.

The Droid X communicates with global positioning system (GPS) satellites to hone in on your current location. It's shown on the map, similar to Figure 14-1. The position is accurate to within a given range, as shown by the blue circle.

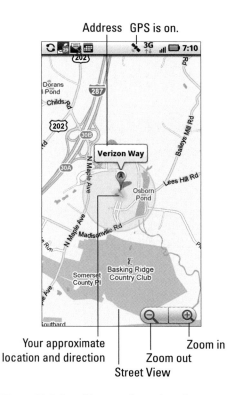

Figure 14-1: An address and your location on a map.

Here are some fun things you can do when viewing the basic street map:

Zoom in: To make the map larger (to move it closer), touch the Zoom In button, double-tap the screen, or spread your fingers on the touchscreen.

Zoom out: To make the map smaller (to see more), touch the Zoom Out button, double-tap the screen, or pinch your fingers on the touchscreen.

Pan and scroll: To see what's to the left or right or at the top or bottom of the map, drag your finger on the touchscreen; the map scrolls in the direction you drag your finger.

The closer you zoom in to the map, the more detail you see, such as street names, address block numbers, and businesses and other sites — but no tiny people.

 To see Satellite view, press the Menu soft button, choose Layers, and then choose Satellite. The map image reloads, shown in both Street and Satellite views, similar to the view shown in Figure 14-2.

Street overlay Landmarks, businesses, and points of interest

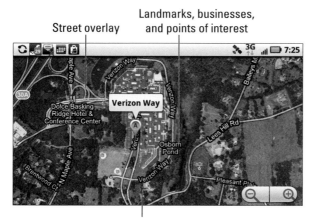

Satellite image

Figure 14-2: The satellite layer.

To return to Street view, press the Menu soft button and choose Layers and then Satellite to peel back the map layer.

- ✔ The Droid X uses GPS, the global positioning system. It's the same technology used by car navigation toys as well as handheld GPS gizmos.

- ✔ When the Droid X is using the GPS, you see the GPS Is On status icon appear.

- ✔ The Compass Arrow (refer to Figure 14-1) shows in which direction the phone is pointing.

- ✔ You can always go back to showing your current location on the map by pressing the Menu soft button and choosing the My Location command.

> ✔ You can add a Traffic layer by pressing the Menu soft button and choosing Layers and then Traffic. Not every location supports the Traffic layer, however.

> ✔ Also see the later section "Locating your address," for details about the Street View feature.

> ✔ The Droid X warns you when various applications access the phone's Location feature. The warning is nothing serious — the phone is just letting you know that software will access the phone's physical location. Some folks may view that action as an invasion of privacy; hence the warnings. I see no issue with letting the phone know where you are, but I understand that not everyone feels that way. If you'd rather not share location information, simply decline access when prompted.

Spiffing up the map with Labs

The Maps app becomes more interesting and conveys more information when you employ the Labs feature. You might find handy the additions that Labs makes to the map, or you might find them annoying. Follow these steps to figure out whether you enjoy the Labs additions:

1. **Open the Maps app.**

2. **Press the Menu soft button.**

3. **Choose More.**

4. **Choose Labs.**

   You see a list of options you can add to the Map display. The app has quite a few of them, and descriptions are provided in the list.

5. **Choose a Labs item to add to the map.**

   The item is added right away, and you can play with it or see it in action.

All features have their benefits, but some of them (Terrain Layer and Traffic, for example) slow things down.

The Scale Bar is useful, especially when you plan to do a lot of walking, as I do.

As Google experiments with the Maps app, you'll find new items added to the Labs list, as well as some items removed. Check the helpful Labs list often to see what's up.

The Android Market app Compass also serves as a virtual compass for the Droid X. See Chapter 19 for more information on the Android Market.

The Droid X Is Your Copilot

The best way to put the Maps app to work is when you're lost or looking for something. You can use Maps to locate people, places, and things. After they've been found, your phone tells you how to get there, turn by turn. So, even when you don't know where you are or where you're going, the Droid X can help.

Locating your address

The Maps app shows your location as a compass arrow on the screen. But *where* is that? I mean, if you need to phone a tow truck, you can't just say, "I'm the blue triangle on the orange slab by the green thing."

Well, you *can* say that, but it probably won't do any good.

To find your current street address, or any street address, long-press a location on the Maps screen. Up pops a bubble, similar to the one shown in Figure 14-3, that gives your approximate address.

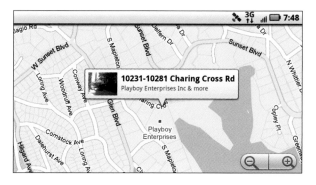

Figure 14-3: Finding an address.

If you touch the address bubble (refer to Figure 14-3), you see a screen full of interesting things you can do, as shown in Figure 14-4.

The What's Nearby command displays a list of nearby businesses or points of interest, some of them shown on the screen (refer to Figure 14-4) and others available by touching the What's Nearby command.

Choose the Search Nearby item to use the Search command to locate businesses, people, or points of interest near the given location.

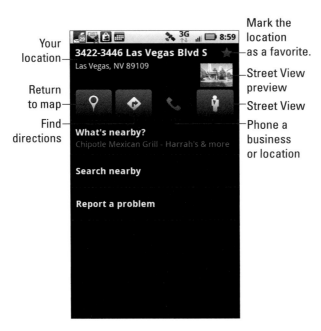

Figure 14-4: Things to do with a location.

The Report a Problem command doesn't connect you with the police; instead, it's used to send information back to Google regarding an improper address or another map malfunction.

What's *really* fun to play with is the Street View command. Choosing this option displays the location from a 360-degree perspective. In Street view, you can browse a locale, pan and tilt, or zoom in on details to familiarize yourself with an area, for example — whether you're familiarizing yourself with a location or planning a burglary.

Press the Back button to return to regular Map view from Street view.

Finding locations on the map

The Maps app can help you find places in the real world, just like the Browser app helps you find places on the Internet. Both operations work basically the same:

Open the Maps app and press the Search soft button. You can type a variety of terms into the Search box, as explained next.

Look for a specific addresses

To locate an address, type it into the Search box; for example:

```
1600 Pennsylvania Ave., Washington, D.C. 20006
```

Touch the Search button on the onscreen keyboard, and that location is then shown on the map. The next step is getting directions, which you can read about in the later section "Getting directions."

- ✔ You don't need to type the entire address. Often times, all you need is the street number and street name and then either the city name or zip code.
- ✔ If you omit the city name or zip code, the Droid X looks for the closest matching address near your current location.

Look for a type of business, restaurant, or point of interest

You may not know an address, but you know when you crave sushi or Tex-Mex or perhaps Ethiopian food. Maybe you need a hotel or gas station. To find a business entity or a point of interest, type its name in the Search box; for example:

```
Movie theater
```

This command flags movie theaters on the current Maps screen or nearby.

Specify your current location, as described earlier in this chapter, to find locations near you. Otherwise, the Maps app looks for places near the area you see on the screen.

Or, you can be specific and look for businesses near a certain location by specifying the city name, district, or zip code, such as

```
Sushi 92123
```

After typing this command and touching the Search button, you see a smattering of sushi restaurants found in my old neighborhood in San Diego and similar to the one shown in Figure 14-5.

Search results
and locations

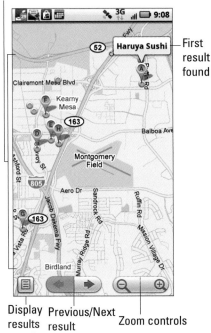

First
result
found

Display Previous/Next
results result
as a list

Zoom controls

Figure 14-5: Search results for sushi in Kearny Mesa.

To see more information about a result, touch its cartoon bubble, such as the one with the Haruya Sushi information (refer to Figure 14-5). The screen that appears offers more information, plus perhaps even a Web site address and phone number. You can press the Get Directions button (refer to Figure 14-4) to get driving directions; see the later section "Getting directions."

✒ Each letter or dot on the screen represents a search result (refer to Figure 14-5).

✒ Use the Zoom controls or spread your fingers to zoom in to the map.

✒ You can create a contact for the location, keeping it as a part of your Contacts list: After touching the location balloon, choose the command Add As a Contact. The contact is created using data known about the business, including its location and phone number and even a Web page address — if that information is available.

Look for a contact's location

You can hone in on where your contacts are located by using the map. This trick works when you've specified an address for the contact — either home or work or another location. If so, the Droid X can easily help you find that location or even give you directions.

The key to finding a contact's location is the little pushpin icon, shown in the margin. Anytime you see that icon, you can touch it to view that location by using the Maps app.

Getting directions

One command associated with locations on the map is Get Directions. Here's how to use it:

1. **Touch a location's cartoon bubble displayed by an address, a contact, or a business or from the result of a map search.**

2. **From the list of options, choose the Get Directions command or touch the Get Directions button.**

   You may be asked whether you want to navigate or get directions. If you choose Navigate, the Droid X goes into Navigation mode; refer to the next section.

   When you choose Get Directions, you see an input screen, similar to the one shown in Figure 14-6. The Droid X already has chosen your current location (shown as My Location in the figure) as the starting point, and the location you searched for, or are viewing on the map, as the destination.

3. **To change the start point, touch the button to the right of the Start Point text box (refer to Figure 14-6).**

   Or, you can type a starting point.

Figure 14-6: Going from here to there.

4. **To change the destination, touch the button to the right of the Destination text box (refer to Figure 14-6).**

5. **Choose your method of transportation: car, public transportation, bicycle, or walking.**

   Not all transportation options are available for all locations.

6. **Touch the Go button.**

   A list of directions appears on the phone's screen.

7. **Follow the directions to get where you want to go.**

The directions appear as a list, which you can follow line by line.

You can choose the Show on Map command to view your trail on the map. Zoom in to see more detail.

You can also choose the Navigate option, which lets your phone dictate the list of directions to you as you travel. See the next section.

Navigating to your destination

When you'd rather not see a list of directions to reach a destination, you can activate the Droid X Navigation mode. In that mode, the phone displays an interactive map that shows your current location and turn-by-turn directions for reaching your final location. Navigation mode also dictates verbally how far you should go and when to turn, for example, and gives you other nagging advice — just like a backseat driver, albeit an accurate one.

Where are your friends?

One Google Maps feature is *Latitude,* a social network program that lets you share your physical location with your friends, also assumed to be using Latitude. Being able to more easily know where your friends are makes it possible to meet up with them — or, I suppose, to avoid them. It's all up to you.

To join Latitude, you press the Menu soft button when viewing a map and then choose the Join Latitude command. Read the information, and then touch the Allow & Share button to continue. If you don't see the Join Latitude command, you've already joined; start Latitude by choosing the Latitude command.

To make Latitude work, you need to add friends to Latitude, and those friends need to use Latitude. After adding Latitude friends, you can share your location with them as well as view their locations on a map. You can also chat with Google Talk, send them email, get directions to their location, and do other interesting things.

To disable Latitude, press the Menu soft button when Latitude is active and choose the Privacy command. Choose the option Turn Off Latitude.

To use Navigation, choose the Navigation option from any list of directions. Or, touch the Navigation icon, shown in the margin.

You can also start the Droid X Navigation mode directly by choosing the Navigation app from the Applications tab. Opening the Navigation app displays a list of options for choosing a destination: You can speak or type a destination, choose a destination from your Contacts list, or navigate to a starred location. A list of locations you've recently looked up also appears, for your convenience.

After choosing Navigation, sit back and have the phone dictate your directions. You can simply listen, or just glance at the phone for an update of where you're heading.

✔ To stop Navigation, press the Menu soft button and choose the Exit Navigation command.

✔ If you tire of hearing the Navigation voice, press the Menu soft button and choose the Mute command.

✔ I refer to the navigation voice as *Gertrude*.

✔ The neat thing about Navigation is that whenever you screw up, a new course is immediately calculated.

✔ A direct link to Navigation is on the Car Home screen — handy for when you're using the Droid X in a car dock in your automobile.

✔ In Navigation mode, the phone uses a lot of battery power. The phone doesn't dim when you travel long distances; the touchscreen remains active. Voice commands also put a drain on battery life. See Chapter 22 for more information on maintaining the phone's battery.

Adding a navigation shortcut to the Home screen

When you visit certain places often — such as home — you can save yourself the time you would spend repeatedly inputting navigation information, by creating a navigation shortcut on the Home screen. Here's how:

1. **Long-press a blank part of the Home screen.**

   You can use any part of the Home screen: left, right, or center.

2. **From the pop-up menu, choose Shortcuts.**

3. **Choose Directions & Navigation.**

4. **Type a contact name, address, destination, or business in the text box.**

   As you type, suggestions appear in a list. You can choose a suggestion to save yourself some typing.

5. **Choose a traveling method.**

   Your options are car, public transportation, bicycle, and on foot.

6. **Scroll down a bit to type a shortcut name.**

7. **Choose an icon for the shortcut.**

8. **Touch the Save button.**

   The Navigation shortcut is placed on the Home screen.

To use the shortcut, simply touch it on the Home screen. Instantly, the Maps app starts and enters Navigation mode, steering you from wherever you are to the location referenced by the shortcut.

- See Chapter 21 for additional information on creating Home screen shortcuts.

- I keep all navigation shortcuts in one place, on the first Home screen to the right.

Say "Cheese"

....

In This Chapter

▶ Using the phone's camera

▶ Taking a still picture

▶ Looking at the picture you just shot

▶ Adding picture effects

▶ Shooting video with the phone

▶ Previewing your video

....

To an alien observing human culture, it would be obvious to suppose that the purpose of photography is to deliver a cultured dairy product to eager people standing still and grinning. Truly, it would amaze me if, while standing under a hot sun with the Chesapeake Bay in the background, a camera actually dispensed some tangy Dubliner or Gruyère.

Of course, saying "Cheese" when having your picture taken has more to do with *cheese* the word than cheese the food. That's because the long — sound in *cheese* supposedly positions the human mouth into a smile, making it look as though everyone in the photograph is having the best time. That isn't a worry for you because you will have read this chapter and understand how to use your Droid X as a camera in a deft and practical manner, thereby keeping your subjects content without the need for some Gouda or Brie.

The Droid X Has a Camera

Before I became a computer nerd, I was a photographer. I had my own darkroom, and I was even crazy enough to develop color slides. As a photographer, I can tell you that the potential for taking pictures is always there. The problem is that you often don't have your camera with you or you're out of film. Fortunately, the Droid X solves both problems.

As a resident of the 21st century, you most likely always have your cellphone with you. Consider it a bonus that the cellphone can double as a camera. It may not be perfect, but it's handy — especially for those times you see a UFO and no one else will ever believe you without a picture as proof.

Taking a picture

To use your Droid X phone as a camera, you need to know that the back of the phone holds the lens. To take a picture, you need to hold the phone away from your face, which I hear is hell to do when you wear bifocals. Before doing that, start the Camera app, whose icon is shown in the margin.

Summon the Camera app from the Applications Tray. After starting the Camera app, you see the main Camera screen, as illustrated in Figure 15-1. The controls shown in the figure eventually disappear, leaving the full screen to preview the image.

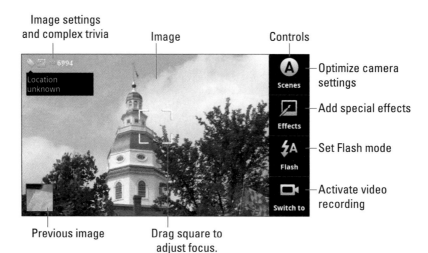

Figure 15-1: Your phone as a camera.

To take a picture, point the camera at the subject and touch the Shutter button, found on the right or top side of the Droid X, depending on whether you're taking a portrait or landscape photograph. (Refer to Figure 1-2, in Chapter 1, for the physical Shutter button's location.)

You can zoom in or out by pressing the Volume Up or Volume Down buttons, respectively. Because the zoom is a *digital zoom*, the image is magnified, as opposed to an optical zoom, which is done by adjusting the camera's lens.

As on other digital cameras, the shutter doesn't snap instantly when you shoot the picture; the camera takes a moment to focus, the flash may go off, and then you hear the shutter sound effect.

For a second, the picture you just snapped appears on the phone's touch screen. Then the phone returns to Camera mode and you can take more pictures.

- ✏ See the next section to find out how to review the image you've just taken.

- ✏ The onscreen controls, shown in Figure 15-1, disappear after a few moments. To see them again, touch the Droid X screen.

- ✏ If you plan to take a lot of pictures, consider placing a shortcut to the Camera app on the Home screen. See Chapter 21 for details.

- ✏ The phone can be used as a camera in either landscape or portrait orientation, though the phone's controls and gizmos are always presented in landscape format (refer to Figure 15-1).

- ✏ The camera focuses automatically, though you can drag the focus square around the touchscreen to specifically adjust the focus (refer to Figure 15-1).

- ✏ You can take as many pictures with your Droid X as you like, as long as you don't run out of storage for them on the phone's MicroSD card.

- ✏ You can use the Gallery to manage images and delete the ones you don't want. See Chapter 16 for more information about the Gallery.

- ✏ You can also delete an image right after you snap the picture; see the next section.

- ✏ The Droid X not only takes a picture but also keeps track of where you were located on Planet Earth when you took the picture. See Chapter 16 for information on reviewing a photograph's location.

- ✏ If your pictures appear blurry, ensure that the camera lens on the back of the Droid X isn't dirty.

- ✏ Refer to Figure 1-3, in Chapter 1, for the location of the camera on the back of the Droid X.

- ✏ The Droid X stores pictures in the JPEG image file format. Images are stored in the DCIM/Camera folder on the MicroSD card; they have the JPG filename extension.

Reviewing the picture

All pictures you take with your camera can be accessed using the Gallery program, which is covered in Chapter 16. Even so, immediately after you take a picture, you're given a chance to review it and other, recent pictures.

To review the image you just took, touch the Previous Image button (refer to Figure 15-1). You see a "camera roll" of recent images. Touch your image to examine it more closely.

After the previous image is shown full-screen, you can examine it in detail: Double-tap or spread your fingers on the touch screen to zoom in; double-tap or pinch the touchscreen to zoom out. Drag your finger to pan the image.

 To do something with the image, press the Menu soft button. You see a screen similar to the one shown in Figure 15-2.

Image preview

Take more pictures

Get rid of the image

Figure 15-2: Picture review.

When the image doesn't meet your liking, touch the Delete button. To remove the image, touch the OK button when prompted.

Touch the Camera button (refer to Figure 15-2) to return to the Camera app and take more pictures.

✔ Deleting an image frees up the space it used on the phone's MicroSD card.

✔ There's no easy or obvious way to undelete an image, so be careful! In fact:

✔ I recommend that you do your deleting and other photo management duties by using the Gallery app, discussed in Chapter 16.

✔ By pressing the Share button, you can instantly share the image with friends on the Internet. You can share by email or text message or by using social networking sites such as Facebook and Twitter, if you have the Droid X configured for use with those apps. Other options, such as sharing with the Picasa photo-sharing Web site, might also appear on the Share button's list.

✓ The Print to Retail option on the Share button allows you to send the image to a photo-processing location near you, where it can be printed.

✓ How you share a photo depends on where you want the image to end up. See Chapter 9 for information on sending multimedia text messages; Chapter 10 covers the Email and Gmail programs, and Chapter 12 delves into Facebook and Twitter.

✓ Use the More button to access additional menu items. One such item, Set As, lets you instantly assign the photo as the Home page *wallpaper* (background image) or to set the image for a contact.

✓ The next time you're face-to-face with a contact, remember to snap that person's photo. Use the picture-review window's Set As button to assign the image as the contact's photo — with the contact's permission, of course.

Adjusting the camera

Your Droid X is more phone than camera — still, it has various camera adjustments you can make. Some adjustment controls are found on the screen when the Camera app first starts, as shown in Figure 15-2. Others are found by pressing the Menu soft button when using the Camera app.

Though you have many camera settings to make, here are a few items worthy of note:

Scenes: Choosing this option lets you preconfigure the Droid X camera for taking certain types of pictures. After touching the Scenes button, swipe the options left or right. Choose one to configure the camera to, ideally, take that type of picture.

Flash Mode: Setting the camera's Flash mode is done by touching the Flash button, shown in Figure 15-1. The camera has three Flash modes to set by touching the button, and confirmed by one of these icons on the touchscreen:

> *Auto Flash:* In this mode, the camera determines whether the flash goes off. Sometimes it does, such as when it's dark, and sometimes it doesn't, such as when you're taking a picture of the sun.
>
> *Flash On:* The flash always blinds your victims.
>
> *Flash Off:* The flash never goes off, even in the dark.

Effects: Add special color effects by touching the Effects button and then swiping left or right through the various effects. After choosing an effect, press the Back soft button to take your picture

Picture Mode: Set options for how to use the camera by pressing the Menu soft button and choosing Picture Modes. You can choose from four ways to use the camera, as described in Figure 15-3.

The Multi-shot option allows the camera to take pictures as long as you press the shutter button. This feature is useful for capturing action pictures, such as in sporting events or when viewing train wrecks.

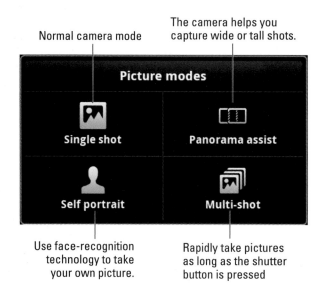

Normal camera mode

The camera helps you capture wide or tall shots.

Use face-recognition technology to take your own picture.

Rapidly take pictures as long as the shutter button is pressed

Figure 15-3: Droid X camera picture modes.

The Panorama Assist option helps you take multiple images that can be laid out in a panorama, either vertically or horizontally. When that option is set, the phone assists you in pointing the camera in the right direction and at the right position to line up the panoramic shots.

✔ To make face detection work, it must be turned on: Press the Menu soft button when using the Camera. Choose Settings, and then choose Face Detection to place a green check mark by that item.

✔ You can force a flash by choosing Flash On mode. That way, dark objects in the foreground show up against a light background, such as when taking a picture of someone in front of a bright window.

You Ought to Be on Video

When the action is hot, when you need to capture more than a moment (and maybe the sounds), you switch the Droid X camera into Video Capture mode. Doing so may not turn you into the next Quentin Tarantino, because I hear he uses an iPhone to make his films.

Recording video

Video chores on the Droid X are handled by the Camcorder app, found on the Applications Tray. You can also enter Video mode by choosing the Switch To button when using the Droid X camera (refer to Figure 15-1).

The Camcorder app looks amazingly similar to the Camera app, with the addition of a time indicator, as illustrated in Figure 15-4.

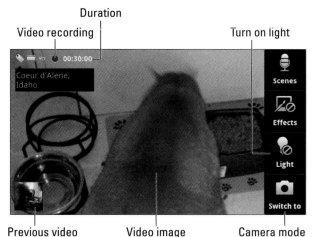

Figure 15-4: Your phone is a video camera.

Start shooting the video by pressing the phone's Shutter button — the same button used to take a picture.

When recording, you see the red dot in the upper left corner of the screen light up, and the recording time is noted (refer to Figure 15-4).

To stop recording, press the Shutter button again.

The video is stored on the phone's MicroSD card. You can watch the video immediately by touching the Previous Video button as covered in the next section. Otherwise, the phone is ready to shoot another video.

- While the phone is recording, a Mute button appears on the touchscreen. Use it to mute the sound.
- Unlike in Camera mode, you cannot use the Droid X volume controls to zoom in or out as you record video.

✔ To ensure that video is recorded in High Definition (HD) mode, press the Menu soft button while using the Camcorder app. Choose Video Modes and then select Fast Motion.

✔ See the next section for more information on previewing a recently shot video.

✔ Chapter 16 covers the Gallery app, used to view and manage videos stored on your phone.

✔ Hold the phone steady! The camera still works when you whip around the phone, but wild gyrations render the video unwatchable.

✔ You can record about ten minutes of video, though that length can be limited by how much storage space is available on the MicroSD card.

✔ The video is stored on the Droid X MicroSD card using the Third Generation Partnership Project video file format. The video files stored on the phone, in the DCIM/Camera folder, have the 3GP filename extension.

Reviewing your movie

To review your video masterpiece, touch the Previous Video button (refer to Figure 15-4). Choose your video from the list (it's the first one shown). Touch the Play button to review the video.

You can use onscreen controls to pause or play the video as well as reverse and fast-forward the scene. The controls disappear as the video plays, but you can touch the screen to bring them back.

 When your video is done playing, you can press the Back soft button to return to the Camcorder app.

✔ The Delete button, shown earlier, in Figure 15-4, can be used to instantly delete the video you just recorded. After touching the Delete button, touch the OK button to confirm deleting the video.

✔ Though deleting a video frees up storage space on the phone's MicroSD card, undeleting or recovering a deleted video is neither easy nor obvious.

✔ You can use the Previous video triangle (refer to Figure 15-4) to page through other videos you've shot. For best reviewing and managing your videos, I recommend using the Gallery app, discussed in Chapter 16.

✔ The Share button can be used to publish your video on the Internet. Options available for sharing include Facebook, Twitter, MMS, Email, Gmail, YouTube, and others.

✔ Refer to Chapter 16 for information on publishing your video to YouTube.

16

The Droid X Louvre

In This Chapter

▶ Viewing images and videos stored on your phone

▶ Finding an image's location

▶ Editing an image

▶ Tagging images and videos

▶ Sending an image by email

▶ Sharing an image with Facebook

▶ Printing an image at a local developer

▶ Publishing a video on YouTube

*S*cience fiction literature promises that there is, somewhere in the universe, a planet full of robots. If so, then one spot you'd have to visit on that planet is its museum. I'm certain that robot art would inspire, humble, and even shock the typical organic life form. Beyond nuts-and-bolts erotica, I suppose that robotic art expresses much about robots' innermost fear of being taken over and dominated by biological creatures like human beings. Perish the thought.

Your Droid X may have nowhere near the sophistication of the robots that dominate various parts of the galaxy, but like those planets, your phone sports a museum. There, you can find pictures and videos, some of which you've taken using the Droid X camera and others you've collected from elsewhere. It's all part of the Gallery, a handy app you can use to view and share images and videos dear to your heart.

A Gallery of Images

Pictures and videos you shoot with your Droid X aren't lost forever. Nope, they're stored on the phone's MicroSD card. After they're stored or created there, you can access them from the Gallery app, where you can view them or edit them or do a number of other interesting things.

Perusing the Gallery

To access images and videos stored on your Droid X, you start the Gallery app. You can find it on the Applications Tray.

When the Gallery opens, you see images organized into categories, as shown in Figure 16-1.

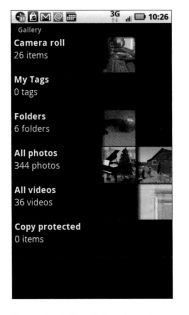

Figure 16-1: The Gallery's main screen.

Here's what you find in each category:

Camera Roll: Images and videos you've taken using the Droid X

My Tags: Images and Videos you've tagged

Folders: All the camera's images and videos, organized by folder — one for Camera images taken with the Droid, one for images downloaded from the Internet, and one for images received via text messaging (MMS), plus folders created by any programs used to synchronize images and videos between the Droid X and a computer

All Photos: Every dang doodle image stored on the phone

All Videos: Every dang doodle video stored on the phone

Copy Protected: Images kept on the phone that cannot be copied

Touch a category to open it and view the pictures or videos it contains. The media is presented in a humongous grid, as shown in Figure 16-2. You can scroll up and down by flicking your finger on the touchscreen.

To view an image or a video, touch it with your finger. The image appears in full size on the screen, and you can tilt the phone to the left to see the image in another orientation.

You can view more images in the album by swiping your finger left and right.

Videos appear with the Play Button icon, shown in the margin. Touching the icon plays the video.

To return to the main category in the Gallery, press the Back soft button.

- ✔ To keep the Gallery handy, considering placing its shortcut icon on the Home screen. Refer to Chapter 21.

- ✔ Refer to Chapter 11 for information on downloading photos from the Internet.

- ✔ See Chapter 13 for more information about doubleTwist, which can be used to copy images and videos from your computer to the Droid X.

- ✔ When previewing an image, you can double-tap the screen to zoom in and then double-tap again to zoom back out.

Finding an image location on a map

In addition to snapping a picture, the Droid X also saves the location where you took the picture. That information is obtained from the phone's GPS, the same tool used to find your location on a map. In fact, you can use the information saved with a picture to see exactly where the picture was taken.

For example, Figure 16-3 shows the location where I took the image shown in Figure 15-1. That location was saved by the phone's GPS technology and is available as part of the picture's data.

Total images and videos

Category   Video   Still image

Figure 16-2: Viewing an album.

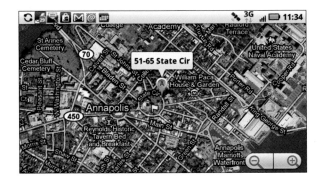

Figure 16-3: A picture's location.

To see where you've taken a picture, follow these steps:

1. **Summon the image in the Gallery.**

2. **Touch the Info button on the touchscreen.**

The Info button is shown in the margin. After you touch that button, information about the picture appears on the screen.

3. **Choose Location.**

   The spot where you took the picture appears in the Maps app.

4. **Touch the Back button to return to the Gallery.**

Not every image has location information. In some cases, the Droid X cannot read the GPS to store the information. When that happens, location information is unavailable.

Working with pictures

The Gallery serves as a way to manage the pictures stored on your Droid X. To individually manipulate an image, summon it in the Gallery by touching the image, as described earlier in this chapter. Press the Menu soft button to see a slate of commands you can use to manipulate the image. Here's what you can do:

Share an image: Send the image elsewhere using the Internet or a text message. See the later section "Sharing your pictures and videos" for details.

Delete an image: Touch the Delete button to remove the image you're viewing. You're prompted before the image is removed; touch the OK button to delete the image.

Use an image for a contact or as wallpaper: Touch the More button and choose the Set As command to apply the image you're viewing to a contact or to set that image as the Home screen wallpaper (background).

The Gallery offers three simple image-editing commands:

Crop: Choose the Edit command, and then Advanced, and then the Crop command to slice out portions of an image, such as when removing an unwanted relative or a former paramour from a family portrait. Figure 16-4 illustrates how to use the cropping tool that appears on the screen. Choose the Apply command to keep the portion of the image that dwells within the orange rectangle. Press the Back soft button to return to the Gallery.

Rotate left, rotate right: Choose the Edit command and then choose Rotate. Use the circle control on the touchscreen to reorient the image. Touch the Save button when you're pleased with the results.

Additional editing commands are available. Find them by pressing the Menu soft button, choosing the Edit command, and then choosing Advanced. I'm truly surprised at the variety and power of the available commands, some of which generally require the power of a full computer to accomplish.

✔ To delete a video, you must first select it. Selecting media is covered in the next section.

✔ Some images might not be available for editing, such as images imported into your phone from shared Picasa albums.

Tagging images

Because images contain visual information, searching and organizing images tend to be haphazard tasks. One method to help you keep your pictures and videos organized is to tag them.

A *tag* is simply a tidbit of text, short and punchy — for example, vacation, Brian, 2009, Wisconsin, or exploding cupcake. By itself, a tag may seem useless, but the key to properly tagging an image is to apply more than one tag. An image tagged with all its descriptions — vacation, Brian, 2009, Wisconsin, and exploding cupcake — is quite descriptive.

Drag around the rectangle.

Resize a corner.

Portion of the image to keep

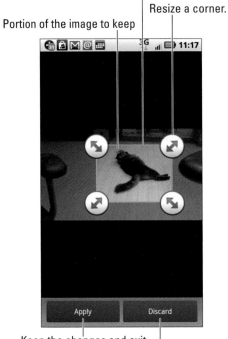

Keep the changes and exit

Keep the image as is

Figure 16-4: Working the crop thing.

To apply a tag to an image in the Gallery, follow these steps:

1. Touch an image to view it by itself on the Droid X touchscreen.

2. Touch the Info button.

Lots of information about the image is displayed, similar to what's shown in Figure 16-5.

Current image tags

Ugly picture filename

Touch to view location

Touch to add tags

2010-07-12_09-22-36_614.jpg

Tags:
Jonah Gookin, summer, Idaho, 2010,
Jeremiah Gookin, vacation

Location:
Lat: 49.69°, Long: -118.81°

Taken on:
July 12, 2010 2:22 AM

Resolution:
4.8MP

File size:
380KB

Other trivia   Image location information

Figure 16-5: Information about an image.

3. Choose Tags.

4. Use the onscreen keyboard to type a tag.

Single word tags work best. If you need to be more descriptive, add more tags.

You can use tags later to search for images. So think of a tag that you would use to find the image if you were doing a search.

As you type, you may see contact names appear. If so, choose that contact name to tag the contact in the image.

5. **Touch the green plus-sign button to add another tag.**

6. **Touch the Done button when you're finished tagging the image.**

The tags you add appear on the image information screen, similar to the one shown in Figure 16-5. They're also used when you perform a search using the Droid X's powerful Search command.

✔ By keeping tags succinct, you can easily sift and sort your images. For example, find all images from 2009 and then all birthday images from 2009.

✔ Many picture-viewing or media management programs on your computer allow for tagging. The tags are usually kept with the picture information so that when you copy or share the images, the tags come along for the ride.

✔ Tagging works only when you remember to do it!

Share Your Pics and Vids with the World

It's socially acceptable to share your phone's images and videos by queuing things up and then handing your phone to another human for their enjoyment. For the friends and relatives you'd rather not interact with personally, you can choose to share the media on your phone in a more digital fashion on the Internet.

Refer to Chapter 13 for information on synchronizing and sharing information between the Droid X and your computer.

Sharing your pictures and videos

Occasionally, you stumble across the Share command when working with photos and videos in the Gallery. This command is used to distribute images and videos from your Droid X to your pals on the Internet.

The menu that appears when you choose the Share command contains various options for sharing media, similar to the one shown in Figure 16-6. You may see more or fewer items on the Share menu, depending on which software you have installed on your Droid X, which Internet services you belong to, and which type of media is being shared.

The following sections describe some of the media items you can choose from the menu and how the media is shared.

Bluetooth

Bluetooth is perhaps the most difficult way to share files, but it's first alphabetically, so I'm forced to talk about it up front. Without boring you: Use a USB cable and directly connect the phone to a computer rather than use Bluetooth for sharing media. See Chapter 13.

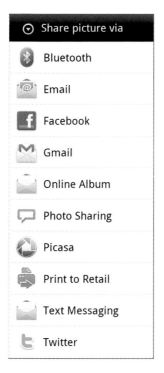

Figure 16-6: Sharing options for media.

The problem with file sharing using Bluetooth on the Droid X is that the devices can pair, but not connect, just fine. Your laptop or a second mobile phone may claim that the Droid X is lacking a *service*. Because this is a software-related issue, it might be repaired in the future. If so, tune into my Web site for updated information:

```
www.wambooli.com/help/phone
```

Email and Gmail

After selecting one or more image or video, choose Email or Gmail from the Share menu to send the media files from your Droid X as a message attachment. Fill in the To, Subject, and Message text boxes as necessary. Touch the Send button to send the media.

✔ You may not be able to send video files as email attachments. That's probably because some video files are humongous. They would not only take too long to send but also might be too big for the recipient's inbox.

✔ As an alternative to sending large video files, consider uploading them to YouTube instead. See the later section "Uploading a video to YouTube."

Facebook

To upload a mobile image to Facebook, choose the Facebook command from the Share menu. Optionally, type (or dictate) a caption. Touch the Upload button. Eventually, the media makes its way to Facebook, for all your friends to enjoy and make rude comments about.

The Facebook option isn't available for sharing videos.

Photo Sharing

The Photo Sharing option is merely a shortcut to sending an image (not a video) to Facebook or your Picasa album. After choosing this option, you see a sharing screen from which you can choose Facebook or Picasa or add a sharing account, such as Photobucket or one of the other free online picture-sharing services.

Picasa

Perhaps the sanest way to share photos is to upload them to Google's Picasa photo-sharing site. Heck, you probably already have a Picasa account synced with your phone, so this option is perhaps the easiest and most obvious to use. Here's how it works:

1. **View a picture in the Gallery.**
2. **Choose Picasa from the Share menu (refer to Figure 16-6).**
3. **Type a caption.**
4. **Optionally, choose your Google account (if you have more than one).**
5. **Choose a Picasa album.**

    You may need to scroll up the top part of the screen a bit to see the Album item, which might be hidden behind the onscreen keyboard.

6. **Touch the Upload button to send the images.**

Because Picasa may automatically sync certain albums with your Droid X, you can end up with two copies of the image on the phone. If so, you can delete the non-Picasa version of the image from its original gallery.

- Picasa is for sharing images only, not video.
- Your Google account automatically comes with access to Picasa. If you haven't yet set things up, visit `picasaweb.google.com` to get started.
- You can share images stored on the Picasa Web site by clicking the Share button found above each photo album.
- To make a Picasa album public, choose the Edit➪Album Properties command, found just above the album. Choose Public from the pop-up menu, by the Share command in the Edit Album Information window.

Print to Retail

Here's a crazy idea: Connect your phone to a local photo developer, such as Costco, and have it send your images electronically so that they can be printed. After choosing the Print to Retail option, you can do exactly that: The Droid X uses its GPS powers to locate a printer near you. You can then fill in the various forms to have your pictures sent and printed.

Text Messaging

Media can be attached to a text message, which then becomes the famous MMS, or multimedia message, that I write about in Chapter 9. After choosing the Messaging sharing option, input the contact name or phone number to which you want to send the media. Optionally, type a brief message. Touch the Send button to send the message.

- Some images and videos may be too large to send as multimedia text messages.

- The Droid X may prompt you to resize an image to properly send it as an MMS.

- Not every cellphone has the ability to receive multimedia text messages.

Twitter

Images are shared on the popular Twitter social networking site by saving the image on a Twitter image-sharing Web site and then tweeting the link to that image. The Twitter app that comes with the Droid uses the TwitPic Web site to share images. After choosing the Twitter option for sharing, you see the TwitPic link in your tweet message. Type additional text (whatever will fit) and then touch the Update button to tweet the pic's link.

YouTube

The YouTube sharing option appears when you've chosen to share a video from the Gallery. See the next section.

Uploading a video to YouTube

The best way to share a video is to upload it to YouTube. As a Google account holder, you also have a YouTube account. You can use the YouTube app on the Droid X along with your account to upload your phone's videos to the Internet, where everyone can see them and make rude comments upon them. Here's how:

1. **Activate the Wi-Fi connection for your Droid X.**

   The best — the only — way to upload a video is to turn on the Wi-Fi connection, which is oodles faster than using the cellphone digital network. See Chapter 13 for information on how to turn on the Wi-Fi connection.

2. **From the Applications Tray, choose the Gallery app.**

3. **View the video you want to upload.**

   Or, simply have the video displayed on the screen.

4. **Press the Menu soft button**

5. **Choose the Share command.**

6. **Choose YouTube.**

7. **Type the video's title.**

8. **Touch the More Details button.**

9. **Optionally, type a description, specify whether to make the video public or private, add tags, or change other settings.**

10. **Touch the Upload button.**

   You return to the Gallery, and the video is uploaded. It continues to upload, even if the phone falls asleep.

To view your video, open the YouTube app in the Applications Tray, press the Menu soft button, and choose the My Account command. If necessary, choose your Google account from the pop-up list. Your video should appear in the My Videos list. If not, choose All My Videos and you'll find it there.

You can share your video by sending its YouTube Web page link to your pals. I confess that using a computer for this operation is easier than using your phone: Log in to YouTube on a computer to view your video. Use the Share button that appears near the video to share it via email or Facebook or other methods.

✐ YouTube often takes a while to process a video after it's uploaded. Allow a few minutes to pass (longer for larger videos) before the video becomes available for viewing.

✐ Wi-Fi access drains battery power, so don't forget to turn it off when you no longer need it after uploading your video.

✐ *Upload* is the official term to describe sending a file from your phone to the Internet.

✐ See Chapter 18 for more information on using YouTube on your Droid X.

17

Your Phone Is Alive
with the Sound of Music

In This Chapter

▶ Checking into music on your Droid X

▶ Listening to a song

▶ Organizing your tunes into playlists

▶ Making a new playlist

▶ Moving music from your computer to your phone

▶ Purchasing music using the Droid X

▶ Using your phone as an FM radio

Anyone familiar with John Cage recognizes that the telephone has always been a musical instrument. Sure, it played only a few tunes — none of them well. I recall having a book of touch-tone melodies you could punch into a phone. My old home number sounded like *Yankee Doodle* when you dialed fast enough.

Beyond being a phone, a map, a camera, and yadda-yadda, your Droid X is a portable music player, similar to that extremely popular gizmo made by a fruit company, something that rhymes with "pie odd." Your Droid X may not have the classic coolness of the Pie Odd, but it plays music just as well — in addition to making phone calls, finding pizza parlors, taking pictures, and yadda-yadda.

Now Hear This!

Your Droid X is ready to entertain you with music whenever you want to hear it. Simply plug in the headphones, summon the Music app, and choose tunes to match your mood. It's truly blissful — well, until someone calls you and the Droid X ceases being a musical instrument and returns to being the ball-and-chain of the modern digital era.

Browsing your music library

Music Headquarters on your phone is the app named, oddly enough, Music. You can start the app by touching its icon found on the Applications Tray. Soon, you discover the main Music browsing screen, shown in Figure 17-1.

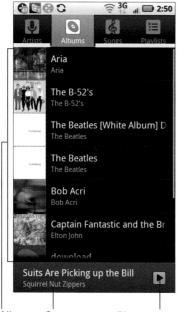

Albums   Current song   Play current song

Figure 17-1: The Music library.

All music stored on your phone can be viewed in four categories:

Artists: Songs are listed by recording artist or group. Choose Artist to see the list of artists. Then choose an artist to see their albums. Choosing an album displays the songs for that album. Some artists may have only one song, not in a particular album.

Albums: Songs are organized by album. Choose an album to list its songs.

Songs: All songs are listed alphabetically.

Playlists: Only songs you've organized into playlists are listed by their playlist names. Choose a playlist name to view songs organized in that playlist.

These categories are merely ways that the music is organized, ways to make the music easier to find when you may know an artist's name but not an album title or you may want to hear a song but not know who recorded it.

A playlist is a list you create yourself to organize songs by favorite, theme, or mood or whatever characteristic you want. The section "Organize Your Music," later in this chapter, discusses playlists.

- Music is stored on the Droid X MicroSD card.

- The size of the MicroSD card limits the total amount of music that can be stored on your phone. Also, consider that storing pictures and videos on your phone horns in on some of the space that can be used to store music.

- See the later section "More Music" for information on putting music into your phone.

- Album artwork generally appears on imported music as well as on music you purchase online. If an album doesn't have artwork, it cannot be manually added or updated.

- When the Droid X can't recognize an artist, it uses the title Unknown Artist. That usually happens with music you copy manually to the Droid X. Music that you purchase, or import or synchronize with a computer, generally retains the artist and album information. (Well, the information is retained as long as it was supplied on the computer or another original source.)

Playing a tune

To listen to music on the Droid X, you first find a song in the library, as described in the preceding section, and then you touch the song title. The song plays in another window, shown in Figure 17-2.

While the song is playing, you're free to do anything else with the phone. In fact, the song continues to play even if the phone goes to sleep. You can just continue listening, a look that's cool wherever you go, because you're wearing ear buds and, obviously, you're a with-it person because you have a portable music player.

After the song is done playing, the next song in the list plays. Touch the Song List button (refer to Figure 17-2) to review the songs in the list; you can even rearrange songs by dragging them in the list.

Figure 17-2: A song is playing.

The next song doesn't play if you have the Shuffle button activated (refer to Figure 17-2). In that case, the phone randomizes the songs in the list, so who knows which one is next?

 The next song also might not play if you have the Repeat option on: The phone has two repeat settings: Repeat all songs in the list and repeat the current song endlessly. When the latter setting is active, the Repeat button appears as depicted in the margin.

To stop the song from playing, touch the Pause button (refer to Figure 17-2).

 When music plays on the phone, a notification icon appears, as shown in the margin. To quickly summon the Music app to see which song is playing, or to pause the song, pull down the notifications and choose the first item, which is the name of the song that's playing.

- Songs may play when you choose them from a list, which skips over the screen you see depicted in Figure 17-2. In that case, choose the song again from the list to see that screen.

- Volume is set by using the Volume switch on the side of the phone: Up is louder, down is quieter.

✔ When you're browsing your music library, you may see a green Play icon, similar to the one in the margin. That icon flags any song that's playing or paused.

✔ Determining which song plays next depends on how you chose the song that's playing. If you choose a song by artist, all songs from that artist play, one after the other. When you choose a song by album, that album plays. Choosing a song from the entire song list causes all songs in the phone to play.

✔ To choose which songs play after each other, create a playlist. See the section "Organize Your Music," later in this chapter.

✔ After the last song in the list plays, the phone stops playing songs — unless you have Repeat on, in which case the list plays again.

✔ You can use the Droid X search abilities to help locate tunes in the phone's music library. You can search by artist name, song title, or album. The key is to press the Search soft button when you're using the Music app. Type all or part of the text you're searching for and touch the Search button on the onscreen keyboard. Choose the song you want to hear from the list that's displayed.

Turning your phone into a deejay

You need to do four things to make your Droid X the soul of your next shindig or soirée:

✔ Connect it to a stereo.

✔ Use the Shuffle command.

✔ Set the Repeat command.

✔ Provide plenty of drinks and snacks.

You can hook the Droid X to any stereo that has line inputs. You need, on one end, an audio cable that has a mini-headphone jack and, on the other end, an audio input that matches your stereo. Look for these cables at stores such as Radio Shack or any stereo store.

After your phone is connected, start the Music app and choose the party playlist you've created. If you want the songs to play in random order, choose the Shuffle command. The Shuffle button (refer to Figure 17-2) appears highlighted when that option is on.

You might also consider choosing the Repeat command so that all songs repeat after they've played.

Enjoy your party, and please drink responsibly.

Organize Your Music

A *playlist* is a collection of tunes you create. You build the list by combining songs from one album or artist or another — whatever music you have on your phone. You can then listen to the playlist and hear the music you want to hear. That's how to organize music on your Droid X.

Reviewing your playlists

Any playlists you've already created, or that have been preset on the Droid X, appear under the Playlists heading on the Music app's main screen. Touching the Playlists heading displays playlists, similar to the ones shown in Figure 17-3.

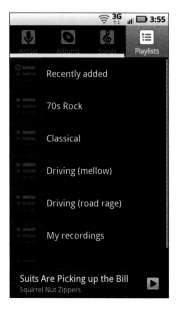

Figure 17-3: Playlists on the Droid X.

To listen to a playlist, long-press the playlist name and choose the Play command from the menu that appears.

You can also touch a playlist name to open the playlist and review the songs that are listed. Then you can choose any song from the list to start listening to that song.

A playlist is a helpful way to organize music when a song's information may not have been completely imported into the Droid X. For example, if you're like me, you probably have a lot of songs by "Unknown Artist." The quick way to remedy that situation is to name a playlist after the artist and then add those unknown songs to the playlist. The next section describes how it's done.

Creating a playlist

To start a new playlist from scratch, you don't just create an empty playlist and then add songs. That might be how things work on your computer, but not on the Droid X. Instead, you need to start by selecting the first tune you want to put on the playlist. Follow these steps:

1. **Play the song you want to use to start a new playlist.**

   You don't have to keep playing the song; feel free to pause the music after the song starts playing.

2. **Press the Menu soft button.**
3. **Choose Add to Playlist.**
4. **Choose New.**
5. **Type the playlist name.**

   Erase whatever silly text already appears in the input field. Type or dictate a new, better playlist name.

6. **Touch the Save button.**

   The new playlist is created and the song you were playing (refer to Step 1) is added to the playlist.

A new playlist has only one song. That's not much of a playlist, unless, of course, the song is by the Grateful Dead. To add more songs to a playlist, follow these steps:

1. **Play the song you want to add to the playlist.**

   You don't have to keep playing the song; feel free to pause the music after the song starts playing.

2. **Press the Menu soft button.**
3. **Choose the Add to Playlist command.**
4. **Choose an existing playlist.**

   You may have to scroll down the list to see all your playlists.

You can continue adding songs to as many playlists as you like. Adding songs to a playlist doesn't noticeably affect the storage capacity of the MicroSD card.

 ✔ Songs in a playlist can be rearranged: Use the tab on the far left end of the song's title in the list to drag the song up or down.

 ✔ To remove a song from a playlist, long-touch the song in the playlist and choose the command Remove from Playlist. Removing a song from a playlist doesn't delete the song from your phone. (See the next section for information on deleting songs from the Music library.)

 ✔ To delete a playlist, long-press its name in the list of playlists. Choose the Delete command. Though the playlist is removed, none of the songs in the playlist has been deleted.

Deleting music

To purge unwanted music from your Droid X, follow these brief, painless steps:

1. **Locate the music that offends you.**

2. **Long-press the musical entry.**

   If you don't want to hear the music, locate the music in a list: Artists, Albums, or Songs.

3. **Choose Delete.**

   A warning message appears.

4. **Touch the OK button.**

   The music is gone.

As the warning says (before Step 4), the music is deleted permanently from the MicroSD card. By deleting music, you free up storage space, and you cannot recover any music you delete. If you want the song back, you have to reinstall or sync it or buy it again, as described in the next section.

More Music

The Droid X may have come with a smattering of tunes preinstalled, or it might have come empty. I don't know which situation is worse: your tolerance of someone else's oddball musical tastes or your enjoyment of silence. Obviously, there's a need for more music, but where does this music come from? Well, there's no need to whip out a pen and notebook or take up the guitar: You can import music from your computer or buy new music from the Amazon MP3 store.

> ✔ Music, like pictures and video, is stored on the phone's MicroSD card. That card has only so much capacity. Though it would be nice to carry around all your music in the Droid X, it's just not practical, so be judicious when adding music to your phone.

> ✔ See Chapter 13 for more information on managing the MicroSD card.

Synchronizing music with your computer

Your computer is the equivalent of the 20th century stereo system — a combination tuner, amplifier, and turntable, plus all your records and CDs. If you've already copied your music collection to your computer, or if you use your computer as your main music storage system, you can share that music with the Droid X.

In Windows, you can use Windows Media Player to synchronize music between your phone and the PC. Here's how it works:

1. **Connect the Droid X to the PC.**

2. **Pull down the USB notification.**

3. **Choose the item Windows Media Sync.**

4. **Touch the OK button.**

5. **On your PC, start the Windows Media Player.**

   You can use most any media program, or "jukebox." These steps are specific to Version 12 of Windows Media Player, though they're similar to the steps you take in any media-playing program.

6. **If necessary, click the Sync tab in Windows Media Player.**

   The Droid X appears in the Sync list on the right side of Windows Media Player, as shown in Figure 17-4.

7. **Drag to the Sync Area the music you want to transfer to the Droid X (refer to Figure 17-4).**

8. **Click the Start Sync button to transfer the music to the Droid X.**

9. **Close the Windows Media Player when you're done transferring music.**

   Or, you can keep it open — whatever.

10. **Unmount the Droid X from the PC's storage system.**

    Refer to Chapter 13 for specific unmounting instructions, also known as turning off USB storage.

Droid X "drive"   Sync tab   Droid

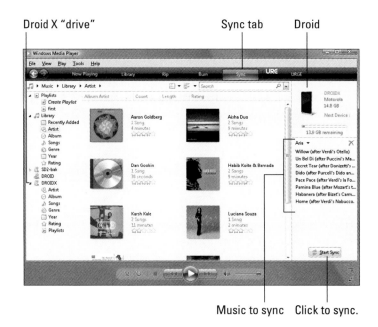

Music to sync   Click to sync.

Figure 17-4: Windows Media Player meets Droid X.

When you have a Macintosh, or you detest Windows Media Player, you can use the doubleTwist program to synchronize music between your Droid X and your computer. Refer to the section about synchronizing with doubleTwist in Chapter 13 for more information.

- ✔ You must mount the Droid X — specifically, its MicroSD card — into your computer's storage system before you can synchronize music.

- ✔ The Droid X can store only so much music! Don't be overzealous when copying over your tunes. In Windows Media Player (refer to Figure 17-4), a capacity thermometer thing shows you how much storage space is used and how much is available on your phone. Pay heed to that indicator!

- ✔ Windows Media Player complains when you try to sync the Droid X to more than one PC. If so, you're warned after Step 6 in this section. It's not a big issue: Just inform Windows Media Player that you intend to sync with the computer for only this session.

- ✔ You cannot use iTunes to synchronize music with the Droid X.

- ✔ Though the USB connection is on for your phone, and the phone's MicroSD card is mounted into the computer's storage system, the Droid X cannot access the MicroSD card. That means you cannot play music (or look at photos or access Contacts, for example) while the MicroSD card is mounted.

> ↙ It's also possible, though extremely unlikely, to manually add music to your phone. By *manually,* I mean mounting the Droid X into the computer's storage system and then copying and pasting music files from your computer to the phone's MicroSD card. The degree of insanity required to make this type of operation fun is so high that anyone attempting the procedure would be incapable of seeing this book on the shelf in any bookstore.

Buying music at the Amazon MP3 store

You don't have the music on your computer. You don't even have the CD to *burn* into your computer! You can't jam an old CD into the Droid X! At this point, a normal person would begin to panic, but because you have this book, you will instead visit the Amazon MP3 store to buy the music you need for your phone.

Before running through the steps, you must have an Amazon account. If you don't have one set up, use your computer to visit www.amazon.com and create one. You also need to keep a credit card on file for the account, which makes purchasing music with the Droid X work O so well.

Follow these steps to buy music for your phone:

1. **Ensure that you're using a Wi-Fi or high-speed digital network connection.**

   When in doubt about the cellular data network, activate the phone's Wi-Fi as described in Chapter 13. You can also refer to Chapter 13 for information on the various cellular data networks and their speeds.

2. **From the Applications Tray, choose the Amazon MP3 app.**

   The Amazon MP3 app connects you with the online Amazon music store, where you can search or browse for tunes to preview and purchase for your Droid X.

3. **Touch the Search button to begin your music quest.**

   Or. you can browse the top-selling songs and albums or browse by category.

4. **Type some search words, such as an album name, a song title, or an artist name.**

   You can also dictate the search text. See Chapter 4 for more dictation information.

   Your search results appear, if any matches are found, as shown in Figure 17-5.

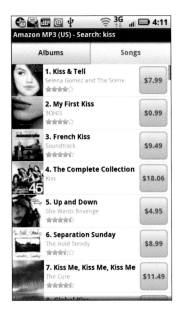

Figure 17-5: Songs found at the Amazon MP3 store.

5. **Touch a result.**

   If the result is an album, you see the contents of the album. Otherwise, a 30-second audio preview plays.

   When the result is an album, choose a song in the album to hear the preview.

   Touch the song again to stop the preview.

6. **To purchase the song, touch the big, orange button with the amount in it.**

   For example, the big, orange button at the top of the list (refer to Figure 17-5) specifies $7.99.

   Touching the button changes the price into the word *BUY*.

7. **Touch the word *BUY*.**

8. **If necessary, you may need to accept the license agreement.**

   This step happens the first time you buy something from the Amazon MP3 store.

9. **Log in to your Amazon.com account: Type your account name or email address and password.**

Your purchase is registered, account authorized, and download started. If they aren't, touch the Retry button to try again.

10. **Wait while the music downloads.**

    Well, actually, you don't have to wait: The music continues to download while you do other things on the phone.

No notification icon appears when the song or album has finished downloading. Notice, however, that the MP3 Store downloading icon vanishes from the notification part of the screen. It's your clue that the new music is in the phone and ready for your ears.

✔ Amazon emails you a bill for your purchase. That's your purchase record, so I advise you to be a good accountant and print it and then input it into your bookkeeping program or personal finance program at once!

✔ You can review your Amazon MP3 store purchases by pressing the Menu soft button in the MP3 Store app and choosing the Downloads command.

✔ You can also buy music using the doubleTwist program. Refer to Chapter 13 for more information on doubleTwist.

Your Phone Is a Radio

With the proper software installed on your Droid X, you don't have to worry about buying or carrying around the right music with you. That's because your phone can also be used as a radio. Think about it: The same technology that kids once carried around with them as *portable transistor radios* in the 1960s can be part of your 21st century phone. What will they think of next?

Listening to FM radio

The Droid X ships with the app named FM Radio, which magically pulls radio signals from the air and puts them into your ear. Kids: That's the only way Mom and Dad listened to music back when we were teenagers.

Start using the FM Radio app by first plugging a headset into your Droid X. (If you forget, the app reminds you.) Then choose the FM Radio app from the Applications Tray.

The first time you use the FM Radio app, you're prompted to scan available stations: Touch the OK button do to so. The Droid X scans all FM frequencies and makes a note of which are active.

After the initial scan, you can use the FM Radio app to listen to broadcast FM radio on your phone. The app's interface is shown in Figure 17-6. Use the controls as illustrated in the figure to change stations or scan for new stations.

 It's possible to listen to the FM Radio app over the Droid's speakers: Press the Menu soft button and choose the Loudspeaker command.

To quit the FM Radio app, press the Menu soft button and choose the command Exit FM.

The FM Radio app uses the headset as an antenna. If you unplug the headset, the FM Radio app closes.

Streaming music from the Internet

Though they're not broadcast radio stations, some sources on the Internet — *Internet radio* — play music. You can listen to that Internet music if you put two apps on your Droid X:

- ✔ Pandora Radio
- ✔ StreamFurious

 Pandora Radio lets you select music based on your mood and customizes what you listen to according to your feedback. The app works like the Internet site www.pandora.com, in case you're familiar with it.

 StreamFurious streams music from various radio stations on the Internet. Though not as customizable as Pandora, it uses less bandwidth.

Both apps are available at the Android Market. They're free, though a paid, *Pro* version of StreamFurious exists.

See Chapter 19 for more information about the Android Market.

FM Radio notification   Current station (preset)

Station presets   Current station (frequency

Scan down   Scan up

Change   Change
frequency   frequency
down   up

Figure 17-6: Listening to the radio on your phone.

Various and Sundry Apps

*T*he Droid X comes prepackaged with a plethora of practical *apps* — tiny programs that can help you and your phone get through your day. These apps can replace other gizmos you would normally carry with you, such as a watch, datebook, or television set. They can provide useful information or offer diverse entertainment. It's all part of the grand scheme of cramming your entire digital life into a teeny little box.

More than a Wall Calendar

Some people have a datebook. Others might write down appointments on business cards or on their palms. These methods might be effective, but they pale in comparison to the power of using your Droid X as your calendar and date keeper. Your phone can easily serve as a reminder of obligations due or delights to come. It all happens thanks to Google Calendar and the Calendar app on your phone.

Understanding the Calendar

The Droid X takes advantage of a feature on the Internet named Google Calendar. If you have a Google account (and I'm certain that you do), you already have a Google Calendar. You can visit the Google Calendar by using your computer to go to this Web page:

```
calendar.google.com
```

If necessary, log in using your Google account. You can use Google Calendar to keep track of dates or meetings or whatever else occupies your time. You can also use your phone to do the same thing, thanks to the Calendar app.

✓ I recommend that you use the Calendar app on your phone to access Google Calendar. It's a better way to access your schedule on the Droid X than using the Browser app to get to Google Calendar on the Web.

✓ Also see the later section "No Need to Alarm You" for information on using the Alarm & Timer app to set alarms on the phone.

✓ The Droid X comes with a Calendar widget you can add to the Home page. (It's a Motorola widget.) The widget is useful for reminding you of upcoming appointments. See Chapter 21 for details on adding widgets to the Home screen.

Browsing dates

To see your schedule or upcoming important events, or just to know which day of the month it is, summon the Calendar app. Touch the Launcher button at the bottom of the Home screen to display a list of all apps on the phone; choose the one named Calendar.

The first screen you see is most likely the monthly calendar view, shown in Figure 18-1. The calendar looks like a typical monthly calendar, with the month and year at the top. Scheduled appointments appear as green highlights on various days.

 To view your appointments by week, press the Menu soft button and choose Week. Or, you can choose the Day command to see your daily schedule. Figure 18-2 shows both Week and Day views in the Calendar.

You can return to the Month view at any time by pressing the Menu soft button and choosing the Month command.

✓ See the later section "Making a new event" for information on reviewing and creating events.

✓ Use Month view to see an overview of what's going on, but use Week or Day view to see your appointments.

✓ I check Week view at the start of the week to remind me of what's coming up.

✓ Different colors flag your events (refer to Figure 18-2) to represent different calendars to which the events are assigned. See the later section "Making a new event" for information on calendars.

✓ Use your finger to flick the Week and Day views up or down to see your entire schedule, from midnight to midnight.

✓ Navigate the days, weeks, or months by flicking the screen with your finger. Months scroll up and down; weeks and days scroll from left to right.

✓ To see the current day highlighted or displayed, press the Menu soft button and choose the Today command.

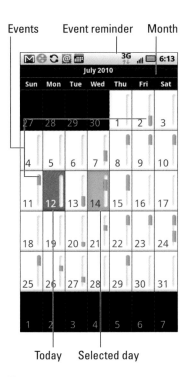

Figure 18-1: The Calendar's month view.

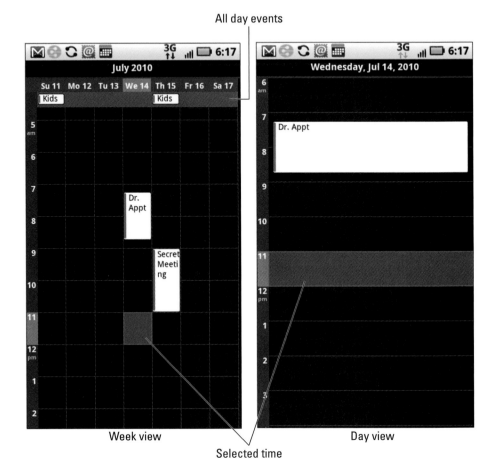

Figure 18-2: The Calendar's week and day views.

Reviewing your schedule

To see more detail about an event, touch it. When you're using Month view, touch the date with the event on it and then choose the event from Day view. Details about the event appear similarly to the ones shown in Figure 18-3.

 To see all upcoming events, you can switch to Agenda view: Press the Menu soft button and choose the Agenda command. Rather than list a traditional calendar, the Agenda screen shows only those dates with events and the events themselves. It's sort of a list.

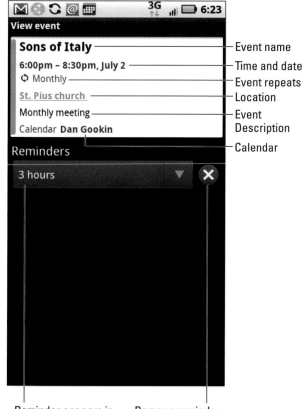

Figure 18-3: Event details.

As with the events in the non-Agenda views, simply touch an event to see more details (refer to Figure 18-3).

- ✔ Not every event has the level of detail shown in Figure 18-3. The minimum amount of information necessary for an event is a name and the date and time.

- ✔ If you touch the event on the calendar too long — if you do a long-press — choose the item View Event from the menu.

- ✔ See the next section for information on event reminders.

Making a new event

The key to making the calendar work is to add events: appointments, things to do, meetings, or full-day events such as birthdays and vacations. To create a new event, follow these steps in the Calendar app:

1. **Select the day for the event.**

   Use Month or Week view and touch the day of the new event.

   To save time, use Day view and touch the hour at which the event starts.

2. **Press the Menu soft button.**

3. **Choose New Event.**

   A screen appears, where you add details about the event.

4. **Type the event name.**

   For example, type Mammogram.

5. **Touch the Who field to add yourself.**

   Your account is named Me on the Droid X.

   You can add other people to the event and they're sent email notifications about the event. If you don't want to bother those folks, don't add them in the Who field.

6. **Use the buttons by Start to set the starting date and time.**

7. **Use the buttons by End to set the ending date and time.**

   When events last all day, like visiting your mother-in-law for an hour, simply touch the All Day button to put a check mark there. All-day events appear at the top of the day when the Calendar is shown in Week view (refer to Figure 18-2).

   At this point, you've entered the minimum amount of information for creating an event. Any details you add are okay but not necessary.

8. **Touch the Save button.**

   The Calendar app creates the event.

You can change an event at any time: Simply summon the event as described in the preceding section, press the Menu soft button while viewing the event, and choose the Edit Event command.

To remove an event, choose an event from the Calendar to view the event details. Press the Menu soft button and choose the Delete Event command. Touch the OK button to confirm.

> ✔ Adding an event location not only tells you where the event will be located but also hooks that information into the Maps app. My advice is to type information into an event's Where field just as though you're

typing information to search for a map. When the event is displayed, the location is a clickable link (refer to Figure 18-3); touch the location link to see where it is on a map.

✔ Google Calendar lets you create multiple calendars, which help you categorize types of events. For example, I have a personal calendar, one for my kids' schedule, one for work, and a travel calendar. Different calendars' events show up in different colors (refer to Figure 18-2).

✔ Use the Repetition button to create repeating events, such as weekly or monthly meetings, anniversaries, and birthdays.

✔ Reminders can be set so that the phone alerts you before an event takes place. The alert can show up as a notification icon (shown in the margin), or it can be an audio alert or a vibrating alert.

✔ To deal with an event notification, pull down the notifications and choose the event. You can touch the Dismiss All button to remove event alerts.

✔ Alert types are set by pressing the Menu soft button in the Calendar app: Choose the More command and then Settings. Use the Select Ringtone option to choose an audio alert. Use the Vibrate option to control whether the phone vibrates to alert you of an impending event.

✔ You can also create events by using the Google Calendar on the Internet. Those events are instantly synced with the calendar on your Droid X phone — *if* you follow my advice in Chapter 2.

Your Phone the Calculator

The Calculator is perhaps the oldest of all traditional cellphone apps. It's probably also the least confusing and frustrating app to use, at least on the Droid X.

Start the Calculator app by choosing its icon from the Applications Tray. The Calculator appears, as shown in Figure 18-4.

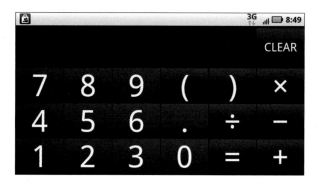

Figure 18-4: The Calculator.

✔ You can swipe the screen (refer to Figure 18-4) to the left to see a panel of strange, advanced mathematical operations you'll probably never use.

✔ Long-press the calculator's text (or results) to cut or copy the results.

✔ I use the Calculator most often to determine the tip at a restaurant. It takes me almost as long to use the Calculator as it does for smarty-pants Barbara to do the 15 percent calculation in her head.

No Need to Alarm You

The Droid X keeps constant and accurate track of the time, which is displayed at the top of the Home screen and also when you first wake up the phone. When you'd rather have the phone wake you up, you can take advantage of the Alarm & Timer app.

Start the Alarm & Timer app by choosing its icon from the Applications Tray. The Alarm Clock is shown in Figure 18-5.

If you see an alarm you want to set, touch the gray square (refer to Figure 18-5) to set that alarm. A green check mark in a square indicates that an alarm is set.

To create your own alarm, follow these steps while using the Alarm Clock app:

1. **Press the Menu soft button.**

2. **Choose Add Alarm.**

3. **Choose Time to set the alarm time.**

   Use the gizmo to set the hour and minute and specify AM or PM. Touch the Set button when you're done setting the time.

4. **Touch the Sound button to choose a ringtone for the alarm — something suitably annoying.**

5. **Specify whether the phone vibrates by placing a check mark next to the Vibrate option.**

6. **Choose whether the alarm repeats.**

   Choose which days of the week you want the alarm to sound.

7. **Choose the Name item to type or dictate a label for the alarm.**

8. **Touch the Done button to create the alarm.**

   The alarm appears in a list on the main Alarm Clock screen, along with any other available alarms.

Alarms must be set or else they will not trigger. To set an alarm, touch it in the alarm list. Place a check mark in the gray box (refer to Figure 18-5).

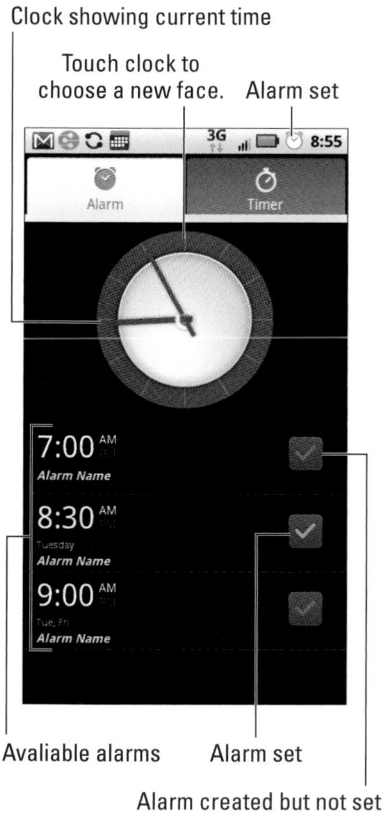

Clock showing current time

Touch clock to
choose a new face.   Alarm set

Avaliable alarms   Alarm set

Alarm created but not set

Figure 18-5: The clock.

✔ For a larger time display, you can add a Clock widget to the Home
screen. Refer to Chapter 21 for more information about widgets on the
Home screen.

✔ Turning off an alarm doesn't delete the alarm.

✔ To remove an alarm, touch it from the list and choose the option Delete
from the bottom of the screen. Touch the OK button to confirm.

✔ The alarm doesn't work when you turn off the phone. The alarm does,
however, go off when the phone is sleeping.

✔ A notification icon appears when an alarm has gone off but has been
ignored.

✔ So tell me: Do alarms go *off* or do they go *on*?

There's No Tube Like YouTube

YouTube is the Internet phenomenon that proves Andy Warhol right: In the future, everyone will be famous for 15 minutes. Or, in the case of YouTube, they'll be famous on the Internet for the duration of a maximum 15-minute video. That's because *YouTube* is *the* place on the Internet for anyone and everyone to share their video creations.

To view the mayhem on YouTube, or to contribute something yourself, start the YouTube app. Like all apps on the Droid X, it can be found on the Applications Tray. The main YouTube screen is depicted in Figure 18-6.

Record and upload a video

Search for videos

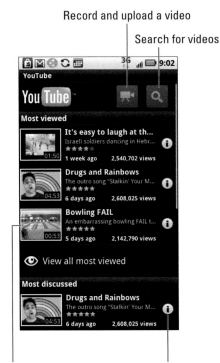

Touch a video to watch.   Find information

Figure 18-6: YouTube.

To view a video, touch its name or icon in the list.

To search for a video, touch the Search button (refer to Figure 18-6). Type or dictate what you want to search for, and then peruse the results.

Videos in the YouTube app play in Landscape mode, so tilt your phone to the left to see the videos in their proper orientation. The videos take up the entire screen; touch the screen to see the onscreen video controls.

Press the Back soft button to return to the main YouTube app after watching a video or if you tire of a video and need to return to the main screen out of boredom.

✍ Use the YouTube app to view YouTube videos, rather than use the Browser app to visit the YouTube Web site.

✍ Because you have a Google account, you also have a YouTube account. I recommend that you log in to your YouTube account when using YouTube on the Droid X: Press the Menu soft button and choose the command My Account. Log in, if necessary. Otherwise, you see your account information, your videos, and any video subscriptions.

✍ Not all YouTube videos are available for viewing on mobile devices.

✍ You can touch the Record & Upload button (refer to Figure 18-6) to shoot and then immediately send a video to YouTube. Refer to Chapter 15 for information on recording video with your Droid X.

Movies in the Palm of Your Hand

Wouldn't it be fun to watch the latest Hollywood hits on your Droid X? Would it be even more fun if the Droid X came with an app that did just that? Would it be "just the best" if watching those films were free?

Well, two out of three ain't bad.

The Droid X comes with the Blockbuster app, which can be used to rent or purchase mainstream movies that you can view right on your phone. The key is to have an account at Blockbuster. When you do, you can follow the direction on the screen after starting the Blockbuster app and get everything singed up and configured. All that's missing is the popcorn.

Even when you don't have a Blockbuster account, you can still use the app to see which films are available.

The Droid X Does Games

For all its seriousness and technology, one of the best uses of a smartphone is to play games. I'm not talking about the silly arcade games (though I admit that they're fun). No, I'm talking about some serious portable gaming.

To whet your appetite, the Droid X comes with a small taste of what the device can do in regard to gaming. It's the NFS Shift app, which is a car-racing game, shown in Figure 18-7.

Figure 18-7: Games on the Droid X.

NFS Shift uses the phone's accelerometer to steer a high-speed race car around various racing tracks from all over the globe. The game also plays stereotypical rock music, which either makes the action more exciting or merely irritates you.

If you want to continue playing NFS Shift, you have to buy it. The program lets you know how much it costs after you complete your first free race.

Of course, gaming isn't limited to NFS Shift. Many games — arcade, action, and puzzle — are to be found in the Android Market. See Chapter 19.

More Apps from the Android Market

I believe that everyone enjoys shopping, especially guys. Don't tell me you've never seen a guy lusting over power tools or pretending to be a well-informed consumer in a cigar store. I admit to being lured by the shopping desire as well. I mean, who doesn't flip through the pages of *SkyMall* magazine and fantasize about impressing their friends at the beach house with that remote control bug zapper?

Happily for everyone, shopping is part of using your Droid X. It's the way you add more apps to the phone's software repository. You have tens of thousands of apps to choose from, which is good news. Better news is that a lot of those apps are free. Everything is available for your perusal at a place called Android Market.

✔ Because the Droid X uses the Android operating system, it can run nearly all applications written for Android.

✔ You can be assured that all apps that appear in the Android Market on your phone can be used with the Droid X. There's no way that you can download or buy something that's incompatible with your phone.

✔ App is short for *application*. It's another word for *software*, which is another word for a program that runs on a computer or on a mobile device, such as your Droid X phone.

Welcome to the Market

Shopping for new software for your Droid X can be done anywhere that you and your phone just happen to be. You don't even need to know what kind of software you want; like many a mindless ambling shopper, you can browse until the touchscreen is blurry with your fingerprints.

✔ You obtain software from the Market by *downloading* it into your phone. That file transfer works best at top speeds; therefore:

✔ I highly recommend that you connect to a Wi-Fi network if you plan to purchase software at the Android Market. See Chapter 13 for details on connecting the Droid X to a Wi-Fi network.

Visiting the Market

New apps await delivery into your phone, like animated vegetables shouting, "Pick me! Pick me!" To get to them, open the Market icon, which can be found on the main Home screen or accessed from the Applications Tray.

After opening the Market app, you see the main screen, similar to the one shown in Figure 19-1. You can browse for apps, games, or special apps from Verizon by touching the appropriate doodad, as shown in the figure.

Find apps by browsing the lists: Choose Apps (refer to Figure 19-1). Then choose a specific category to browse. You can sort apps by their popularity; separate categories exist for paid, free, and newer apps.

When you know an app's name or an app's category or even what the app does, searching for the app works fastest: Touch the Search button at the top of the Market screen (refer to Figure 19-1). Type all or part of the app's name or perhaps a description. Touch the keyboard's Search button to begin your search.

Browse for games   Search for apps

Browse all apps   Special Verizon apps

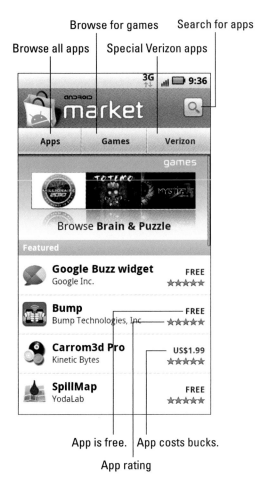

App is free. | App costs bucks.

App rating

Figure 19-1: Android Market.

To see more information about an app, touch it. Touching the app doesn't buy it, but instead displays a more detailed description, screen shots, and comments, plus links to see additional apps or contact the developer.

✔ The first time you enter the Android Market, you have to accept the terms of service; touch the Accept button.

✔ Pay attention to an app's ratings. Ratings are added by people who use the apps, like you and me. Having more stars is better. You can see additional information, including individual user reviews, by choosing the app.

- In addition to getting apps, you can download widgets for the Home screen as well as wallpapers for the Droid X. Just search the Android Market for *widget* or *live wallpaper*.

- See Chapter 21 for more information on widgets and live wallpapers.

Getting a free app

After you locate an app you want, the next step is to download it. Follow these steps:

1. **If possible, activate the phone's Wi-Fi connection.**

   Downloads complete much faster over the Wi-Fi connection than over the digital cellular connection. See Chapter 13 for information on connecting your Droid X phone to a Wi-Fi network.

2. **Open the Market app.**

3. **Locate the app you want and open its description.**

   Refer to the preceding section for details. If you're just starting out, consider getting one of the V CAST apps in the Verizon category. (Most of them are free.)

4. **Touch the Install button.**

   The Install button is found at the bottom of the app's list o' details. Free apps feature an Install button. Paid apps have a Buy button. (See the next section for information on buying an app.)

   After touching the Install button, you're alerted to any services that the app uses. The alert isn't a warning, and it doesn't mean anything bad. It's just that the developer is being honest with you about what the app does on your phone.

5. **Touch the OK button to begin the download.**

   You return to the main Market screen as the app downloads. It continues to download while you do other things on your phone.

    After the download is successful, the phone's status bar shows a new icon, as shown in the margin. That's the Successful Install notification.

6. **Pull down the notifications.**

   See Chapter 3 for details, in case you've never pulled down notifications.

7. **Choose the app from the list of notifications.**

   The app is listed by its app name, with the text `Successfully Installed` beneath it.

At this point, what happens next depends on the app you've downloaded. For example, you may have to agree to a license agreement. If so, touch the I Agree button. Additional setup may involve signing in to an account or creating a profile, for example.

After the initial setup is complete, or if no setup is necessary, you can start using the app.

- Don't forget to turn off Wi-Fi after downloading your app; Wi-Fi is a drain on the phone's battery.

- The new app's icon is placed on the Applications Tray, along with all the other apps on the Droid X.

- Yes, when you add an app, it shuffles all icons on the Applications Tray — no way around that.

- You can also place a shortcut icon for the app on the Home screen. See Chapter 21.

- The Android market has many wonderful apps you can download. Chapter 25 lists some that I recommend, all of which are free.

Buying an app

Some great free apps are available, but many of the apps you dearly want probably cost money. It's not a lot of money, especially compared to the price of computer software. In fact, it seems odd to sit and stew over whether paying 99 cents for a game is "worth it."

I recommend that you download a free app first, to familiarize yourself with the process.

When you're ready to pay for an app, follow these steps:

1. **Activate the phone's Wi-Fi connection.**

2. **Open the Market app.**

3. **Browse or search for the app you want, and choose the app to display its description.**

   Review the app's price. It's priced in dollars, euros, pounds, or yen. You can buy an app priced in another currency; your credit card or cellphone bill is charged the proper amount.

4. **Touch the Buy button.**

   If you don't have a Google Checkout account, you're prompted to set one up. Follow the directions on the screen.

5. **Choose the payment method.**

   You can choose to use an existing credit card, add a new card, or — most conveniently — add the purchase to your cellular bill.

   If you choose to add a new card, you're required to fill in all information about the card, including the billing address.

6. **Touch the Buy Now button.**

   The Buy Now button has the app's price listed.

   After you touch the Buy button, the app is downloaded. You can wait or do something else with the phone while the app is downloading.

The app may require additional setup steps, confirmation information, or other options.

The app can be accessed from the Applications Tray, just like all other apps available on your Droid X.

Eventually, you receive an email message from Google Checkout, confirming your purchase. The message explains how you can get a refund from your purchase within 24 hours. The section "Removing installed software," later in this chapter, discusses how it's done.

Be sure to disable the phone's Wi-Fi after downloading the app, because Wi-Fi is an additional drain on the phone's battery.

Manage Your Applications

The Market is not only where you buy apps — it's also the place you return to for performing app management. That task includes reviewing apps you've downloaded, updating apps, and removing apps you no longer want or that you severely hate.

Reviewing your downloads

If you're like me, and if I'm like anyone, you probably sport a whole host of apps on your Droid X. It's kind of fun to download new software and give your phone new abilities. To review the apps you've acquired, follow these steps:

1. **Start the Market app.**

2. **Press the Menu soft button.**

3. **Choose Downloads.**

4. **Scroll your downloaded apps.**

The list of downloaded apps should look similar to the one shown in Figure 19-2.

Besides reviewing the list, you can do two things with an installed app: Update it or remove it. The following two sections describe how each operation is done.

The Downloads list is accurate in that it represents apps you've downloaded. Some apps in the list, however, might not be installed on your Droid X: They were downloaded, installed, and then removed. To review all apps installed on the phone, see the section "Controlling your apps," later in this chapter.

Updates available

App successfully downloaded

Figure 19-2: Apps downloaded for the Droid X.

Updating an app

One nice thing about using the Android Market to get new software is that the Market also notifies you of new versions of the programs you download. Whenever a new version of any app is available, you see the Updates Available notification icon, shown in the margin.

Locate apps that need updating by pulling down the phone's notifications and choosing Updates Available. Or, you can visit the Downloads list, as described in the preceding section.

To update an app, obey these steps:

1. **Turn on the phone's Wi-Fi access, if it's available.**

   Updates are downloaded from the Internet, which means the faster your phone can connect, the more quickly the updates are made.

2. **Choose the updated app; touch it to open more details.**

   For example, touch an app with the Updates Available flag (refer to Figure 19-2).

3. **Touch the Update button.**

4. **Touch the OK button to heed the warning.**

   The update means that an entirely new version of the app is downloaded and installed, which replaces the installed version. That's okay.

5. **Optionally, read any services that the app uses on your phone and then touch the OK button.**

   The update is downloaded.

As when you initially install the app, you're free to do other things with the phone while the update is downloading. When downloading is complete, the Successful Install notification appears, as shown in the margin. You can then start using your updated app or continue applying updates by repeating the steps in this section.

After the download is complete, pull down the notifications and select the downloaded app from the notification list. When you first start the updated app, you may be asked to agree (again) to the licensing terms; touch the I Agree button. After that, you can start using the app.

✓ Future releases of the Android operating system will feature an Update All button, which updates, all at one time, all apps that have pending updates. If so, in Step 3 touch the Update All button to get all your apps up-to-date.

✔ The Android operating system update might also apply an Update Automatically option for your apps. When selected, the apps automatically download their updates when available.

Removing installed software

There are a few reasons why you'd want to remove installed software. The first, most odiously, is that you just don't like a program or it does something so hideously annoying that you find removal of the app to be emotionally satisfying. The second is that you have a better program that does the same thing. The third reason is to free up a modicum of storage on the phone's internal storage area or MicroSD card.

Whatever the reason, removing an app from your Droid X works like this:

1. **Start the Market app.**
2. **Press the Menu soft button.**
3. **Choose the Downloads heading to summon a list of all software you've downloaded into your phone.**

   Refer to Figure 19-2.

4. **Touch the app that offends you.**
5. **Touch the Uninstall button.**
6. **Touch the OK button to confirm.**

   The app is removed.

7. **Fill in the survey to specify why you removed the app.**

   Be honest, or be as honest as you can given the short list of reasons.

8. **Touch OK.**

   The app is gone!

The app continues to appear on the Downloads list even after it's been removed. After all, you downloaded it once. That doesn't mean that the app is installed. To review apps installed on the Droid X, see the next section.

✔ In most cases, if you uninstall a paid app before 24 hours has passed, your credit card or account is fully refunded.

✔ You can always reinstall paid apps that you've uninstalled. You aren't charged twice for doing so.

Controlling your apps

The Droid X has a technical place where you can review and manage all apps you've installed on your phone. To visit that place, follow these steps:

1. **From the Applications Tray, choose Settings.**

2. **Choose Applications.**

3. **Choose Manage Applications.**

   A complete list of all applications installed on your phone is displayed. Unlike the Downloads list in the Market app, only installed applications appear in the list.

4. **Touch an application name.**

   Additional details and controls for the application are displayed, similar to the ones shown in Figure 19-3.

5. **Touch the Back button when you're done being baffled by the information.**

   You can also just touch the Home soft button to immediately escape to the Home screen.

You can use the Application Info screen (refer to Figure 19-3) to uninstall an app, similar to the steps described in the preceding section. This technique works for some older Android apps that don't appear on the Downloads list.

Refer to the information in the Storage section to determine how much space the app is using on the phone's internal storage or MicroSD card.

If the app is consuming a huge amount of space when compared with other apps and you seldom use the app, consider it a candidate for deletion.

The Force Stop button is used to halt a program that runs amok. For example, I had to stop an older Android app that continually made noise and offered no option to exit. It was a relieving experience. See Chapter 22 for more details on shutting down apps run amok.

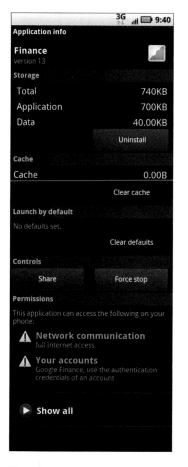

Figure 19-3: Detailed app information.

Part V
Off the Hook

The 5th Wave   By Rich Tennant

"So, what kind of roaming capabilities does this thing have?"

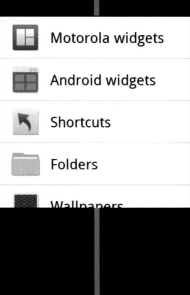

*H*ave you ever noticed that cell phones lack dials and hooks, yet we continue to say things like "dial the phone" or "hang up"? It's tradition, kind of like calling that minor bump over a car's tire a *fender* or referring to that place we send teenagers as high *school*. They're just terms that carry over from an earlier time when the words we use today actually meant something.

You can't take your Droid X off the hook any more than you can use a crank to start your Prius. Still, you can take your Droid X places that an old timey phone wouldn't dare dream of going. There are also various chores associated with using a modern cell phone, duties and obligations beyond those necessary for the operation of a candlestick phone. Those tasks are covered in this part of the book.

Out and About

*C*ordless phones were all the rage in the 1980s. Owning one was something you boasted about, proudly telling the person you were talking with that you were "going cordless." Never mind that the range was terrible and objects such as walls and refrigerators hindered the signal or that the neighbor's baby monitor would pick up your call. Nope, taking the phone with you, even for a short distance, was cool.

Cellphones go everywhere, of course. They have no wires, so your use of the Droid X is limited to only where it can find a signal — which is just about anywhere in the world. Yes, it's true: You can wander the Gobi Desert with your Droid X. It may not be able to receive a signal, but you can be out there, wandering.

Where the Droid X Roams

The word *roam* takes on an entirely new meaning when applied to a cellphone. It means that your phone receives a cell signal whenever you're outside your cellphone carrier's operating area. In that case, your phone is *roaming*.

Roaming sounds handy, but there's a catch: It almost always involves a surcharge for using another cellular service — an *unpleasant* surcharge.

The Droid X alerts you whenever you're roaming. You see a Roaming icon appear at the top of the screen, in the status area. That icon tells you that you're outside the regular signal area, possibly using another cellular provider's network.

There's little you can do to avoid incurring roaming surcharges when making or receiving phone calls. Well, yes: You can wait until you're back in an area serviced by your primary cellular provider. You can, however, altogether avoid using the other network's data services while roaming. Follow these steps:

 1. **From the Applications Tray, choose the Settings icon.**

 2. **Choose Data Manager.**

 3. **Choose Data Delivery.**

     If Data Roaming is activated for your phone, you see a warning: Dismiss the warning or choose the option that disables Data roaming. Otherwise:

 4. **Ensure that the Data Roaming option isn't selected.**

     Remove the green check mark by the Data Roaming option.

The phone can still access the Internet over the Wi-Fi connection when you're roaming. Setting up a Wi-Fi connection doesn't make you incur extra charges, unless you have to pay to get on the wireless network. See Chapter 13 for more information about Wi-Fi.

Another network service you might want to disable while roaming has to do with MMS (Multimedia Messaging System), more commonly known as text messages. To avoid surcharges from another cellular network for downloading an MMS message, follow these steps:

 1. **Open the Text Messaging app.**

 2. **If the screen shows a specific conversation, press the Back soft button to return to the main messaging screen.**

     (It's the screen that lists all your conversations.)

 3. **Touch the Menu soft button.**

 4. **Choose Messaging Settings.**

 5. **Remove the green check mark by Auto-Retrieve.**

     Or, if the item isn't selected, you're good to go — literally.

For more information about multimedia text messages, refer to Chapter 9.

When the phone is roaming, you may see the text *Emergency Calls Only* displayed on the locked screen.

Airplane Mode

As anyone knows who has been flying recently, using a cellular phone while on an airborne plane is strictly forbidden. That's because, if you did, the navigation system would completely screw up, the plane would invert, and everyone onboard would die in a spectacular crash on the ground, in a massive fireball suitable for the 5 o'clock Eyewitness News. It would be breathtaking.

Seriously, you're not supposed to use a cellphone when flying. Specifically, you're not allowed to make calls in the air. You can, however, use your Droid X to listen to music, play games, or do anything else that doesn't require a cellular connection. The secret is to place the phone in *Airplane mode*.

The most convenient way to put the Droid X in Airplane mode is to press and hold the Power button. From the menu, choose Airplane Mode. You don't even need to unlock the phone to perform this operation.

The most inconvenient way to put the Droid X into Airplane mode is to follow these steps:

1. **From the Applications Tray, choose the Settings icon.**

2. **Choose Wireless & Networking**

3. **Touch the square by Airplane Mode to set the green check mark.**

    When the green check mark is visible, Airplane mode is active.

When the phone is in Airplane mode, a special icon appears in the status area, as shown in the margin. You might also see the text *No Service* appear on the phone's locked screen.

To exit Airplane mode, repeat the steps in this section but remove the green check mark by touching the square next to Airplane Mode.

  ✓ Officially, the Droid X should be powered *off* when the plane is taking off or landing. See Chapter 2 for information on turning off the phone.

  ✓ You can compose email while the phone is in Airplane mode. The messages aren't sent until you disable Airplane mode and connect again with a data network.

✔ Bluetooth networking is disabled when you activate the Droid X Airplane mode. See Chapter 13 for more information on Bluetooth.

✔ Many airlines now feature wireless networking onboard. You can turn on wireless networking for the Droid X and use a wireless network in the air. Simply activate the Droid X Wi-Fi, per the directions in Chapter 13, after placing the phone in Airplane mode — well, after the flight attendant tells you that it's okay to do so.

Droid X air travel tips

I don't consider myself a frequent flyer, but I travel several times a year. I do it often enough that I wish the airports had separate lines for security: one for seasoned travelers, one for families, and one, of course, for frickin' idiots. The last category would have to be disguised by placing a Bonus Coupons sign or Free Snacks banner over the metal detector. That would weed 'em out.

Here are some of my cellphone and airline travel tips:

✔ **Charge your phone before you leave.** This tip probably goes without saying, but you'll be happier with a full cellphone charge to start your journey.

✔ **Take a cellphone charger with you.** Many airports feature USB chargers, so you might need just a USB-to-micro USB cable. Still, why risk it? Bring the entire charger with you.

✔ **At the security checkpoint, place your phone in a bin.** Add to the bin any of your other electronic devices, keys, or metal shards. I know from experience that keeping your cellphone in your pocket most definitely sets off airport metal detectors.

✔ **When the flight attendant asks you to *turn off* your cellphone for take-off and landing,** obey the command. That's *turn off,* as in power off the phone or shut it down. It doesn't mean placing the phone in Airplane mode. Turn it off.

✔ **Use the phone's Calendar app to keep track of flights.** The event title serves as the airline and flight number. For the event time, I insert the take-off and landing schedules. For the location, I add the origin and destination airport codes. Referencing the phone from your airplane seat or in a busy terminal is much handier than fussing with travel papers. See Chapter 18 for more information on the Calendar.

✔ **Remember that some airlines may eventually feature Android apps you can use while traveling.** Rather than hang on to a boarding pass printed by your computer, you just present your phone to the scanner. (At the time this book went to press, no airline apps were available for the Droid X, but I predict that you'll soon see a lot of them. Refer to Chapter 19 for information on finding apps in the Android Market.)

✔ **Some apps you can use to organize your travel details are similar to, but more sophisticated than, using the Calendar app.** Visit the Android Market and search for *travel* or *airlines* to find a host of apps.

International Calling

You can use your cellphone not only to dial up folks who live in other countries but you can also take your cellphone overseas and use it in another country. Neither task is as difficult as properly posing for a passport photo, but it can become frustrating and expensive when you don't know your way around.

Dialing an international number

A phone is a bell that anyone in the world can ring. To prove it, all you need is the phone number of anyone in the world. Dial that number using your Droid X and, as long as you both speak the same language, you're talking! Or, if you're not talking, you're the United Nations!

To make an international call with the Droid X, you merely need to know the foreign phone number. That number includes the international country-code prefix, followed by the number.

Before dialing the international country-code prefix, you must dial a plus sign (+) on the Droid X. The + is the *country exit code,* which must be dialed in order to exit the national phone system and access the international phone system. For example, to dial Finland on your Droid X, you dial +358 and then the number in Finland. The +358 is the exit code plus the international code for Finland, 358.

To produce the + code in an international phone number, press and hold the 0 key on the Droid X dialpad. Then input the country prefix and the phone number. Touch the Dial button (the green phone icon) to complete the call.

- ✔ In most cases, dialing an international number involves a time zone difference. Before you dial, be aware of what time it is in the country or location you're calling.

- ✔ Dialing internationally also involves surcharges, unless your cellphone plan already provides for international dialing.

- ✔ The + character is used on the Droid X to represent the country exit code, which must be dialed before you can access an international number. In the United States, the exit code is 011. (In the United Kingdom, it's 00.) So, if you're using a landline to dial Russia from the United States, you dial 011 to escape from the United States and then 7, the country code for Russia. Then dial the rest of the number. You don't have to do that on the Droid X, because + is always the country exit code, and it replaces the 011 for U.S. users.

✔ The + character isn't a number separator. When you see an international number listed as 011+20+???????, do not insert the + character in the number. Instead, dial +20 and then the rest of the number.

✔ International calls fail for a number of reasons. One of the most common is that the recipient's phone company or service blocks incoming international calls.

✔ Another reason that international calls fail is the zero reason: Often times, you must leave out any zero in the phone number that follows the country code. So, if the country code is 254 for Kenya and the phone number starts with 012, you dial +254 for Kenya and then 12 and the rest of the number. Omit the leading zero.

✔ You can also send text messages to international cellphones. It works the same as making a traditional phone call: Input the international number into the Messaging app. See Chapter 9 for more information on text messaging.

✔ Know which type of phone you're calling internationally — cellphone or landline. The reason is that an international call to a cellphone often involves a surcharge that doesn't apply to a landline.

Making international calls with Skype Mobile

Your Droid X comes with the Skype Mobile app, which can be used to make inexpensive international calls. It's an excellent option, especially when your cellular contract doesn't provide for international calling.

If you don't yet have a Skype account, use your computer to create one. You need that account to use Skype Mobile. Set up the account by first obtaining the Skype program for your computer: Visit www.skype.com to get started. Further, you must have Skype Credit to make the international call. That credit can be purchased from within the Skype program on your computer.

The Skype Mobile app is found in the Applications Tray. After starting it, log in with your Skype ID and password.

You can't make an international call unless you've created a contact with an international number. The contact must be a Skype Mobile contact, shown on the Contacts tab on the Skype Mobile Screen, illustrated in Figure 20-1.

To make an international call, touch the Call Phones tab at the top of the screen. Punch in the number, including the + sign for international access as described in this chapter and as shown in Figure 20-1. Touch the Contact button to make the call.

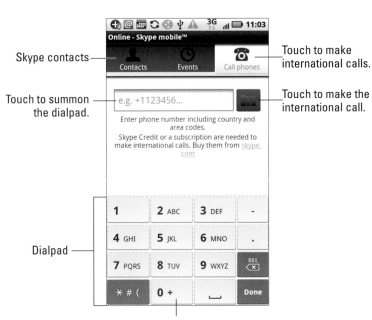

Skype contacts —

Touch to summon the dialpad.

Dialpad —

Touch to make international calls.

Touch to make the international call.

Press and hold to put a + in the number.

Figure 20-1: Calling internationally with Skype Mobile.

After the call is connected with Skype Mobile, the Droid X touchscreen looks similar to the way it looks when you regularly place calls. You can use the phone dialpad, if necessary, mute the call, put it on speaker, and so on.

When you're finished with the call, touch the End button.

✔ You're always signed into Skype Mobile unless you sign out. Pressing the Home button to switch away from the app doesn't log you out of Skype.

✔ To log out of Skype Mobile, press the Menu soft button, choose More and then choose Sign Out.

✔ The first time you use the Skype Mobile app, you're required to read various information and agree to the licensing terms.

✔ At the time this book went to press, Skype Mobile required a digital cellular signal; it doesn't work over a Wi-Fi connection

✔ Check with your cellular provider to see whether you're charged connection minutes for using Skype Mobile. Even though the international call is free, you might still be dinged for the minutes you use on Skype to make the call.

Taking your Droid X abroad

The easiest way to use a cellphone abroad is to rent or buy a cellphone in the country where you plan to stay. I'm serious: Often, international roaming charges are so high that it's just cheaper to get a throwaway cellphone wherever you go, especially if you plan to stay there for a while.

When you opt to use your Droid X rather than buy a local phone, things should run smoothly — *if* a compatible cellular service is in your location. (The Droid X uses the CDMA cellular network.) The foreign carrier accepts incoming and outgoing calls from your phone and cheerfully charges you the international roaming rate.

The key to determining whether your Droid X is usable in a foreign country is to turn it on. The name of that country's compatible cellular service should show up at the top of the phone, where Verizon Wireless (or whatever your carrier is) appears on the Droid X main screen. (See Figure 2-1, in Chapter 2.)

✔ You receive calls on your cellphone internationally as long as the Droid X can access the network. Your friends need only dial your cellphone number as they normally do; the phone system automatically forwards your calls to wherever you are in the world.

✔ The person calling you doesn't pay extra when you're off romping the globe with your Droid X. Nope — *you* pay extra for the call.

Customize Your Phone

In This Chapter

▶ Changing the Home screen background

▶ Working with icons and widgets on the Home screen

▶ Using folders for Home screen organization

▶ Adding security

▶ Silencing the phone's noise

▶ Enabling automatic answer and redial

▶ Modifying phone settings

▶ Setting accessibility options

T hough some people love to customize things, most people don't even bother. I suppose they could be afraid that they'll break something, but most people in my travels who refuse to customize anything simply profess contentment with the boring status quo. (Okay, they don't use the word *boring*.) Or, maybe they don't know how easily they can customize something technical, such as the Droid X phone.

The key to understanding customization is to accept that the Droid X is *your* phone. You can change the way it looks, how it works, and where it finds apps, plus a bunch of other interesting tasks, all designed to make it your own phone.

It's Your Home Screen

The Droid X sports a roomy Home screen. It's really *seven* Home screens. Of course, the phone comes preconfigured with lots of icons and widgets adorning all seven of the Home screens. You can customize them by removing those widgets and icons, especially those you seldom use, and replacing them with icons and widgets you use. You can also add folders to organize things, and you can even put a new wallpaper on the Home screen. Truly, you can make the Home screen look just the way you want.

For the most part, the key to changing the Home screen is the *long-press:* Press and hold your finger on a blank part of the Home screen (not on an icon). You see a pop-up menu appear, as shown in Figure 21-1. From that menu, you can begin your Home screen customization adventure, as discussed in this section.

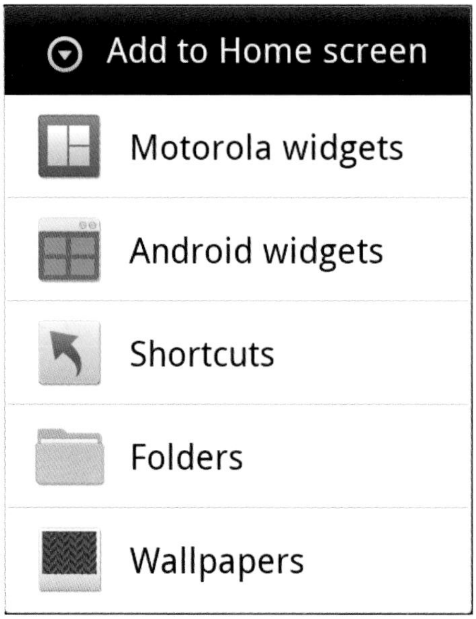

| ⊙ Add to Home screen |
| Motorola widgets |
| Android widgets |
| Shortcuts |
| Folders |
| Wallpapers |

Figure 21-1: The Add to Home Screen menu.

Changing wallpaper

The Home screen has two types of backgrounds, or wallpapers: traditional and live. Live wallpapers are the animated ones. A not-so-live wallpaper can be any image, such as a picture from the Gallery.

To set a new wallpaper for the Home screen, obey these steps:

1. **Long-press the Home screen.**

   Ensure that you're long-pressing on a blank part of the Home screen.

   The Add to Home Screen menu appears, as shown in Figure 21-1.

2. **Choose Wallpapers.**

   Another menu appears, with three options (refer to Figure 21-2).

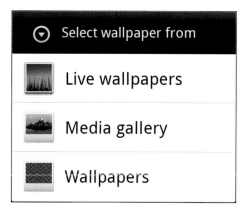

Figure 21-2: Selecting wallpaper.

3. **Select an option based on the type of wallpaper.**

   Your choices are

   > *Live Wallpapers:* Choose an animated or interactive wallpaper from a list.

   > *Media Gallery:* Choose a still image stored in the Gallery app.

   > *Wallpapers:* Choose a wallpaper from a range of stunning images (no nudity).

4. **Choose the wallpaper you want from the list.**

   For the Media Gallery option, you see a preview of the wallpaper where you can select and crop part of the image.

   For certain Live Wallpapers, a Settings button may appear. The settings let you customize certain aspects of the interactive wallpaper.

5. **Touch the Save or Set Wallpaper button to confirm your selection.**

   The new wallpaper takes over the Home screen.

Live wallpaper is interactive, usually featuring some form of animation. Otherwise, the wallpaper image scrolls slightly as you swipe from one Home screen to another.

✔ You cannot long-press on a home screen that is already full of icons and widgets. The reason? There is nothing else you can add to that screen.

✔ The Zedge app has some interesting wallpaper features. Check it out at the Android Market; see Chapter 19.

✔ See Chapter 16 for more information about the Gallery, including information on how cropping an image works.

Adding apps to the Home screen

You need not live with the unbearable proposition that you're stuck with only the apps supplied on the Home screen. Nope — you're free to add your own apps. Just follow these steps:

1. **Touch the Launcher button to hunt down the app you want to add to the Home screen.**

2. **Press — and keep pressing— an app's icon.**

   After a moment, you return to the Home screen with the app's icon still stuck under your finger.

3. **Slide your finger — still pressed down — left or right to go to a left or right part of the Home screen.**

   Seven Home screens are on the Droid X.

4. **Position your finger — still pressed down — on the spot where you want the app's icon to be placed.**

5. **Release your finger.**

   A copy of the app's icon is placed on the Home screen. There's no need to clean your fingertip after completing these steps.

The app hasn't moved: What you see is a copy. You can still find the app on the Applications Tray, but now the app is — more conveniently — available on the Home screen.

- ✔ Keep your favorite apps, those you use most often, on the Home screen.

- ✔ You cannot drop an app in a spot where the Home screen is already full of apps or widgets. Try using a blank Home screen.

- ✔ When the Home screen gets too full, you can organize your apps into folders. See the later section "Organizing apps into folders."

Slapping down widgets

Just as you can add apps to the Home screen, you can add widgets. A *widget* works like a tiny interactive or informative application, often providing a gateway into another app on the Droid X.

The Droid X comes with a bazillion widgets already affixed to the Home screen. You can place even more widgets on the Home screen by following these steps:

1. **Long-press the Home screen.**

2. **Choose Motorola Widgets or Android Widgets from the Add to Home Screen menu.**

3. From the list, choose the widget you want to add.

The widget is plopped on the Home screen.

The variety of available widgets depends on the applications you have installed. Some applications come with widgets, some don't.

- ✓ The Motorola Widget category contains widgets customized for your Verizon Droid X phone. The Android Widget category contains widgets available to users of any Android phone. If you can't find the widget you want in one category, repeat Steps 1 and 2 to look in the other.

- ✓ You cannot install a widget when the Home screen has no room for it. Choose another Home screen, or remove icons or widgets from the current Home screen.

- ✓ To remove a widget, see the later section "Rearranging and removing icons and widgets."

Creating shortcuts

A shortcut is a doodad you can place on the Home screen that's neither an app nor a widget. Instead, a *shortcut* is a handy way to get at a feature or an informational tidbit stored in the phone without having to endure complex gyrations.

For example, I have a shortcut on my Home screen that uses the Maps app Navigation feature to help me return to my house. I don't use the app when I'm running from the police, either.

To add a shortcut, long-press the Home screen and choose the Shortcuts command from the Add to Home Screen menu (refer to Figure 21-1). What happens next depends on which shortcut you choose.

For example, when you choose a bookmark, you add a Web page bookmark to the Home screen. Touch that shortcut to open the Browser app and visit that Web page.

Choose a Contact shortcut to display contact information for a specific person, The Droid X has shortcuts for Music and the Maps app (Direction & Navigation), plus, shortcuts for various apps are installed on your phone.

A nerdy shortcut to add is the Settings shortcut. After choosing this item, you can select from a number of on–off options that can appear on the Home Screen as widgets.

 The AnyCut app is useful for creating certain shortcuts that the Droid X cannot create by itself, such as a shortcut to direct-dial a contact. Check out AnyCut at the Android Market; see Chapter 19.

Rearranging and removing icons and widgets

Icons and widgets aren't fastened to the Home screen. If they are, it's day-old chewing gum that binds them, considering how easily can you rearrange and remove unwanted items from the Home screen.

Press and hold an icon on the Home screen to move it. Eventually, the icon seems to lift and break free, as shown in Figure 21-3.

Icon being pressed (appears larger)

Launcher button changes to trash

Figure 21-3: Moving an icon about.

You can drag a free icon to another position on the Home screen or to another Home screen, or you can drag it to the Trash icon that appears at the bottom of the Home screen, replacing the Launcher button (refer to Figure 21-3).

Widgets can also be moved around or removed in the same manner as icons.

  ✔ Dragging a Home screen icon or widget to the Trash removes the icon or widget from the Home screen. It doesn't uninstall the application or widget; the app can still be found on the Applications Tray, and the widget can once again be added to the Home screen.

  ✔ When an icon hovers over the Trash, ready to be deleted, its color changes to red.

    ✔ See Chapter 19 for information on uninstalling applications.

    ✔ Your clue that an icon or widget is free and clear to navigate is that the Launcher button changes to the Trash icon (refer to Figure 21-3).

Organizing apps into folders

When you run out of room on the Home screen, or you feel like adding an extra level of Home screen organization, you can create a folder. The _folder_ is used to store icons, similar to the way folders on your computer store files. The result is the same for both: organization.

Create a folder by following these steps:

1. **Long-press the Home screen.**

2. **Choose the Folders command.**

   A list appears, showing many different types of folders you can create on the Home screen. The number of items in the list depends on the various apps you have installed and whether the app allows you to create handy Home screen folders.

3. **Select New Folder from the list.**

   The new folder icon appears on the Home screen. You probably want to rename it.

4. **Touch the folder icon to open it and show its contents.**

   New folders are empty, of course. Figure 21-4 shows a folder into which I've copied various game apps.

5. **Long-press the folder window's title.**

   Refer to Figure 21-4 for the location. When you press too briefly, the folder closes. Start over again in Step 4.

6. **Type or dictate a new folder name.**

   Touch the folder's Name field to summon the onscreen keyboard.

7. **Touch the OK button to lock in the new name.**

   Optionally, close the folder by touching its X button. Refer to Figure 21-4 for the location of the X button.

Drag icons to move them into the folder, just as you drag icons around the Home screen. Or, you can drag icons from the Applications Tray into the folder. You simply need to "drop" the icon over the folder to copy it into the folder.

To move an icon out of a folder, long-press the icon. The folder closes, and then you can drag the icon to a new position on the Home screen or drag it to the Trash.

Delete folders by dragging them to the Trash.

Touch to close.

Press and hold
to change name.

Folder contents

Figure 21-4: A folder for games and fun.

Droid X Security

The Droid X comes with a lock, a simple touchscreen gizmo you slide to the right to unlock the phone and gain access to its information and features. For most folks, that lock is secure enough. For many others, the lock is about as effective as using wet tissue paper for armor.

You can add two additional types of security locks to your phone: A pattern lock and a passcode lock. The details are provided in this section.

Before the lock can be used, you have to ensure that the Screen lock is enabled on your Droid X. Follow these steps:

1. **From the Home screen, press the Menu soft button.**

2. **Choose Settings.**

3. **Choose Location & Security.**

4. Place a green check mark by the Security Lock item.

If the green check mark is there already, you're set to go. Otherwise, touch the gray box to place a check mark there.

When the Screen Lock item is unchecked, you no longer see the main unlocking screen for the Droid X; pressing the Power button summons the Home screen, not the unlocking screen.

Further, without the Screen Lock in place, you cannot add the extra levels of security covered in the next two sections.

✔ The security you add affects the way you turn on and wake up your phone. See Chapter 2 for details.

✔ Future releases of the Android operating system may add an additional security feature: a password lock. It works similarly to the passcode lock, though you can use a variety of characters in the password.

Creating an unlock pattern

One of the best ways to secure your phone and its information is to create an *unlock pattern*. This pattern must be duplicated (or followed) to unlock the phone and make calls, though unlocking isn't required for answering the phone.

Here's how to set the unlock pattern:

1. From the Home screen, press the Menu soft button.

2. Choose Settings.

3. Choose Location & Security.

4. Choose Security Lock.

The Security Lock item is unavailable when the Screen Lock item hasn't been selected.

5. Choose Security Lock Type.

6. Select Pattern Lock.

If you haven't yet set a pattern, you see some directions and the Next button. Keep touching the Next button, or let yourself be amused by the animation, and eventually you see the screen where you set the unlock pattern, shown in Figure 21-5.

I started here.

Keep dragging with your finger

Pattern so far

Figure 21-5: Setting an unlock pattern.

7. **Draw the unlock pattern with one of your stubby fingers.**

   Or, use one of your elegant fingers. Honestly, I don't know how nice your fingers are. Use Figure 21-5 as your guide.

   You can hit each dot only once in the pattern.

8. **Touch the Continue button.**

9. **Draw the pattern again to confirm that you have more than a goldfish memory and can repeat yourself.**

   According to research paid for with your tax dollars, goldfish have a two-second memory. If you're a goldfish and can't remember your pattern, touch the Cancel button and start over again in Step 4.

10. **Touch the Confirm button.**

    Assuming that you didn't screw up, you're done.

If you did screw up, you have to repeat the steps in this section.

The pattern lock is required whenever you turn on the phone or awaken it from Snooze mode. Chapter 2 describes how to use the unlock pattern.

To remove the pattern, follow Steps 1 through 5 in the preceding list and choose None from the Security Lock Type menu. Confirm the unlock pattern and it's disabled.

- ✔ The unlock pattern can be as simple or complex as you like. I'm a big fan of simple.

- ✔ Wash your hands! Smudge marks on the display can betray your pattern.

- ✔ The unlock pattern can be overridden when USB Debugging is enabled. Unless you're writing software for the Droid X, however, odds are good that you'll never have USB Debugging turned on.

Setting a passcode

I suppose that using a *passcode,* or a series of punched-in numbers, is more left-brained than using a pattern lock. So, if you have no trouble remembering numbers or you do have trouble remembering patterns, and you want more security on your Droid X, consider adding a passcode.

To add a passcode, follow Steps 1 through 5 in the preceding section and then choose Passcode Lock. You see an input screen, similar to Figure 21-6.

Enter at least four numbers for the passcode. Touch the check mark button to confirm the passcode or the X button to cancel (refer to Figure 21-6).

Do it again: After entering the passcode the first time, you're asked to repeat yourself. You need to assure the Droid X that you haven't just forgotten the number you input.

The passcode is required when you turn on or wake up the Droid X.

To disable the passcode, follow Steps 1 through 5 in the preceding section. Choose the item None from the Security Lock Type menu. You need to punch in the passcode one more time to confirm.

As with the unlocking pattern, placing the Droid X into Debugging mode can disable the passcode, which shouldn't be anything for you to worry about.

Backup and erase

Passcode goes here.

Confirm/Accept

Cancel

Figure 21-6: Entering a passcode.

Various Phone Adjustments

The Droid X has many options and settings for you to adjust. You can fix things that annoy you or make things better to please you. The whole idea is to make the phone more usable for you.

Stopping the noise!

The Droid X features a bag of tricks designed to silence the phone. These techniques can come in very handy, especially when a cellphone's digital noise can be outright annoying.

Double-Tap to Silence: You can configure the Droid X so that a quick double-tap on the touchscreen mutes the phone's ringer. Follow these steps:

1. **On the Home screen, press the Menu soft button.**

2. **Choose Settings.**

3. **Choose Sound or Sound & Display.**

   Newer versions of the Android operating system use the Sound category; older versions use Sound and Display.

4. **Place a check mark by Double-Tap to Silence.**

   The item is found at the bottom of the list.

Vibration Mode: You can make the phone vibrate for all incoming calls, which works in addition to any ringtone you've set (and still works when you've silenced the phone). To activate Vibration mode, follow these steps:

1. **Press the Launcher button on the Home screen to display the Applications Tray.**

2. **Choose the Settings app.**

3. **Choose Sound or Sound & Display.**

4. **Place a check mark by Phone Vibrate.**

Silent Mode: Silent mode disables all sounds from the phone, except for music, YouTube, and other types of media, as well as alarms that have been set by the Alarm & Timer and Calendar apps.

To enter Silent mode, follow Steps 1 through 3 in the previous set of steps, but place the check mark by the item Silent Mode.

Face Down to Shut Up: A quick way to silence an annoying Droid X is to turn it over and place it face-down on the tabletop. That trick works only when you've followed these steps:

1. **On the Home screen, press the Menu soft button.**

2. **Choose Settings.**

3. **Choose Sound or Sound & Display.**

4. **Place a check mark by Smart Profile: Face Down.**

Try to avoid the temptation to slam the phone down on the table. Seriously: Just turning it over, face-down, is all you need.

Performing automatic phone tricks

Two phone settings on the Droid X might come in handy: Auto Answer and Auto Retry. Both options are found on the Call Settings screen: Start the Settings icon from the Applications tray and choose the Call Settings item.

By placing a check mark by Auto Answer, you direct the Droid X to automatically answer the phone whenever the headset is attached. The assumption is that you're using the phone, listening to music for example, when a call comes in. When the Auto Answer item is on, the phone call is answered automatically.

By placing a check mark by Auto Retry, you direct the phone to automatically redial a number when the call doesn't go through. Obviously, this feature is ideal for radio show call-in contests.

Changing various settings

Here are a smattering of settings you can adjust on the phone — all made from, logically, the Settings screen. To get there from the Home screen, press the Menu soft button and choose the Settings command.

You can also view the Settings screen by choosing the Settings app on the Applications Tray.

Screen brightness: Choose Display or, if you have an older version of the Android operating system, choose Sound & Display. Scroll down to choose Brightness. Move the slider on the screen to specify how bright the display appears.

Place a check mark by Automatic Brightness to have the Droid X's internal eyeball examine the lighting situation and set the brightness accordingly.

Screen timeout: Choose Display (or Sound & Display) and then scroll down to choose Screen Timeout. Select a timeout value from the list. This duration specifies when the phone goes into Snooze mode.

Ringer volume: Choose Sound or Sound & Display and then choose Ringer Volume. Use the slider to specify how loud the phone rings for incoming calls. You can also separately set the volume for notifications. Touch OK when you're done.

Keep the phone awake when plugged in: Choose Applications and then choose Development. Place a check mark by the option Stay Awake.

Adjust the onscreen keyboard: Choose Language & Keyboard and then choose Multi-Touch Keyboard. A smattering of interesting options appears — options you can set when they please you or deactivate when they annoy you.

Setting the Home soft button double-tap function

As master of your Droid X, you can determine what happens when you press the Home soft button twice. It's called the Double Tap Home Launch function. As the Droid X comes out of the box (as least my Droid X), pressing the Home soft button twice quickly summons the Voice Commands app. You can change that behavior, so that pressing the Home button twice does a variety of interesting or useful things.

To modify the Double Tap Home Launch function, heed these steps:

1. **From the Applications Tray, open the Settings app.**
2. **Choose Applications.**
3. **Choose Double Tap Home Launch.**
4. **Select a new function from the pop-up list.**

   For example, you can choose Dialer to summon the Phone app whenever you press the Home button twice.

A handy option to choose for Double Tap Home Launch is the Camera. I find that setting extremely useful, even more so than having the Camera app's shortcut on the Home screen. That's because you end up using the Droid X's physical buttons when you take pictures, and pressing the Home soft button twice fits into that paradigm.

One of the Double Tap Home Launch functions is called Happenings. Rather than take you back to the 1960s, it merely displays the Social Networking app's status updates window.

Using accessibility settings

If you find the Droid X not meeting your needs or you notice that some features don't work well for you, consider taking advantage of some of the phone's accessibility features. Follow these steps:

1. **While at the Home screen, press the Menu soft button.**
2. **Choose Settings.**
3. **Choose Accessibility.**
4. **Place a check mark by the Accessibility option.**

   Two options become available when Accessibility is on:

Zoom Mode: A magnification window appears on the touchscreen, allowing you to better see teensy information.

Screen Reader: Touching items on the screen directs the phone to read that text.

5. Touch the OK button after reading the scary warning.

The accessibility feature is active.

6. Repeat Steps 4 and 5 to activate other features.

To disable any accessibility settings, repeat these steps and remove check marks in Step 4. Or, just uncheck the Accessibility setting to disable them all. Touch OK to confirm.

When Screen Reader is activated, you double-tap items on the touchscreen to activate them.

Maintenance and Troubleshooting

1'm a stickler for maintenance, as one of the few people who even bothers to read lawn equipment manuals so that I can properly winterize every year. In fact, I feel dirty when I put away the lawn mower without properly draining the oil and removing the spark plug. It was the winter of 2007.

The Droid X doesn't require that you change its oil, and you probably don't need to winterize your phone. You do, however, have a few maintenance duties to consider, as well as some troubleshooting advice I have to offer for times of cellphone woe. It's all wrapped up in this chapter.

Battery Care and Feeding

Perhaps the most important item you can monitor and maintain on your cellphone is its battery. The battery supplies the necessary electrical juice by which the phone operates. Without battery power, your Droid X is about as useful as a tin can and string for communications. Keep an eye on the battery.

Monitoring the battery

The Droid X displays the current battery status at the top of the screen, in the status area, next to the time. The icons used to display battery status are shown in Figure 22-1.

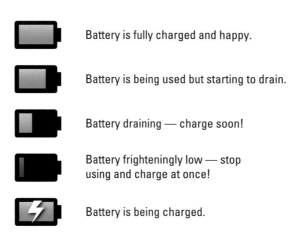

Battery is fully charged and happy.

Battery is being used but starting to drain.

Battery draining — charge soon!

Battery frighteningly low — stop using and charge at once!

Battery is being charged.

Figure 22-1: Battery status icons.

You might also see an icon for a dead or missing battery, but for some reason I can't get my phone to turn on and display that icon.

You can check the specific battery level by following these steps:

1. **From the Home screen, touch the Menu button.**
2. **Choose Settings.**
3. **Choose About Phone.**
4. **Choose Status.**

The top two items on the Status screen offer information about the battery:

Battery Status: This setting explains what's going on with the battery. It might say Full when the battery is full or Charging when the battery is being charged, or you might see other text, depending on how desperate the phone is for power.

Battery Level: This setting reveals a percentage value, describing how much of the battery is charged. A value of 100 percent indicates a fully charged battery. A value of 110 percent means that someone can't do math.

Later sections in this chapter describe activities that consume battery power and how to deal with battery issues.

- Heed those low-battery warnings! The phone sounds a notification whenever the battery gets low. (See the orange battery icon shown in Figure 22-1). The phone sounds another notification when the battery gets *very* low. (See the red battery icon in Figure 22-1).

- When the battery is too low, the phone shuts itself off.

- In addition to the status icons, the Droid X notification light turns a scary shade of red when battery juice is dreadfully low.

- The notification light glows green when the battery is full or glows yellow-orange when the battery is charging.

- The best way to deal with a low battery is to connect the phone to a power source: Either plug the phone into a wall socket or connect the phone to a computer by using a USB cable. The phone charges itself immediately; plus, you can use the phone while it's charging.

- You don't have to fully charge the phone to use it. If you have only 20 minutes to charge and the phone goes back up to only a 70 percent battery level, that's great. Well, it's not great, but it's far better than a 20 percent battery level.

- When the battery gets very low, you see a pop-up message on the screen, urging you to plug it in *at once!*

- Battery percentage values are best-guess estimates. Just because you talked for two hours and the battery shows 50 percent doesn't mean that you're guaranteed two more hours of talking. Odds are good that you have much less than two hours. In fact, as the percentage value gets low, the battery appears to drain faster.

Determining what is sucking up power

A nifty screen on the Droid X reviews which activities have been consuming power when the phone is operating from its battery. The informative screen is shown in Figure 22-2. To get to that screen, follow these steps:

1. **From the Home screen, touch the Menu button.**

2. **Choose Settings.**

3. **Choose Battery Manager.**

4. **Choose Battery Use.**

    You see a screen similar to the one shown in Figure 22-2.

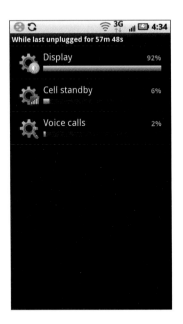

Figure 22-2: Things that drain the battery.

The number and variety of items listed on the Battery Use screen depend on what you've been doing with your phone between charges and how many different programs you're using.

Carefully note which applications consume the most battery power. If possible, curb your use of those programs to conserve the juice. For example, I could have saved 2 percent by not phoning that all-night friend's chat line. Refer to Figure 22-2.

Managing battery performance

The Droid X features Battery Profile settings to help you manage the phone's power consumption. Similar to managing power on a computer, you can configure your phone to use one of three power modes:

Performance mode: In this mode, nothing is held back, no timeouts are set, and phone operates using all its capabilities. Performance mode has no power restrictions. It is, essentially, *no* power management.

Smart mode: In this mode you get to customize the battery-saving options. You can set time-out values and make other changes to customize the way the Droid X conserves power.

Battery Saver mode: In this most restrictive mode, the phone may even turn off its digital cellular connection to save power. Just about anything that can be held back or have a time-out applied is restricted in Battery Saver mode.

To set a battery profile on your Droid X, follow these steps:

1. **From the Home screen, touch the Menu button.**

2. **Choose Settings.**

3. **Choose Battery Manager.**

4. **Choose Battery Profile.**

5. **Choose a battery profile from the list.**

When you select Smart mode, you can choose the Battery Profile Options to see another screen full of various battery options, timeouts, and additional settings that can be customized. Figure 22-3 describes what's up.

The Droid ships with Smart mode enabled.

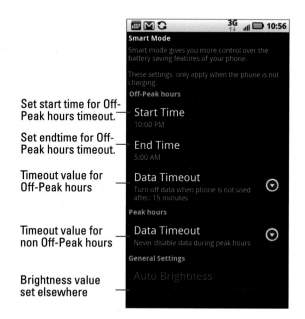

Set start time for Off-Peak hours timeout.

Set endtime for Off-Peak hours timeout.

Timeout value for Off-Peak hours

Timeout value for non Off-Peak hours

Brightness value set elsewhere

Figure 22-3: Battery settings for Smart mode.

Saving battery life

Here's a smattering of things you can do to help prolong battery life in your Droid X:

Turn off vibration options. The phone's vibration is caused by a teensy motor. Though you don't see much battery savings by disabling the vibration options, it's better than no savings. To turn off vibration, follow these steps:

1. **From the Home screen, touch the Menu button.**
2. **Choose Settings.**
3. **Choose Sound or Sound & Display.**

   Some versions of the Android operating system name the category Sound, and others name it Sound & Display.

4. **Remove the check mark by the Phone Vibrate option.**
5. **Remove the check mark by Haptic Feedback.**

   The Haptic Feedback option is what causes the phone to vibrate when you touch the soft buttons.

Additionally, consider lowering the volume of notifications, which also saves a modicum of battery life, though in my travels I've missed important notifications by setting the volume too low.

Dim the screen. If you look at Figure 22-2 (earlier in this chapter), you see that the display sucks down quite a lot of battery power. Though a dim screen can be more difficult to see, especially outdoors, it definitely saves on battery life.

Battery replacement

Unlike on some cellphones, you can easily replace the battery in the Droid X. Chapter 1 discusses how to install and remove the battery. It's cinchy! But the real questions come when you need to replace the battery and have to decide what to replace it with.

Under normal usage, the battery in the Droid X should last at least as long as the typical two-year cellular contract. The battery is probably good for about four years if you treat it properly. Even so, at some point the battery will fail: The battery charge decreases and, eventually, the battery doesn't even hold a charge.

Ensure that any replacement battery you buy is compatible with the Droid X. A BH5X battery from Motorola (the phone's manufacturer) works best. Otherwise, ensure that the battery is a 3.7V battery designed for the Droid X. Avoid buying batteries for your electronics at swap meets or from the back of trucks in grocery store parking lots.

You set the screen brightness from the Settings app: Choose Display or Sound & Display, and then choose Brightness.

Turn off Bluetooth. When you're not using Bluetooth, turn it off. Or, when you *really* need that cyborg Bluetooth ear thing, try to keep your phone plugged in. See Chapter 13 for information on turning off Bluetooth, though you can do it quickly from the Power Control widget.

Turn off Wi-Fi. Wi-Fi networking on the Droid X keeps you on the Internet at top speeds but drains the battery. Because I tend to use Wi-Fi when I'm in one place, I keep my phone plugged in. Otherwise, the battery drains like my bank account at Christmas. Refer to Chapter 13 for information on turning off the phone's Wi-Fi.

Disable automatic syncing. The Droid X syncs quite often. In fact, it surprises me when I update something on the Internet and find the phone updated almost instantly. When you need to save battery power and frequent updates aren't urgent (such as when you're spending a day traveling), disable automatic syncing by following these steps:

1. **From the Home screen, touch the Menu button.**
2. **Choose Settings.**
3. **Choose Accounts.**
4. **Choose your Google account.**
5. **Remove the green check mark by each item.**

When saving battery juice isn't important, remember to repeat these steps to reenable background and automatic synchronization.

Regular Phone Maintenance

The Droid X gives you only two tasks that you can do for regular maintenance on the phone: Keep it clean, which is probably something you're doing already, and keep important information backed up.

Keeping it clean

You probably already keep your phone clean. I must use my sleeve to wipe the touch screen at least a dozen times a day. Of course, better than your sleeve is something called a microfiber cloth. This item can be found at any computer- or office-supply store.

- ✔ Never use any liquid to clean the touch screen — especially ammonia or alcohol. Those substances damage the touch screen.

- ✔ If the screen keeps getting dirty, consider adding a screen protector. This specially designed cover prevents the screen from getting scratched or dirty but also lets you use your finger on the touchscreen. Be sure that the screen protector is designed for use with the Droid X.

- ✔ You can also find customized Droid X cellphone cases, belt clips, and protectors, though I've found that those add-on items are purely for decorative or fashion purposes and don't even prevent serious damage if you drop the phone.

Backing up your phone

A *backup* is a safety copy of the information on your Droid X. That includes the contact information, music, photos, video, and apps you've installed, plus any settings you've made to customize your phone. Copying that information to another source is one way to keep the information safe, in case anything happens to the phone.

On your Google account, information is backed up automatically. That information includes your Contacts list, Gmail, and Calendar app appointments. Because the Droid X automatically syncs that information with the Internet, a backup is always present.

To confirm that your Google account information is being backed up, heed these steps:

1. **From the Home screen, touch the Launcher button.**
2. **Choose My Accounts.**
3. **Choose your Google account.**
4. **Ensure that a green check mark appears by every option.**

    When no check mark is there, touch the gray square to add one.

If you have more than one Google account synchronized with the Droid X, repeat these steps for each account.

Beyond your Google account, which is automatically backed up, you can use the Verizon app Backup Assistant to create, on the Verizon computers, a safety copy of *all* your phone's contact information.

To use Backup Assistant, you must configure it on your Droid X, plus you must create an account on the Verizon Web site.

Where to find phone information

Who knows what evil lurks inside the heart of your phone? Well, the phone itself knows. You can view information about the battery, phone number, mobile network, and uptime, plus other information. To see that trivia, summon the Settings app and choose About Phone and then Status.

For specific information about your account, such as minutes used and data transmitted, you have to visit the cellular service's Web site. In the United States, the Droid X is supported by the Verizon Wireless network at the time this book goes to press. The Web site is www. verizonwireless.com. You need to set up or access your account, which then leads you to information about your phone usage and billing and other trivia.

Configure Backup Assistant by starting the app from the Applications Tray: Accept the licensing terms and conditions, create a PIN, and follow the directions to set up the account. Touch the Sync Now button to start the backup.

On a computer, you can visit the Verizon Web site to complete the process:

```
www.verizonwireless.com/backupassistant
```

Create an account by following the directions on the site. After the account is created and you log in, you can access the backup copy of the contact information on your Droid X.

There's no native way to back up the data on the Droid X MicroSD card. That backup would include all data on your phone — even photos, videos, and music. To do this type of backup, you must manually copy the information from the MicroSD card to another location, such as your computer. That backup, or safety, copy of the information on the MicroSD card lets you restore those files to the MicroSD, in case anything bad happens to the phone.

For more information on copying the information from the MicroSD card, refer to a reference document for your computer's operating system that covers copying files. Because the Droid X can be mounted to your computer's storage system like an external storage device (a USB drive), the operation isn't overly complex, though it requires more explanation than I have room for in this tome.

Updating the system

Every so often, a new version of your phone's operating system becomes available. It's an *Android update* because Android is the name of the Droid X operating system, not because your phone is some type of robot.

When an automatic update occurs, you see an alert or a message appear on the phone, indicating that a system upgrade is available. You have three choices:

- Install Now
- Install Later
- More Info

My advice is to choose Install Now and get it over with — unless you have something (a call, a message, or another urgent item) pending on the phone, in which case you can choose Install Later and be bothered by the message again.

You can manually check for updates: From the Settings screen, choose About Phone and then choose System Updates. When your system is up-to-date, the screen tells you so. Otherwise, you find directions for updating the system.

Help and Troubleshooting

Things aren't as bad as they were in the old days. Back then, you could try two sources for help: the atrocious manual that came with your electronic device or a phone call to the guy who wrote the atrocious manual. It was unpleasant. Today, things are better. You have many resources for solving issues with your gizmos, including the Droid X.

Getting help

The Droid X comes with a modicum of assistance for your weary times of woe. Granted, its advice and delivery method aren't as informative or entertaining as the book you hold in your hands. But it's something!

To get help, open the Help Center app, found on the Applications Tray. You see four categories:

Guided Tours: Videos to help you use your phone

Tips and Tricks: Suggestions for doing things you may not know about

Users Guide: Documentation for the Droid X

FAQs: Frequently asked questions and their answers

Choosing some of the items displays information stored on your phone. For other categories, you're whisked off to the Internet for details.

Some of the information presented is pretty good, but also pretty basic. It's also, at its core, simply what would have once been printed and bundled with the Droid X: the dratted manual.

Fixing random and annoying problems

Aren't all problems annoying? There isn't really such a thing as a welcome problem, unless the problem is welcome because it diverts attention from another, preexisting problem. And random problems? If problems were predictable, they would serve in office. Or maybe they already are?

Here are some typical problems and my suggestions for a solution:

General trouble: For just about any problem or minor quirk, consider restarting the phone: Turn off the phone, and then turn it on again. That procedure will most likely fix a majority of the annoying and quirky problems you encounter with the Droid X.

When restarting doesn't work, consider turning off the Droid X and removing its battery. Wait about 15 seconds, and then return the battery to the phone and turn on the phone again.

Check the data connection: Sometimes, the data connection drops but the phone connection stays active. Check the status bar. If you see bars, you have a phone signal. When you don't see the G, E, 3G, or Wi-Fi icon, the phone has no data signal.

Sometimes, the data signal just drops for a minute or two. Wait around and it comes back. If it doesn't, the cellular data network might be down, or you may just be in an area with lousy service. Consider changing your location.

For wireless connections, you have to ensure that the Wi-Fi is set up properly and working. That usually involves pestering the person who configured the Wi-Fi signal or made it available, such as the cheerful person in the green apron who serves you coffee.

Music begins to play while you're on the phone: I find this quirk most annoying. For some reason, you start to hear music playing while you're in a conversation on the phone. I actually wonder why the phone's software doesn't disable music from even being able to play while the phone is in use.

Anyway, it might seem like stopping the music is impossible. It's not: Press the Home soft button to go to the Home screen. (You might have to unlock the phone.). Pull down the notifications and choose the Music Playing notification. Press the Pause button to pause the music.

The MicroSD card is busy: Most often, the MicroSD card is busy because you've connected the Droid X to a computer and the computer is accessing the phone's storage system. To unbusy the MicroSD card, unmount the phone or stop the USB storage. See Chapter 13.

When the MicroSD card remains busy, consider restarting the phone, as described earlier in this section.

An app has run amok: Sometimes, apps that misbehave let you know. You see a warning on the screen announcing the app's stubborn disposition. Touch the Force Close button to shut down the errant app.

When you don't see a warning or when an app appears to be unduly obstinate, you can shut 'er down the manual way, by following these steps:

1. **From the Applications Tray, choose the Settings icon.**
2. **Choose Applications.**
3. **Choose Manage Applications.**
4. **Choose the application that's causing you distress.**

   For example, a program doesn't start or says that it's busy or has some other issue.
5. **Touch the Force Stop button.**

   The program stops, if it's running.

After stopping the program, try opening it again to see whether it works. If the program continues to run amok, contact its developer: Open the Market app and choose Downloads. Open the app you're having trouble with and choose the option Send Email to Developer. Send the developer a message describing the problem.

Reset the phone's software (a drastic measure). When all else fails, you can do the drastic thing and reset all the phone's software, essentially returning it to the state it was in when it first arrived. Obviously, you need not perform this step lightly. In fact, consider finding support (see the next section) before you start:

1. **From the Home screen, touch the Menu button.**
2. **Choose Settings.**
3. **Choose Privacy.**

4. **Choose Factory Data Reset.**

5. **Touch the Reset Phone button.**

   You'll se a final, scary warning.

6. **Touch the Erase Everything button.**

   All the information you've set or stored on the phone is purged.

Again, *do not* follow these steps unless you're certain that they will fix the problem or you're under orders to do so from someone in Tech Support.

Getting support

The easiest way to find support for the Droid X is to dial 611. You're greeted by a cheerful Verizon employee, or an automated robot system, who will gladly help you with various phone issues.

On the Internet, you can find support at these Web sites:

www.motorola.com

market.android.com/support

http://support.vzw.com/clc

Droid X Q&A

I love Q&A! That's because not only is it an effective way to express certain problems and solutions but some of the questions might also cover things I've been wanting to ask.

"The touchscreen doesn't work!"

A touchscreen, such as the one used on the Droid X, requires a human finger for proper interaction. The phone interprets a slight static charge between the human finger and the phone to determine where the touch screen is being touched.

You cannot use the touch screen when you're wearing gloves, unless they're specially designed, static-carrying gloves that claim to work on touchscreens. Batman wears this type of glove, so it probably exists in real life.

The touchscreen might also fail when the battery power is low or when the phone has been physically damaged.

"The keyboard is too small!"

It's not that the keyboard is too small — it's that you're a human being and not a marsupial. Your fingers are too big!

You can rotate the phone to landscape orientation to see a larger onscreen keyboard. Not every app may feature a landscape-orientation keyboard. When one does, you'll find typing on the wider onscreen keyboard much easier than normal.

"The battery doesn't charge"

Start from the source: Is the wall socket providing power? Is the cord plugged in? The cable may be damaged, so try another cable.

When charging from a USB port on a computer, ensure that the computer is turned on. Most computers don't provide USB power when they're turned off.

"The phone gets so hot that it turns itself off!"

Yikes! An overheating phone can be a nasty problem. Judge how hot the phone is by seeing whether you can hold it in your hand: When the phone is too hot to hold, it's too hot. If you're using the phone to warm up your coffee, the phone is too hot.

Turn off the phone. Take out the battery and let it cool.

If the overheating problem continues, have the phone looked at for potential repair. The battery might need to be replaced.

Do not continue to use a phone that's too hot! The heat damages the phone's electronics. It can also start a fire.

"The phone doesn't do Landscape mode!"

Not every app takes advantage of the Droid X's ability to orient itself in Landscape mode. For example, the Home screen doesn't "do landscape." One program that definitely does Landscape mode is Browser, shown in Chapter 11. So, just because an app doesn't enter Landscape mode doesn't mean that it *can't* enter Landscape mode.

The Droid X has a setting you can check to confirm that landscape orientation is active: From the Applications Tray, choose Settings and then choose the Display or Sound & Display category. Ensure that a check mark appears by the item Orientation. If not, touch the square to put a green check mark there.

Part VI
The Part of Tens

The 5th Wave — By Rich Tennant

"Well, here's what happened—I forgot to put it on my AK Notepad."

Market

Music

Sudoku Daily

Settings

*1*t's been traditional that all *For Dummies* books end with a Part of Tens, where the chapters in that part each contain or discuss ten items. The original plan was for a Part of Twenties, but most authors found that too arduous a chore to write. They would complain that it was easy to find ten things to write about, often only having to fabricate three or four of them, but for twenty things they just couldn't consistently make up the extra dozen or so items.

Ten seems like a good, round number, especially for concocting lists. The chapters found in this part of the book contain useful lists, tips, shortcuts, and suggestions, all neatly organized into ten items each. And in most of the chapters, I didn't have to fabricate extra items just to round up the list.

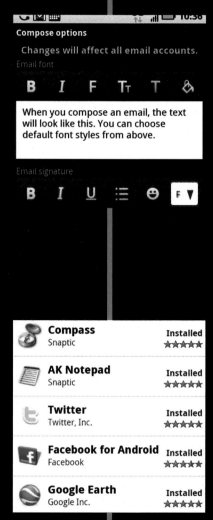

Ten Tips, Tricks, and Shortcuts

I'm sure that Pavlov was impressed with his dog. Every time the bell rang, the dog would salivate. And I'm sure that Pavlov's dog was impressed that every time his master's phone rang, the esteemed psychologist would rush in to answer the thing.

Oh, aren't we all classically conditioned to do things — perhaps often to our detriment? For example, you do many things with your phone out of habit. Yet I've discovered a few tips and tricks that make using the Droid X better. Ten of them are placed in this chapter.

Summon a Recently Opened App

I have to kick myself in the head every time I return to the Applications Tray to, once again, scroll the list o' icons to dig up an app I just opened. Why bother? Because I can press and hold the Home soft button to instantly see a list of recently opened apps, similar to the one shown in Figure 23-1.

Figure 23-1: Recently opened apps.

Pressing and holding the Home soft button works no matter what you're doing with the phone; you don't necessarily have to view the Home screen to see the list of recently opened apps.

Updates to the Android operating system may list more apps than the six recent apps shown in Figure 23-1.

Formatted Email

The email I receive from cellphones all have the same telltale formatting: Boring. That's because most cellphone email programs lack any formatting abilities. What you send is plain text.

```
Yawn.
```

On the Droid, however, you can format your email all nice and fancy. Figure 23-2 describes what's up with the email composition screen, used by the Email app.

You can even create a template of sorts, kind of like preformatting your Droid X email messages. Follow these steps:

1. **Start the Email program.**

2. **If necessary, choose an email account.**

   For example, if you see the combined inbox, choose a specific account.

 3. **Press the Menu soft button.**

4. **Choose Email Settings.**
5. **Choose Compose Options.**

   You can set the email font for all outgoing messages by making changes in the top part of the screen: Use the controls illustrated in Figure 23-3 to manipulate the preset text in the window.

6. **When you're content, touch the Done button.**

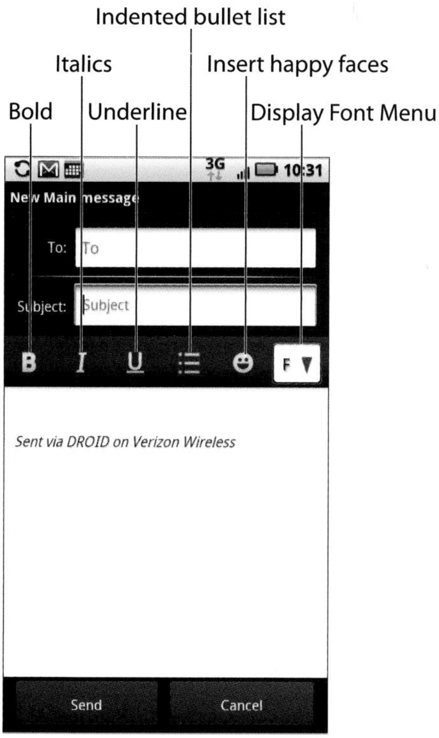
Indented bullet list
Italics
Insert happy faces
Bold
Underline
Display Font Menu
10:31
New Main message
To:
To
Subject:
Subject
Sent via DROID on Verizon Wireless
Send
Cancel

Figure 23-2: Formatting your email.

Text formatting can also be applied to your email signature, as shown in Figure 23-3. In fact, you can edit your email signature as illustrated in the figure.

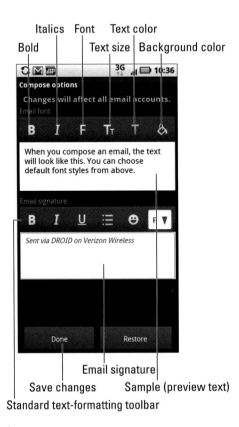

Italics   Font   Text color
Bold   Text size | Background color

Email signature|
Save changes   Sample (preview text)
Standard text-formatting toolbar

Figure 23-3: Setting the standard email text format.

- ✔ Touch a format button once to turn the format on, and again to turn it off.

- ✔ Multiple formats can be applied to your text.

- ✔ When a text format has been chosen, it appears outlined in red.

- ✔ The Font menu (refer to Figure 23-2) contains four items that deal with the text font in your messages: *F* to select the font type; *Tt* to select the text size; *T* to select the text foreground color; and a paint bucket to set the background color.

- ✔ Text formatting is applied to new text you write or to selected blocks of text. See Chapter 4 for information on selecting text.

- ✔ See Chapter 10 for more information about email on your Droid X.

Stop Unneeded Services

Some things may be going on in your Droid X that you don't need or even suspect. These things are computer activities, usually the monitoring of information or the phone's status. The technical term for these activities is *services*.

When a service has started that you don't want, or have been requested to stop, you can halt the service. Here's how:

1. **While at the Home screen, press the Menu soft button.**
2. **Choose Settings.**
3. **Choose Applications.**
4. **Choose Running Services.**
5. **Touch a service to stop it.**

   Most likely, it's a service you recognize that you don't need, or a service you've been directed to disable from another source or authority.

   As an example, I've stopped the Skype Mobile service from running because I don't need it. I've also stopped the Blockbuster service for the same reason.

6. **Touch the Stop button to halt the service.**

When you stop a service, you free phone resources used by that service. These resources include memory and processor power. The result of stopping unneeded services can be improved performance.

The service starts up again the next time you start the phone. The only way to halt a specific service for all eternity is to uninstall the program associated with that service, which is a drastic step.

Do not randomly disable services. Many of them are required for the Droid X to do its job, or for programs you use to carry out their tasks. If you disable a service you don't recognize and the phone begins to act funny, turn the phone off and then on again to fix the problem.

Set Keyboard Feedback

Typing on a touch screen keyboard isn't easy. Along with the screen being tiny (or your fingers being big), it's difficult to tell what you're typing. You can add some feedback to the typing process. Heed these steps:

1. **While at the Home screen, press the Menu soft button.**

2. **Choose Settings.**

3. **Choose Language & Keyboard.**

4. **Choose Multi-Touch Keyboard.**

5. **Put a check mark by the option Vibrate On Keypress.**

   This option causes physical feedback when you press a "key" on the onscreen keyboard.

6. **Put a check mark by the option Sound On Keypress.**

   The Droid X makes a sound when you type on the onscreen keyboard. Clackity-clack-clak.

Of the two options, I prefer Sound On Keypress. The phone makes a different sound for the character keys and the space key, which reminds me of my ancient typewriter.

  ✔ Yeah, *keypress* is two words: key press.

  ✔ Obviously, these steps don't apply to using Swype. See Chapter 4 for information on using the Swype keyboard.

Add a Word to the Dictionary

Betcha didn't know that the Droid X has a dictionary. The dictionary is used to keep track of words you type using the onscreen keyboard — words that may not be recognized as being spelled properly.

To add a word to the Droid X dictionary, long-press the word after you type it. From the menu that appears, choose the Add *"Word"* to Dictionary command, where *Word* is the word you want to add.

When using the onscreen keyboard, you can choose the word when it appears in the list of suggestions, as shown in Figure 23-4. Long-press the word, as shown in the figure, to add it to the dictionary. The confirmation that appears is your clue that the word has been added.

To review the contents of the dictionary, open the Settings app and choose Language & Keyboard and then User Dictionary. You see a list of words you've added. Touch a word to edit it or to delete it from the dictionary.

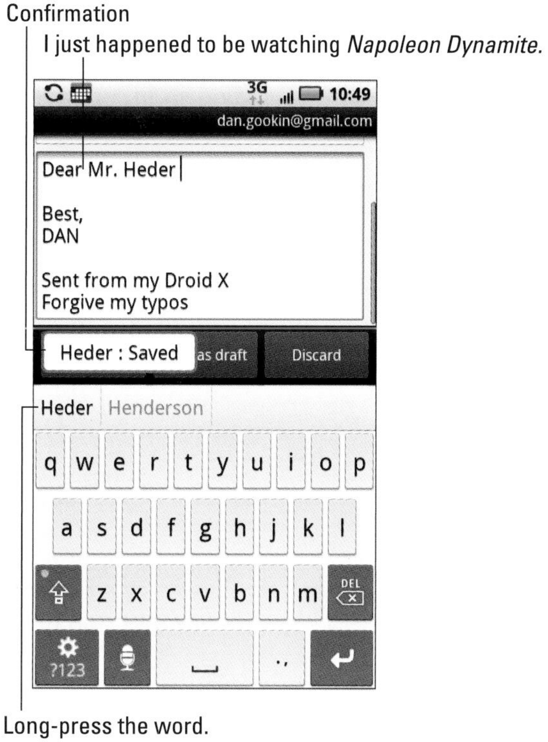

Confirmation
I just happened to be watching *Napoleon Dynamite.*

Long-press the word.

Figure 23-4: Adding a word to the dictionary.

Set Vibration with the Volume Control

A quick way to activate Vibrate mode on the Droid X is to press the Volume button until the Volume setting decreases one notch before Silent. That notch is Vibrate. Figure 23-5 illustrates what you see on the screen.

The Volume control is located on the right side of the phone, as illustrated in Figure 1-2, over in Chapter 1.

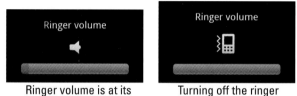

Ringer volume is at its lowest notch.

Turning off the ringer volume activates vibration.

Figure 23-5: Setting vibration with the volume control.

Create a Direct-Dial Screen Widget

For the numbers you dial most frequently, use the Favorites list, as described in Chapter 8. For your überfavorites, you use Home screen widgets. Here's how to create a direct-dial contact widget on the Home screen for the people you call frequently:

1. **Long-press the Home screen.**

2. **Choose Motorola Widgets.**

3. **Choose Quick Contact Tasks.**

4. **Choose the contact you want to direct-dial.**

5. **Choose the phone number, if the contact has multiple phones.**

   Choose the number from the top portion of the contact's information, in the Call category.

6. **Touch the Done button.**

The contact's phone number, and picture (if they have one) appears on the Home screen as a widget. Touching the phone icon on the widget summons a dialing menu; if you touch the check box, you enable one-touch dialing for that contact.

The Quick Contact widget can be resized: Long-press it and then drag the corners around with your finger to resize. You can make the Quick Contact widget as large or as small as you like. I prefer smaller, especially when the contact has an ugly picture attached.

Create a Direct Text-Message Widget

Just as you can create a direct-dial shortcut (shown in the preceding section), you can create an icon to directly text-message a contact. The difference is that you choose a phone number from the Text Message list in Step 5 rather than from the Call category.

The widget that appears on the Home screen can be used to instantly send that contact a text message. Simply touch the icon and start typing with your thumbs.

See Chapter 9 for more information about text messaging.

Find Your Lost Cellphone

Someday, you're going to lose your Droid X. It might be for a panic-filled few seconds, or it might be forever. Aside from welding a chain to your phone, I have a software solution to suggest.

Various cellphone locator services are available, specifically for phones (such as the Droid X) that feature GPS and communicate with satellites. Multiple apps are also available at the Android Market that can help you locate and, you hope, recover a wandering phone.

I've tried a few of the programs and can't recommend any of them over the others. Some you can try are

- LocService
- Mobile Defense
- Mobile Phone Locator Lite
- Phoning Pigeon

At the time this book goes to press, Mobile Defense is a closed beta. Hopefully, soon it will be released.

Most of these services require that you set up a Web page account to assist in locating your phone. They also enable services that send updates to the Internet. The updates assist in tracking your phone, in case it becomes lost or stolen.

Check my Wambooli Web site for any updates regarding apps that help you locate a lost phone:

```
www.wambooli.com/help/phone
```

Enter Location Information for Your Events

When you create an event for the Calendar app, be sure to enter the event's location. You can type either an address (if you know it) or the name of the location. The key is to type the text as you would in the Map app when searching for a location. That way, you can touch the event location and the Droid X displays it on the touchscreen. Finding an address couldn't be easier.

- See Chapter 14 for more information about the Maps app.
- See Chapter 18 for details about the Calendar.

Ten Things to Remember

*O*h, if *only* there were just ten things to remember. My guess is that you have more like a bazillion things to remember, which is why people keep forgetting things. I mean, beyond your wallet, car keys, glasses, cellphone, home address, PIN number, spouse's name, and various account names and passwords on the Internet, what else could you possibly need to remember?

Okay! There are *lots* of things to remember, most of which you don't remember that you remember. For your Droid X, I've narrowed the list to ten items that I recommend you not forget. When I suddenly remember the eleventh thing, I'll panic and contact my publisher, but by then it will be too late. Visit my Web site for more things to remember and Droid X updates: www.wambooli.com.

Lock the Phone on a Call

Whether you dialed out or someone dialed in, after you start talking, lock the phone: Press the Power button atop the Droid X. By doing so, you ensure that the touch screen is disabled and the call isn't unintentionally disconnected.

Of course, the call can still be disconnected by a dropped signal or the other party getting all huffy and hanging up on you, but by locking the phone, you should prevent a stray finger or your pocket from disconnecting (or muting) the phone.

Landscape Orientation

Too many times I find myself using the phone and cursing my stubby fingers. Then I slap myself in the forehead and tilt the phone to the left. Yes sir, landscape orientation comes to the rescue. Some applications give you a wider screen view, larger keyboard, and more room to touch buttons in landscape orientation.

Not every app supports landscape orientation.

Use Text Magnification

When you need to pinpoint where to place the cursor in text, use the little target icon shown in the margin. When that target icon appears, you can press and hold the touchscreen to see a wee li'l magnification window. Use that window to help you position the cursor.

The magnification trick comes in especially handy when editing text. See Chapter 4 for additional information.

Use the Keyboard Suggestions

Don't forget to take advantage of the suggestions that appear above the onscreen keyboard when you're typing text. In fact, you don't even need to touch a suggestion; to replace your text with the highlighted suggestion, simply touch the onscreen keyboard's space key. Zap! The word appears.

✔ The setting that directs the keyboard to make suggestions work is Show Suggestions. To ensure that the setting is active, open the Settings app and choose Language & Keyboard and then Multi-Touch Keyboard.

✔ Refer to Figure 4-6 (from Chapter 4) to see how the onscreen keyboard suggestions work.

Things That Consume Lots of Battery Juice

Three items on the Droid X suck down battery power faster than a teenage wannabe-vampire consumes Clamato juice:

✔ Wi-Fi networking

✔ Bluetooth

✔ Navigation

Both Wi-Fi networking and Bluetooth require extra power for their wireless networking. When you need that speed or connectivity, they're great! I try to plug my phone into a power source when I'm accessing Wi-Fi or using Bluetooth. Otherwise, I disconnect from those networks as soon as I'm done, to save power.

Navigation is certainly handy, but because the phone's touchscreen is on the entire time and dictating text to you, the battery drains rapidly. If possible, try to plug the phone into the car's power socket when you're navigating. If you can't, keep an eye on the battery meter.

See Chapter 22 for more information on managing the Droid X battery.

Check for Roaming

Roaming can be expensive. The last non-smartphone (dumbphone?) I owned racked up $180 in roaming charges the month before I switched to a better cellular plan. Even though you too may have a good cell plan, keep an eye on the phone's status bar. Ensure that when you're making a call, you don't see the Roaming status icon on the status bar atop the touchscreen.

Well, yes, it's okay to make a call when you're roaming. My advice is to remember to *check* for the icon, not to avoid it. If possible, try to make your phone calls when you're back in your cellular service's coverage area. If you can't, make the phone call but keep in mind that you will be charged roaming fees. They ain't cheap.

Use + When Dialing Internationally

I suppose most folks are careful when dialing an international number. On the Droid X, you can use the + key to replace the country's exit code. In the United States, that code is `011`. So, whenever you see an international number listed as `011-xxx-xxxxxxx`, you can instead dial `+xxx-xxxxxx`, where the x characters represent the number to dial.

See Chapter 20 for more information on international dialing.

Properly Access the MicroSD Card

To access the Droid X storage area using your computer, you must properly mount the phone's MicroSD card. After the card is mounted, you can use your computer to access files — music, videos, still pictures, contacts, and other types of information — stored on your phone.

When the MicroSD card is mounted on a computer storage system, you cannot access the card using the phone. If you try, you see a message explaining that the MicroSD card is busy.

When you're done accessing the MicroSD card from your computer, be sure to stop USB storage: Pull down the USB notification and choose Charge Only. Touch the OK button. (See Chapter 13 for more details.)

> ✔ Future releases of the Android operating system may change the way the USB connection is made on your Droid X. See my Web site for more information:
>
>   www.wambooli.com/help/phone

> ✔ Do not simply unplug the phone from the USB cable when the computer is accessing the MicroSD card. If you do, you can damage the MicroSD card and lose all information stored there.

Snap a Pic of That Contact

Here's something I always forget: Whenever you're near one of your contacts, take the person's picture. Sure, some people are bashful, but most folks are flattered. The idea is to build up your Contacts list so that all contacts have photos. That makes receiving a call much more interesting when you see the caller's picture displayed, especially a silly or embarrassing picture.

When taking the picture, be sure to show it to the person before you assign it to the contact. Let them decide whether it's good enough. Or, if you just want to be rude, assign a crummy-looking picture. Heck, you don't even have to do that: Just take a random picture of anything and assign it to a contact. But, seriously, keep in mind that the phone can take a contact's picture the next time you meet up with that person.

See Chapter 15 for more information on using the Droid X camera and assigning a picture to a contact.

The Search Command

Google is known worldwide for its searching abilities. By gum, the word *Google* is now synonymous for searching. So, please don't forget that the Droid X, which uses the Google Android operating system, has a powerful Search command.

The search command is not only powerful but also available all over. The Search soft button can be pressed at any time, in just about any program to search for information, locations, people — you name it. It's handy. It's everywhere. Use it.

Ten Worthy Apps

In This Chapter

▶ AK Notepad
▶ Barcode Scanner
▶ Dolphin Browser
▶ Google Finance
▶ Movies
▶ Paper Toss
▶ Quick Settings
▶ Ringdroid
▶ SportsTap
▶ Voice Recorder
▶ Zedge

*W*elcome to the most controversial chapter of this book! It's an almost impossible task to narrow the list of more than 65,000 Android apps for the Droid X into the 10 most noteworthy.

I know for certain that I haven't tried all 65,000 apps. Still, I feel I should pass along some suggestions and ideas for what I've found to be my favorites.

I'm open to adding to this list, for future versions of this book as well as on my Web page, at www. wambooli.com. Feel free to send me suggestions. Until then, here are what I feel are ten apps worthy of your attention.

All these apps are free. Find them at the Android Market. See Chapter 19.

AK Notepad

 One program that the Droid X is missing out of the box is a notepad. A good choice for an app to fill that void is AK Notepad: You can type or dictate short messages and memos, which I find handy.

For example, before a recent visit to the hardware store, I made (dictated) a list of what I needed by using AK Notepad. I also keep some important items as notes, things that I often forget or don't care to remember, such as frequent flyer numbers, my dress shirt and suit size (like I ever need that info), and other important notes I might need handy but not cluttering my brain.

Perhaps the most important note you can make is one containing your contact information. A note labeled In Case You Find This Phone on my Droid X contains information about me in case I ever lose my phone and someone is decent enough to search it for my information. (Also see Chapter 23 for information on finding lost phones.)

Barcode Scanner

Many apps from the Android Market can be quickly accessed by scanning their barcode information. Scanning with what? Why, your Droid X, of course!

By using an app such as Barcode Scanner, you can instantly read in and translate barcodes to product descriptions, Web page links, or links directly to apps in the Android Market.

Though you can find similar barcode-scanning apps, I find Barcode Scanner the easiest to use: Run the app. Point the phone's camera at a bar code and, in a few moments, you see a link or an option for what to do next. For getting an app, the Open Browser option takes you to the Android Market, where obtaining the app is just a few touches away.

Using the Barcode Scanner in this chapter

Throughout this chapter, you find barcode icons. After installing the Barcode Scanner app (or a similar app), use your Droid X to scan the barcodes. Choose the button Open Browser to download the recommended app from the Android Market.

Additional app recommendations and their barcodes are found all over the Internet, in magazines, and on my Android phone support page at www.wambooli.com/help/phone.

Dolphin Browser

Though I don't mind the Browser app that comes with the Droid X, it's universally despised by many Android phone owners. A better and more popular alternative is Dolphin Browser.

Like many popular computer browsers, Dolphin Browser features a tabbed interface, which works much better than the silly multiple window interface of the standard Browser app on the Droid X.

The Dolphin Browser also sports many handy tools, which you can access by pressing the Menu soft key. Unlike other Android apps, the tools pop up on a menu you can see on the screen.

If you grow fond of the Dolphin Browser, use the directions from Chapter 21 for replacing a copy of the Browser app's icon with the Dolphin Browser on the Droid X main Home screen.

Google Finance

The Google Finance app is an excellent market-tracking tool for folks who are obsessed with the stock market or want to keep an eye on their portfolios. The app offers you an overview of the market and updates to your stocks, as well as links to financial news.

To get the most from this app, configure Google Finance on the Web, using your computer. You can create lists of stocks to watch, which are then instantly synchronized with your Droid X. You can visit Google Finance on the Web at

```
www.google.com/finance
```

As with other Google services, Google Finance is provided to you for free, as part of your Google account.

Movies

The Movies app is the Droid X gateway to Hollywood. It lists currently running films and films that are opening, and it has links to your local theaters with showtimes and other information. It's also tied into the popular Rotten Tomatoes Web site for reviews and feedback. If you enjoy going to the movies, you'll find the Movies app a valuable addition to your Droid X.

Paper Toss

 Yeah, it's a game. The object is simple: Toss a crumpled piece of paper into a trashcan. The trashcan appears in varying locales and at different distances. Your nemesis is a circulating fan, which affects the arc of your throw. My record is ten in a row. And I love the polite "golf clapping" that takes place after each successful shot. It's a clever and addicting game.

Quick Settings

 The Droid X has many settings and even more places buried on the phone where you have to go to change those settings: Brightness. Volume. Bluetooth. Wi-Fi. That's not a challenge when you install the Quick Settings app.

With its simple idea, what Quick Settings does is place all common phone settings on one screen. You can turn settings on or off or make adjustments without having to venture down into the deep, dark recesses of the Settings screens. This app is pure genius.

Ringdroid

 The Ringdroid app lets you customize and create ringtones for the Droid X. You can either snip a segment of music already on your phone or use the phone to record your own ringtone. This one-purpose app does its only job very well.

SportsTap

 I admit to not being a sports nut, so it's difficult for me to identify with the craving to have the latest scores, news, and schedules. The sports nuts in my life, however, tell me that the very best app for that purpose is a handy thing named SportsTap.

Rather than blather on about something I'm not into, just take my advice and obtain SportsTap. I believe you'll be thrilled.

Voice Recorder

 The Droid X can record your voice or other sounds, and the Voice Recorder is a good app for performing that task. It has an elegant and simple interface: Touch the big Record button to start recording. Make a note for yourself or record a friend doing his Daffy Duck impression.

Previous recordings are stored in a list on the Voice Recorder's main screen. Each recording is shown with its title, the date and time of the recording, and the recording duration.

Zedge

 Yeah, Zedge is the eleventh item, but it's a good one: The Zedge program is a helpful resource for finding wallpapers and ringtones for the Droid X. It's a sharing app, so you can access wallpapers and ringtones created by other Android phone users as well as share your own.

Zedge features an easy-to-use interface, plus lots of helpful information on what it does and how it works.

Index